Teaching Language and Content to Linguistically and Culturally Diverse Students: Principles, Ideas, and Materials

A Volume in:
Language Studies in Education
Series Editor: Terry A. Osborn

Teaching Language and Content to Linguistically and Culturally Diverse Students: Principles, Ideas, and Materials

by

Yu Ren Dong
Queens College, CUNY

INFORMATION AGE
PUBLISHING

80 Mason Street
Greenwich, Connecticut 06830

Library of Congress Cataloging-in-Publication Data

Dong, Yu Ren.
  Teaching language and content to linguistically and culturally diverse
students : principles, ideas, and materials / by Yu Ren Dong.
     p. cm. – (Language studies in education)
  Includes bibliographical references.
  ISBN 1-59311-088-X (pbk.) – ISBN 1-59311-089-8 (hardcover)
  1. English language–Study and teaching (Secondary)–Foreign speakers.
  2. Interdisciplinary approach in education. 3. Second language
  acquisition. 4. Multicultural education. I. Title. II. Series.
  PE1128.A2D624 2004
  428'.0071'2–dc22
                            2003025914

Printed in the United States of America

CONTENTS

Dedication   vii

Acknowledgments   ix

Credits   xi

Introduction   xii

1   Second-Language Acquisition for Adolescents   1

2   Listening to English-Language Learners' Stories and Adjusting Teaching to their Backgrounds and Needs   19

3   Assessing and Evaluating ELL Students' in Mainstream Classes   41

4   Tapping into English-Language Learners' Prior Knowledge   67

5   Teaching Disciplinary Specific Vocabulary to English-language learners   97

6   Second Language Reading Instruction in Mainstream Classes   125

7   Second Language Writing Instruction in Mainstream Classes   167

8   Second Language Listening/Speaking Instruction in Mainstream Classes   207

Appendix A: Topic Oriented Mathematical Non-fiction Reading   229

Appendix B: Multicultural Literature   233

Appendix C: ESL Related Internet Resources   239

References   241

Subject Index   255

DEDICATION

In memory of my father, Ke Chang Dong
1929-2003
who set me on the journey of learning and
pushed me forward with his insights and stories

ACKNOWLEDGMENTS

This book has developed over the years with the help of public school teachers and administrators, and public school students. I owe a debt of gratitude to those schools and classroom teachers, especially the science assistant principals at Newtown High School and Long Island City High School, and their science and ESL teachers who welcomed me into their classrooms and who unconditionally shared their insights and resources with me. Thanks also to the English language learners at these two high schools who actively participated and whose journeys to a new culture have provided valuable insights into our understanding of second language acquisition for academic success.

Part of the research findings reported in this book was sponsored by a CUNY PSC research grant and my gratitude to their support cannot be overstated enough. I have taught Language, Literacy, and Culture in Education and Reading and Writing for Diverse Learners courses to mainstream teachers over the years. Many graduate students who took these courses with me responded positively and they considered these courses important parts of their professional development. Many of their teaching strategies and reflections have provided the sparks for ideas contributing to our teaching subject matter knowledge to English language learners. I thank them all. My thanks also go out to the many colleagues who read and edited parts of my manuscript. They are Suzanne Abruzzo, Frances Curcio, John Walsh, and Myra Zarnowski.

Finally, I want to thank my husband and our son for their constant support and loving encouragement, and especially my husband's technical assistance throughout this long and arduous process. My son was in 11th grade when this project began. As I watched him graduate from high school and go to college over the years, I gained clearer insights into the minds of the high school students I observed.

CREDITS

Pages 13-14. From *Crossing customs: International students write on U.S. college life and culture*. (Eds.) by Andrew Garrod & Jay Davis, 1999, New York: Falmer Press. Reprinted with permission of Taylor & Francis, Inc., Routledge, Inc., Garland Science.

Pages 75-77. From *Crest of peacock: Non-European roots of mathematics* by Ghaverghese Joseph, 2000, Princeton, NJ: Princeton University Press. Reprinted with permission of Princeton University Press.

Page 76. *From Africa counts* by Claudia Zaslavsky, Chicago, IL: Lawrence Hill Books. Reprinted with permission of Lawrence Hill Books.

Page 126, 131-132, 133, 134, 174. From *Biology: The study of life* by William D. Schraer & Herbert J. Stoltze, 1995, Upper Saddle River, NJ: Prentice Hall. Reprinted with permission of Pearson Prentice Hall.

Page 144, 180. From *Integrated mathematics: Course II* (2nd Ed.) by Edward P. Keenan & Isidore Dressler, 1990, New York: AMSCO School Publications, Inc. Reprinted with permission of AMSCO School Publications.

Pages 154-155. From "A celebration of grandfathers" by Rudolfo Anaya, 1983, in *Homecoming*, Evanson, IL: McDougal Littell. Reprinted with permission of Susan Bergholz Literary Services.

Page 156-157, 159, 164, 198, 200. From *History of the world* by Perry, et al., 1995, Evanson, IL: McDougal Littell Inc. Reprinted with permission of McDougal Littell Inc.

Pages 162-163. From *Narrative of the life of Frederick Douglass* (Ed.) by Blassingame, McKivigan, and Hinks, 2001, New Haven, CT: Yale University Press. Reprinted with permission of Yale University Press.

Pages 164-165. From *They thought they were free: The Germans, 1933-45* by Mayer, Milton, 1955. Chicago, IL: The University of Chicago Press. Reprinted with permission of The University of Chicago Press.

Page 175. From *If the earth were a few feet in diameter* by Joe Miller, 1998, Greenwich, CT: The Greenwich Workshop Press. Reprinted with permission of Joe Miller.

Page 187. From *Between angels: Poems* by Stephen Dunn, 1989, New York: Alfred A. Knopf, Inc. Reprinted with permission of W. W. Norton & Company.

Pages 224-225. From *25 Mini-plays: World history*, Erin Fry, 2000, New York: Scholastic Inc. Reprinted with permission of Scholastic Inc.

INTRODUCTION

When asked about her childhood, Qian Wen, a Chinese student newly arrived in an American high school, revealed her love for nature back home:

> When I was young back home in my country in Mainland China, I would go out in the park close to my house, catching grasshoppers, butterflies, dragon-flies, and lady bugs with my peers during the summer break. We collected these bugs and took them home and put them in different jars. We fed them with leaves and water and observed them. I don't remember what we found out but I do remember the thrill that I had over collecting those colorful dragonflies. Once I found a blue-tailed dragonfly. It took me quite a while to follow her and finally I caught her. That made a hit among my peers and also created several fascinating questions: How come dragonflies fly so fast? Why can dragonflies catch things to eat while flying? Why does a dragonfly have a small body but two large eyes?

Qian Wen wants to major in biology in college and be a doctor in the future. As I traveled from school to school, from class to class, watching and listening to these students, I learned that Qian Wen's love and dream were also shared by many students whose native language is not English. At the same time, these students noted an overwhelming concern for

Teaching Language and Content to Linguistically and Culturally Diverse Students:
Principles, Ideas, and Materials; pages vii–xii.
A Volume in: Language Studies in Education
Copyright © 2004 by Information Age Publishing, Inc.
All rights of reproduction in any form reserved.
ISBN: 1-59311-088-X (paper), 1-59311-089-8 (cloth)

their subject matter knowledge learning. In comparison to their ESL classes, they considered biology and social studies as the most difficult subjects, like learning another foreign language besides English. They were overwhelmed by a large number of vocabulary words from these disciplines and a broader coverage of subjects, struggled with the reading and the writing assignments, and were pressured by the tests. They told me that even though they spent more time on these subjects than their ESL learning, still they received much lower grades. A report from the New York City Board of Education (2000) shows a passing rate in Regents biology (a content exam for high school graduation) in 1999 for English proficient students as 43.5 percent, while a passing rate for non-native English speaking students as only 19.9 percent. What is happening in these content classes? How do mainstream teachers work with students like Qian Wen? What prevents these motivated and intelligent students from achieving?

During the 1997 and 1998 school year, I began to observe high school content classes, both mainstream and ESL self-contained classes (classes composed of all English language learners), such as ESL biology, ESL social studies, and ESL math. I talked to the teachers, the assistant principals in these departments, and the students. I read the textbooks and the curriculum guidelines, and the tests. I collected students' homework, notes, and test results. Sitting in these classes I became a high school student once again, learning biology and social studies as I did as a teenager. In my year-long exploration, I found wonderful teaching but also many frustrations like the following:

SCENE I

I was observing some English language learners in their math classes. One math teacher, Mr. Beach, was very curious about my coming to his class each day to watch those who speak exotic languages. Although he told me that he had few students with limited English proficiency, in fact one third of his class were ESL students. I saw him calling on only native English speaking students to answer questions or to go to the board to write the solution to a problem. Several students told me that, although they might not speak as well as their native English speaking peers, they at least wanted to go to the board to write answers. When asked about those silenced English language learners, Mr. Beach revealed that they should write more and speak less. If these students prefer to be quiet and do their work, he was not going to bother them to speak up or do anything in class.

SCENE II

Mr. Smith shook his head when I asked him about the recent test results for his ESL biology class. Two-thirds of his class did not pass the first marking period. One reason for their failure to pass, according to Mr. Smith, was that they were not ready for his class. His reasoning was this:

> From a personal point of view, if I went to Spain and I didn't speak Spanish, I would think that I have to learn Spanish before sitting in a biology class. Many ESL kids in my class are very slow functioning in language and I am not focusing on language skills because I am concentrating on biology. That's presumably the point of their being in the biology class. Therefore, they shouldn't really be taking biology until they are ready.

SCENE III

Susan has been teaching for 20 years. She has witnessed an influx of immigrant students over the years in her inner city high school, which, according to her, was getting worse and worse because fewer students could speak fluent English. In my observations of her class, I noticed that Susan talked a lot and wrote very little. She also gave no positive feedback to the students. She stood in front of the room, holding the textbook up and giving directions or explaining things in a rapid pace. One day after her class, I asked her about her students and her teaching.

Dong: Some students told me that they enjoyed doing the lab.

Susan: Really? They don't ask questions and they don't say anything. They just sit there with those confused faces.

Dong: Do you think that they understand those directions and questions asked on the lab report?

Susan: Probably not, unfortunately. But I cannot slow down the curriculum. We have to finish.

Dong: Are there any other ways to make these directions and questions understandable? For example, if you simplify the words for them or write them on the board?

Susan: As much as I would like to, I have not learned how. I have been teaching for over 20 years in this school, and my way of teaching worked before and it should be working now.

Unfortunately, these examples of misconceptions and lack of sensitivity when dealing with students for whom English is not their native language, are not isolated incidents. The indifference of many teachers seems to contrast sharply with these students' eagerness for learning and their quest for success. The approaches these teachers are taking, including benign neglect, an over-emphasis on a language requirement, or a one-method-fits-all methodology, do not address the needs of their second language learners or provide an equal opportunity to learn. However, teachers are not the only ones to blame. Despite the fact that the student body in American schools has radically changed over the past decade, and despite the fact that the literature about teaching English as a second language and about bilingual instruction matures over 20 years, still, prospective and in-service teachers very often have had very little, if any, preparation for teaching second language students.

In recent years, we have seen a continuous influx of immigrant students into American public schools in general and New York City public high schools in particular. In New York City alone, there has been a steady increase in the number of English language learners (ELL) in recent years. For example, the total number of high school English language learners, who received ESL/Bilingual education, increased from 39,602 in 1999 to 41,201 in 2001 (New York City Board of Education, 2003). However, the ELL students' performance on the Regents exams was much lower comparing to their English proficient peers. According to New York City Board of Education (2003), only 31.3 percent of the ELL students graduated from high school passing the English Regents exam in class of 2001, while their English proficient peers had a higher passing rate (59.5%). In other academic areas, such as biology, global history, etc., ELL students also had a much lower passing rate compared to their English proficient peers. Because of an increased number of students for whom English is not their native language in high schools and tougher standards for high school graduation, the education of English language learners is no longer solely the responsibility of language teachers, but all teachers. All teachers need guidance in how to integrate language and content in their classrooms to enable these students to succeed.

With the continuous growth of students who are limited in English proficiency, more and more mainstream teachers find themselves having difficulties in understanding their students' backgrounds and skills and developing teaching methods to work with these students. There have been limited resources to prepare teachers for this student population, and a dearth of appropriate textbooks dealing in a systematic way with both ESL oriented teaching and content area subject matter. The textbooks written with an ESL orientation tend to group the content areas in a broad category, such as social studies or science and cover the whole range of K-12 (Adamson, 1993; Cantoni-Harvey, 1987; Carrasquillo & Rodriguez, 1995, Crandall, 1987; Echevarria & Graves, 1998; Gunderson, 1991; Peitzman & Gadda, 1994; Richard-Amato & Snow, 1992; Samway & McKeon, 1999). Disciplinary specific curriculum is only mentioned in passing. These books have been written by ESL language professionals who address the language component of the issue but lacked experience in content curriculum and content teaching. In teacher education, we have books preparing secondary content teachers but giving little apparent recognition to English language learners, assuming that future teachers will be working with native speakers of English. Therefore, it is time to combine the strengths of the two fields and take a serious look at the disciplinary specific curriculum at the high school level and design teaching practices that are both content challenging and ESL responsive.

This book is written with this purpose in mind. My purpose for writing this book is to discuss what constitutes effective instruction for students for whom English is not their native language. As an English as a second language educator who prepares prospective teachers for their work with a diverse student body, including non-native English speaking students, I hope this book will provide one point of departure for bridging the gulf between subjects and provoke conversations among all teachers as they reflect on their practice as their classrooms become more linguistically and culturally diverse.

I was fortunate to meet with a group of young and dedicated content teachers who saw diversity in their classroom not as a problem but as a resource and who tried out different methods and techniques to work with their students. Also influential in my work were a few supportive assistant principals who welcomed my research with open arms and shared with me both their successes and problems in dealing with a diverse student population. Many English language learners in these classrooms taught by these teachers flourished. They talked, responded, and interacted. They touched, felt, smelled in addition to watching, reading, writing, and listening. They sought, explored, and inquired. Biology and social studies were still tough subjects, but their teacher presented them in such a stimulating and comprehensible way and provided these students with many exciting and challenging experiences and language support both inside and outside of school. All that made these students feel that they had a chance of success. This experience enables me to see culturally responsive teaching in action.

This book is intended for high school content teachers, preservice teachers who prepare to teach in a subject matter area, college faculty involved in both pre-service and in-service teacher preparation programs, curriculum developers, and policy makers in teacher education. In this book they will find teaching principles as well as concrete ideas for teaching content subject matter knowledge to diverse students. Taking biology, global studies, English literature, or math as a content example, many ideas and strategies described in the book can be applied to other content area teaching also.

DESCRIPTION OF CONTENTS

This book is organized into eight chapters. Chapter One, "Second Language Acquisition for Adolescents" lays out a theoretical framework for understanding second language adolescent learners' second language, literacy, and culture acquisition and learning. It reviews research in the field of second language acquisition and bilingual education and discuss social, cultural, language, cognitive, and psychological developments of second language adolescents in schools. Focusing on school based second language acquisition and learning, the chapter discusses critical issues facing public school mainstream teachers today.

Chapter Two, "Listening to English Language Learners' Stories and Adjusting Teaching to Their Backgrounds and Needs" offers vignettes of eight English language learners and insights into mainstream teachers' working with these students for their academic, social, and language development.

Chapter Three "Assessing and Evaluating ELL Learners in Mainstream Classes" discusses difficult issues of evaluation and offers effective instructional and assessment tools for English language learners' language and content knowledge development. Regent's exams and ELA exams are used to analyze examine language and cultural appropriateness in standardized testing. It provides a guideline and examples for preparing English language learners for challenging high school graduation testing and makes suggestions for assessing English language learners' academic performance in daily instruction.

Chapter Four "Tapping into English language Learners' Prior Knowledge" offers teaching ideas for how mainstream teachers could identify and build upon English language learners' prior knowledge in English, mathematics, science, and social studies.

With each chapter focusing on specific language and literacy skills, such as vocabulary, reading, writing, listening/speaking, Chapters Five, Six, Seven, and Eight, provide ideas and strategies that can be used to make teaching concepts comprehensible, relevant, and meaningful to non-native English speaking students. There are four parts within each chapter, each addressing a different area of content knowledge, including English, mathematics, science, and social studies. After the discussion and description of each teaching idea or strategy, a sample student production is presented. Suggestions about teaching materials and resources are offered in the appendices.

CHAPTER 1

SECOND LANGUAGE ACQUISITION FOR ADOLESCENTS

HOW DOES AN ADOLESCENT ACQUIRE A SECOND LANGUAGE?

As native English speakers, we acquired our native language when we were young. Using English is such a natural part of our everyday lives that we seldom pause and examine how we became fluent. We speak, listen, read, and write in English with such an effortless and pleasant ease that it is hard to imagine anyone having difficulty with it. We take language for granted until we start to learn a second language, or travel abroad, or witness non-native English speaking students in our own classrooms who struggle with the language that we have acquired so easily, automatically, and unconsciously. Why is second language acquisition so difficult, so consuming, and so conscious? How does an adolescent acquire a second language? Researchers have been asking these questions for many years. What research has shown is that second language acquisition shares similarities

Teaching Language and Content to Linguistically and Culturally Diverse Students:
Principles, Ideas, and Materials; pages 1–18.
A Volume in: Language Studies in Education
Copyright © 2004 by Information Age Publishing, Inc.
All rights of reproduction in any form reserved.
ISBN: 1-59311-088-X (paper), 1-59311-089-8 (cloth)

with first language acquisition but that it differs from first language acquisition in significant ways.

Similar to first language acquisition, second language acquisition involves the language learner, whether a child or a teen or an adult, interacts with people who speak that language in a meaningful way. In second language acquisition, as in the first, the learner is often in silence at the beginning (Krashen, 1982). However, that silence does not mean that s/he is tuned off or acting dumb; rather it is a time when s/he is making active meaning of the new language and the new environment through listening and observing. Gradually, the learner utters a sound or a word in the new language. Then, s/he begins to produce phrases and sentences. Research in both first and second language has shown that language learners go through similar stages in their language development, specifically their learning of grammatical structures.

In first language acquisition, by the time a child reaches school age, s/he has already acquired a complex oral language for communication purposes. During the years of elementary school, middle school, and high school, the child's native language acquisition continues and expands to the acquisition of the written language (reading and writing), and to the power to use the language to think in the complex academic content areas, such as math, science, literature, and social studies. Cummins (1980, 1984) made a distinction in these two types of language acquisition: one is the acquisition of Basic Interpersonal Communication Skills (BICS) and the other is the acquisition of Cognitive Academic Language Proficiency (CALP). Young children or adult learners of a second language for communication purposes, according to Cummins, might only need to acquire BICS. However, school-aged children have to acquire CALP as well. These students who come to US schools, for example, high schools either in the beginning of the school year or in the middle of the school year, do not have the luxury of time while first language learners have to acquire the oral language first and then the written language. Rather, they face a situation where they have to acquire both oral and written language simultaneously in order to meet graduation requirements. Many second language students are placed in ESL classes two or three periods a day and spend the rest of their school day in the content classes which demand they use the language they are trying to acquire to learn academic content. A 14-year-old English language learner who has just arrived in the US faces the enormous challenges of gaining proficiency in a second language and completing, in the new language, content area courses needed to graduate from high school all within four years.

The distinction between BICS and CALP is important in raising our awareness of acquisition of different types of second language, which very often is not obvious. How long does it take English language learners to acquire CALP? Collier (1987, 1989), using scores obtained from standardized tests in reading, language arts, mathematics, science, and social studies, noted after examining school records of thousands of English language learners, ranging from elementary to high school, students who had schooling back in their home countries and were motivated to acquire a second language would take possibly 5-7 years to catch up with their native peers in CALP. How long does it take to acquire BICS? In comparison to CALP, researchers such as Cummins (1981, 1984) and Collier (1987, 1989) have found that very often BICS takes a shorter time to acquire (1-2 years) within a rich language environment and the learner's actively seeking out for interactions in the new language. However, when the language environment is not rich enough or the learner does not seek out and interact with native peers, BICS might take a longer time to acquire. Leki (1992) cited the example of international students who developed high proficiency of CALP, but could not carry on daily conversations with a native speaker. In inner city public schools, students who live in a home environment where English is not the dominant language and where daily communicative activities can be conducted using their native language would not acquire the second language as fast as might be expected.

There are two implications for teaching based on these research findings. One, we cannot wait until students have developed BICS before they start to acquire CALP. We cannot misplace one for the other. Mr. Smith's misconception (see the introduction) lies in that he took students' lack of conversational proficiency in English (BICS) as an indicator of their overall proficiency in English (BICS & CALP) or as a prerequisite for the students' readiness for the acquisition of CALP. Just the fact that students could not participate in class or communicate adequately in English does not necessarily mean that they are not eligible for the acquisition of CALP.

Two, students' fluency in BICS is not the equivalent of their fluency in CALP. Students showing the ability to communicate adequately in English does not mean that they have caught up with their native peers in CALP on standardized tests as well. If students enter American schools in grade nine and we do not provide them with the opportunity to acquire CALP, they will run out of time to learn CALP before they have to leave school. As Mohan (1986) noted,

> ESL students need to acquire English, as well as learn difficult subject matter through English. There may have been little continuity in their educational experiences in their home country, yet at the end of their secondary education, their level of academic achievement in English and their level of subject matter knowledge will be judged by comparison with English speaking students. (p. 3)

Therefore, there is an urgent need for all teachers, language and content, to take the responsibility of educating second language students by providing these students with access to the content curriculum and the opportunity to acquire both BICS and CALP.

WHAT CAN WE DO TO PROMOTE SECOND LANGUAGE LEARNERS' LANGUAGE ACQUISITION AND LEARNING OF ACADEMIC CONTENT?

In recent years, we have seen a shift in focus of second language teaching from a traditional satellite type of ESL language instruction to an integrated language and content (math, science, literature, and social studies) instruction (Adamson, 1993; Cantoni-Harvey, 1987; Carrasquillo & Rodriguez, 1996; Chamot & O'Malley, 1994; Echevarria & Graves, 1998; Gunderson, 1991; Enright & McCloskey, 1988; Peitzman & Gadda, 1994; Richard-Amato & Snow, 1992). This shift in teaching is supported by two second language acquisition principles. Two of these principles were proposed by Stephen Krashen (1982): One is called Input Principle and the other the Affective Filter Principle. According to Krashen, second language acquisition becomes successful only when the learner is exposed to comprehensible input, the input that is meaningful, sufficient, and relevant to the student at the level a little above the learner's current language and cognitive level. Krashen's hypothesis parallels with Vygotsky's zone of proximal development (1978) in that both acknowledge the rich learning context and the necessary challenge required to motivate the learner to acquire language. An Affective Filter refers to the level of anxiety that the language learner possesses while learning a new language. The degree of the affective filter can be influenced by factors both from within the learner, such as the learner's motivation, self-confidence, attitudes, and personality, and from the environment, such as classroom learning tasks, teacher input, peer influence, etc. For example, an introverted student or the student who has a negative attitude toward the new language and the new culture is not likely to participate in classroom discussions and make an active use of the new language. Also, if the teacher's input exceeds the student's language level or it is not related to the student, it will induce much anxiety from the learner, therefore overwhelming or frustrating the learner. A classroom environment with a low affective filter indicates a conducive environment where the learner has low anxiety and therefore is motivated to make sense of the input and more likely to learn actively and use the new language.

Traditionally, high school content has been taught with the expectation that students have already learned about the subject in their middle school years and have had appropriate cultural knowledge base and vocabulary. For example, biology textbooks at the high school level are written based on the assumption that students have grown up in the American culture and will understand and learn the content which is presented in scientifically appropriate ways and written for grade appropriate reading. However, with the increasing diversity of the student population across the nation, these assumptions and expectations have to be re-examined. Second Language learning principles, such as Krashen's Input principle and Affective

Filter principle, indicate that in order to promote content learning for all students, textbook designers, administrators, and teachers need to address the issues of language and culture and English language learners' needs in their secondary education. In order to help our students to catch up to or keep up with their native English speaking peers, all teachers must teach both content and language at the same time. Without care taken for these students' language development, such as their current level of language proficiency and language difficulties they are dealing with, we are not going to make our input comprehensible, thus increasing the level of class-room affective filter. In such a setting, we will not be providing equal access to educational opportunities for English language learners.

WHAT ROLE DOES CULTURE PLAY IN ADOLESCENTS' SECOND LANGUAGE ACQUISITION?

One of my student teachers at the student teaching seminar wrote about this incident which occurred in her ESL class:

> Eliza had only been here for a few months and was doing wonderfully. How-ever, some days she just put her head down on the desk and started crying. Although I asked her, she did not wish to talk about what was wrong. But I learned from her aunt that she was here with her aunt's family and her par-ents were still back home in Dominican. One day students were asked what they would buy if they had $1,000. As I was going around the room helping students, I saw most of them writing about things like cars, clothes, houses, etc. But when I came to Eliza, her paper had only one sentence: "I would buy an airplane ticket to Dominican Republic and never come back."

Eliza's writing gives us a glimpse of an acculturation process in second language acquisition for adolescents. The process of second language acquisition is also a process of acculturation, a gradual adaptation to the new culture. Unlike first language learners acquiring a language in the native culture, second language learners are acquiring a new language away from their native culture. Many immigrant students come over to the US with relatives or siblings and are separated from their parents as in Eliza's case. Very often this unstable and confusing situation adds to the difficulty in their second language acquisition and acculturation. Different from first language learners, second language learners especially teenagers and adults, have already acquired their first language, a set of cultural val-ues and beliefs, and literacy skills. Therefore, they come to learn a second language by constantly comparing and contrasting their native language with the new language, their prior cultural, and educational experiences with the new experiences. On the whole, second language learners go through four stages of acculturation paralleling their second language acquisition process. Acton and Felix (1986) labeled the four stages as tourist, survivor, immigrant, and citizen. In the first two stages of acculturation, second language learners first experience the excitement and newness of just being in a new country, seeing different people and things. During these two stages, second language learners acquire their BICS. However, that newness and excitement wear off when the second language learners experience overwhelming differences and confusions in the new language and the new culture. Their affective filter goes up and culture shock comes in and they experience extreme homesickness, loneliness, anger, frustration, sadness, and even some physical discomfort. At this point, they view the new culture with dissatisfaction or even hostility and they tend to withdraw to their inner self or to their fellow country students for comfort and solace. According to second language researchers, this is called the acculturation threshold, in that students either progress into the next stage of acculturation and language acquisition or remain in the same stage and fail to move on to the next stage. Eliza is obviously suffering from cultural shock.

The role that sociocultural factors play in second language acquisition was emphasized by Schumann (1978) in his acculturation hypothesis. Schumann observed the second language and culture acquisition of Alberto, an adult immigrant from Costa Rica for a period of ten months. Schumann found that second language acquisition to a large degree depended on the learner's social and psychological distance from the new culture, and the difference between the learner's native culture and the target culture. This distance is determined by the degree of willingness or the motivation on the part of the learner to learn about the new culture, the degree of openness given from the new culture. Alberto learned English just to get by for his basic survival. Being in the US as a manual worker, he interacted only with his Spanish speaking friends. He found comfort and solace in his Spanish speaking community and had no motivation for learning English or for acculturating into the American mainstream culture, even though there were English classes and English TV programs available to him. As a result, Alberto's English remained minimal and showed no progress. Studying Alberto's language acquisition and acculturation process led Schumann to believe that the acculturation process was vital in second language acquisition. When the social and psychological distance was large, the learner would not pass the early stages in second language acquisition. An ideal language and culture acquisition environment, as described by Schumann, has these characteristics: an environment that has a shorter the social distance between the second culture and the target culture; a desire in both the second language learner and the people in the target culture for the second language learner to acculturate; and a receiving culture which has an open and positive attitude toward people from other cultures.

However, in dealing with diverse students coming from different cultures, the classroom teacher is so busy covering the curriculum and preparing students for the upcoming tests that s/he is seldom aware of the students' social and psychological distance. An example shown below illustrates that the social and psychological distance can be created by certain topics in biology. A Bangladeshi student was struggling with learning about human sexual functions in her biology class.

> Sexual reproduction is difficult to learn because in my country, in high school, we were not allowed to talk about the sexual stuff until the students have become 18 . . . I don't know how to approach these kinds of things. My parents have never given a mention to me about this. I was so stressed out during those days of biology classes. (A Bangladeshi female student)

Her teacher was obviously unaware of her dilemma and puzzled by her low performance, interpreting it as lack of effort and motivation on the part of the student. As shown in the above example, the curriculum set-up and lack of knowledge about students' culture on the part of the teacher can exacerbate the difficulty of language acquisition, enlarge the social distance, and prolong the acculturation and language acquisition process. Acton and Felix's acculturation stages and Schumann's acculturation hypothesis have implications for teaching English language learners in public schools. Knowing the four stages of the acculturation process will help teachers who work with second language learners to understand and assess some of the early behaviors and attitudes that these students exhibit and to strategize to ease the difficulty in the students' acculturation. Also, knowing the best environment in which acculturation and second language acquisition takes place, teachers can create a classroom environment that is open, non-threatening, and positive for both native English speaking students and non-native English speaking students. As a two-way street, the acculturation process takes place not only through the second language learner's active interaction with the target culture, but also by people from the target culture embracing the people from other cultures and offering opportunities and resources for them to learn and use the new language and be a part of the target culture. It is incumbent upon teachers who work with a diverse student body to create classroom environments conducive to language and culture acquisition.

WHAT ROLE DOES ENGLISH LANGUAGE LEARNERS' NATIVE LANGUAGE AND PRIOR LITERACY EXPERIENCES PLAY IN THEIR SECOND LANGUAGE ACQUISITION?

In working with non-native English speaking students or in learning another language ourselves, we are all very aware of the fact that different languages have different sound systems and words to describe, explain, and express meanings and thoughts. These experiences lead us to ask, what role does native language play in second language acquisition? Look at the following examples:

Hebrew:	kaniti bair / et hagluya
Non-native English:	I bought downtown the postcard.
English:	I bought the postcard downtown.
Spanish:	se habla espanol?
Non-native English:	He speaks Spanish?
English:	Does he speak Spanish?
Chinese:	wo kanjian na ge mai dong xi de nu ren.
Non-native English:	I saw the buy stuff woman.
English:	I saw the woman who bought the stuff.
Arabic:	Baytuhu qadimun.
Non-native English:	his house old
English:	His house is old.

What do these examples tell us about the impact that the native language has on the second language learner's production of English? Looking closely at non-native English, we can easily trace the way of forming sentences back to the native language. The above examples illustrate that an English language learner's native language influences acquisition of a second language. Researchers in second language acquisition have found that these influences are not always negative. Instead, they often reflect the learner's efforts to use prior knowledge about the language that they know in order to learn a new language. When the sounds, words, or the sentence structure of the learner's native language share something in common with the new language, this active drawing on one's prior knowledge will help the learner's second language acquisition tremendously. However, when the sounds, words, or the sentence structure differ widely between the two languages, or the sounds, words, or the sentence structure of the second language do not exist in the learner's native language, confusion and mistakes will arise to make second language acquisition difficult (Brown, 1987; Eckman, 1977; Lightbown & Spada, 1993). Research comparing and contrasting second language learners' literacy learning both in the native language and in English has shown that this transfer from the native language can reveal deep and subtle culturally mediated ways of thinking and writing.

An intriguing discussion of the impact of the native language and thought processes can be traced back to the Whorfian Hypothesis documented by Carroll (1956). Based on their study of the Hopi language in

Eskimo tribes, the linguist Edward Sapir and his student Benjamin Whorf claimed that language and culture were closely interrelated, shaping and being shaped by one another. Language reflects culturally specific ways of looking at the world and making sense of the world. Comparing English and Chinese, for example, the English word "uncle" can refer to either the father's brother or the mother's brother, while Chinese use different words to differentiate the father's brother or the mother's brother. The same is true for the terms used to describe other human relationships.

English	*Chinese*
aunt	da yi (mother's older sister)
	xiao yi (mother's younger sister)
	da gu (father's older sister)
	xiao gu (father's younger sister)
cousin	biao jie (mother's sister's daughter older than the speaker)
	biao mei (mother's sister's daughter younger than the speaker)
	tang jie (father's sister's daughter older than the speaker)
	tang mei (father's sister's daughter younger than the speaker)
	biao ge (mother's sister's son older than the speaker)
	biao di (mother's sister's son younger than the speaker)
	tang ge (father's sister's son older than the speaker)
	tang di (father's sister's son younger than the speaker)

While there are no English equivalent translations, there are different terms used in Chinese to refer to the following relationships:

a. mother's sister's daughter's son
b. mother's brother's son's daughter
c. mother's mother's brother's son
d. mother's father's sister's daughter's son

While a native Chinese speaker will learn early the close and tight kinship organizations through learning the kinship terminology, however, these detailed break-downs of the relationships may baffle a native English speaker, whose language does not have such as elaborate terminology for the kinship system, and as a result, it might make Chinese kinship terms more difficult to learn for a native English speaker.

Some of the prototypical examples used in biology, such as blue jay or gray fish, are very much culture bound, too. For instance, in high-school biology textbooks in China, the prototypical example used is a woodpecker and Chinese students would have no clue of what a blue jay is unless the teacher is aware of this difference and use this difference to connect it with students' prior knowledge.

Research on the effects of culturally mediated ways of thinking and language use on adolescents' and adults' second language learning was expanded by Kaplan's ground breaking study in 1966, entitled "Cultural Thought Patterns in Intercultural Education." Kaplan was concerned with the fact that "Foreign students who have mastered syntactic structures have still demonstrated inability to compose adequate themes, term papers, theses, and dissertations" (p. 3). Influenced by the Whorfian Hypothesis, Kaplan proposed a contrastive rhetoric hypothesis after analyzing hundreds of non-native English speaking college students' essays in English. The theme of his hypothesis is that different cultures have different ways of thinking, thus they have different ways of writing. Therefore, the 'foreignness' in foreign students' writing in English is the result of not only language problems but also interference from their native thinking patterns. To illustrate these patterns, Kaplan offered diagrams describing paragraph organizations of an academic essay written in different languages. An English pattern is described by him as direct and linear in a deductive fashion, which has grown out of Platonic-Aristotelian philosophical and rhetorical origins. The Semitic pattern, referring to Arabic languages, is characterized as parallelism, favoring coordination over subordination. The diagram of the Romance pattern, referring to Spanish and French, is marked by a tolerance for digression from time to time. The diagram for the Russian pattern also allows for some digression from the main point. The Oriental pattern, referring to Chinese, Japanese, and Korean, is illustrated by an indirect approach to the main topic, characterized by an obliqueness of the main point until the very end of an essay.

In her year of teaching college students how to write in English in mainland China, Matalene (1985) attributed the Chinese way of writing to cultural values deeply rooted in Confucian and Marxist philosophies. She argued that, as the Chinese culture values uniformity and social harmony, children who grow up in that culture have already internalized those ways of thinking into their ways of writing. They had acquired a different set of reader expectations, and they transferred what they learned so well in Chinese into their writing in English. Therefore, it was natural to express one's views by referring to the traditional and culturally accepted patterns and echoing the Party line. Matalene's reflection on her students' writing and her own way of writing shed light on what is logical or illogical, direct or indirect in thinking and writing:

> Our own rhetorical values are profoundly affected by the fact that we are post-Romantic Westerners, teaching and writing in the humanities. As such, we value originality and individuality, what we call the "Authentic Voice." We encourage self-expression and stylistic innovation. In persuasive discourse, we subscribe to Aristotle's dictum, "State your case and prove it," and we expect to be provided with premises and conclusions connected by inductive or deductive reasoning. We call this a "logical" argument. . . . But Western

rhetoric is only Western. As we commit ourselves to reinventing our own rhetorical tradition, we need to understand the limits as well as the virtues of that tradition. And as our world becomes a global village in which ethnocentrism is a less and less appropriate response, we need to understand and appreciate rhetorical systems that are different from our own. (p. 790)

The above discussion on the impact of culture on language, thought, and literacy adds to our understanding of English language learners' reading and writing difficulties in our classrooms. Besides other influences, native language and cultural influences may explain some of these difficulties. Since many second language learners come to our classrooms already trained in some of the approaches and strategies used in reading and writing in their native language, they may not be aware of American academic ways of reading and writing. Instead of assuming that their students understand standard directions in English, teachers need to be aware of mismatches of cultural values and different ways of reading and writing (Buchanan, 1990). In dealing with reading and writing tasks in content areas, some of the writing norms and conventions have to be taught explicitly. For example, the norm of backing up one's claim with citations is an obvious academic practice to many American teachers. However, it is not that obvious to many students from cultures, such as China, where more emphasis is placed on using the works of others to learn and on imitation rather than on citing others' works in students' written work. Also, for some students from cultures where critical reading is not encouraged or taught, the students may simply summarize or even commit plagiarism. Finally, classroom talks are varied from culture to culture (Sullivan, 1996). In Chinese, Korean, and Japanese cultures, the teacher is an authority and the teacher's talk is the only talk delivered in the classroom. Students are taught to be silent (Hasegawa & Gundykunst, 1998; Jones, 1999) and silence is valued rather than an indication of lack of motivation or ignorance. Knowing about the students' culture will sensitize all of us to the issues of language and culture and schooling.

WHAT ROLE DOES DEVELOPMENTAL PSYCHOLOGY PLAY IN ADOLESCENTS' SECOND LANGUAGE ACQUISITION?

Despite differences in English language learners' cultural, educational, and language backgrounds, these students do share one thing in common with their native peers, that is, they are all teenagers going through similar cognitive developmental, social, and biological changes in their lives. As Piaget's (1947, 1972) child's intellectual development theory noted, a teenager of 14, 15, or 16 years of age is undergoing a cognitive change moving from the concrete operational stage to the formal operational stage and then to the abstraction and formal thinking stage. Students at this age are eager to learn new things, to attempt to define their identity, to experiment with new possibilities, to discover contradictions, and to question the authority. Their physical and cognitive maturation can facilitate their language acquisition. One major development in their language use is marked by their use of language ranging from literal and affective oriented responses to interpretive and abstract thinking related responses. In second language acquisition, several research studies (Ausubel, 1964; Cummins, 1981; Horwitz, 1983; Oller & Nagato, 1974) have provided evidence to argue that older second language learners, such as adolescents, are better language learners than younger children. Although it is true that younger children can acquire a second language with ease and speed and without any accent, however, when Cognitive Academic Language Proficiency (CALP) is concerned, teenagers demonstrate their strengths and have an edge over younger children. Teenagers have already acquired many concepts in their native language. In learning the second language, they do not need to learn each concept all over again; instead, they only need to learn a different name or phrase for the concept that they know through actively drawing on their previous language, cultural, and educational experiences. Also, since teenagers have already developed their cognitive abilities through formal education or through life experience, they are much better in making generalizations, applying abstract concepts to suitable exemplars, and solving problems. Some researchers such as Genesee (1976) have found that there is a correlation between intelligence and the development of second language reading, grammar, writing, and vocabulary, even though intelligence is not related to oral communication skills. In all these situations, teenagers are better second language learners in comparison to younger children. Even though second language learners speak broken English, which makes them look childish or ignorant, their cognitive level is at a similar stage as their native peers, moving from the concrete level to the abstract level of cognitive development. Their general ability to function abstractly can be transferable to elements initiated by the teacher. These transferable elements can be enhanced by using visual aids, by making a connection between the task at hand and students' lives, and by concrete and intuitive examples of the abstraction. Chamot and O'Malley (1994) gave an example of a high school English language learner's encountering a task in science. Although in the beginning the student was overwhelmed by the task, after some probing questions asked by the teacher, the student realized that she had already learned about this in her native country, even though she had learned it in Spanish. The teacher's probing questions triggered the student's transfer of her knowledge and skills in Spanish to the learning environment in English.

On the other hand, this new emerging self for many adolescents can hinder their language acquisition because of their being highly self-consciousness about themselves, their eagerness to be part of a group, and their intolerance of ambiguities and contradictions (Derwing, et al., 1999). They might hide their language deficiency or feeling of inferiority might result in their failure to venture out to actively seek language learning opportunities. Like their native peers, teens at this age also go through the period of "imaginary audience," agonizing over what others perceive them to be both physically and mentally. The following is an example of a Pakistani teen's, account of an embarrassing moment in his first year in the new culture:

> There I was in America at the age of thirteen in the middle of my 8th grade. I was the only person in that middle school who couldn't say a single word in English. I found it as an insult, and a disappointment. Soon I was admitted to Bryant Cullen High School as a freshman. I had to walk home every day because the school did not support school buses. Well, one day I was walking behind some students who looked like thugs or bad people. By accident, I stepped onto one guy's foot. The apology was right on my tongue, but I was unable to spit it out quickly. Before I could say anything, somebody stepped on my foot. When I turned and looked, I realized that he was the guy whose foot I stepped on. He talked really fast and I could not make out what he was saying. But judging by his facial expressions and body language I knew that he was pretty angry at what I did and especially at that I did not apologize to him. One of the boys said something like "Are you blind?" I understood "Are you" but I did not know the word "blind", so I murmured "yes." All of a sudden, they all started laughing and clapping their hands. I did not know what was going on but I sensed that they were making fun of me. I was so mad. The next day I could still feel everyone at school was laughing at my inability to speak English.

Obviously the over-self-consciousness and in the adolescent years can make language acquisition especially challenging for these students. It is especially true for English language learners who feel being constantly judged and evaluated because of their outsider status and language barrier. Even a good intention on the part of the teacher might not receive a good outcome. Here is an example of a Bosnia student's, Almin Hodzic's telling of how he was spotlighted by the teacher to share with the class his trauma due to the war in his home country.

> I remember my first social studies class in which my well-meaning teacher took me in front of my class to explain what was happening in Bosnia. I did not know where to start. It seems that she asked too much. Where do I start? The firing line? The concentration camp? What do I tell them about me? Even when I finally figured that I should explain the history of the conflict, I did not have linguistic skill to do it. Finally, I decided to draw on the chalkboard a picture of the city encircled by Serbian soldiers. But since I did not know how to say "surrounded" I just repeated, "Serbs around, Serbs around and then boom, boom." I used my whole body to try to explain. Even though my teacher constantly smiled to indicate that she understood, I was sure that

the students had no idea what I meant. I could see their confused faces, wide eyes and open mouths. I just remembered that I was in a sweat after this class, and even though I was extremely frustrated, I still smiled. Inside, I was ready to cry. Perhaps I felt this way because this was the first time I ever looked back at my experiences during the war or perhaps because I had an uncomfortable feeling of being different. Maybe I just did not want to be put on the spot and made to talk. Or maybe I just wanted to keep my memory of the horrors inside of me. (from *Crossing customs: International students write on US college life and culture*, pp. 181-182, Garrod A., & Davis, J. 1999, NY: Falmer Press.)

In Scene One in the introduction, we meet a teacher who neglects his English language learners' class participation due to their language status. In the above example, the teacher pays attention to English language learners and invites them to tell the class something they know best. However, in dealing with teenage second language learners, even a good intention on the part of the teacher may not receive a good outcome because of the characteristics of teenagers. All this reveals a complex task for a teacher today in dealing with teenage second language students. Teachers who have been trained to use only one method or to teach only one type of students, as shown in Susan's case in the introduction, must adapt their instruction to the students' needs, sensitize their instruction, and expand their teaching repertoire in order to meet the challenge of the profession in the 21st century. This is especially critical in dealing with students who have just gone through the trauma of a terrorist attack as shown below.

I was once in a terrorist attack. It was almost three months after my 16th birthday when my girlfriend and I celebrated our six-month friendship. We were with three friends and we didn't know what to do. My girlfriend suggested that we should go to Tel-Aviv, and we took the first bus to Tel-Aviv, line 47 of "Dah". When we came to Tel-Aviv we saw a coffee shop right in front of the station. We went to this coffee shop because we didn't have anything else to do. We just wanted to pass the time. A good friend of mine called me. His name is Martin. He told me that there was a party on the Lilehblum and he could let us in for free. We asked the waitress for our bill. We waited for almost 10 minutes to get the bill. Martin called again and asked where we are, and I told him that we were on our way. When we went out from the coffee shop a bus passed us. It was line 47 of "Dah." We heard the bus stop in the bus station, and we heard the doors open, then we heard a big "Boom." It was a long loud sound, and then a complete silence. We couldn't hear anything not even the cars. After a few seconds the shouting began. Men, women, and children began shouting and cry. There was a smell of smoke powder. After a couple of minutes the police and the fire department came. People start to come out and look at the place. Nobody from my company got hurt. But a glass chip got in my back. Eight people were killed that night. (A 9th grader from Israel)

With an increased number of English language learners in the nation's schools, often these learners are no longer the minority any more but the majority student population. In many New York City public high schools for example, students placed in an ESL program are very often placed in the ESL self-contained classes for content instruction. In other words, they will not only attend ESL language classes, but also ESL biology classes, ESL social studies classes, etc. Many English language learners whom I talked to over the years are concerned about their future and have this general feeling of a stigma attached to being an English language learner. The following comments of English language learners illustrate this kind of dissatisfaction and concern:

> Everything [I take] is ESL. That's why I am very sad . . . I like to go to the regular class. A lot of students make fun of me because of my failure to test out of ESL classes. Also, by testing out I can go into a good college, I heard . . . A lot of people who are here for a shorter period of time, such as a year and a half were able to go to the regular class. But I couldn't, and that made me very upset. (by a Bangladeshi male student)

> Back in the Philippines, I took Tagalog, my native language. But English was my subject language. I have learned English since Kindergarten. But I am still placed in ESL classes. I don't know why. What is more is that we are treated like we don't have any intelligence. What we learned in ESL is like what we learned in kindergarten. Teachers here don't know that what we had learned back home was far more and far advanced in science and math than American students in the same grade. I was very insulted by all this. (by a Philippine male student)

> It was hard to make friends here because each class has different people in it. In my school back in Poland, all the students have all their classes together for all four years of high school. It's easier to make friends that way. Also, we don't need to run around to find our classrooms between breaks because we have the same classroom all day and the teacher comes to us to teach. So that chaos between breaks really threw me off the first few weeks when I came here. (by a Polish female student)

The above discussion of the cultural, language, educational, and cognitive developmental aspects of second language learning points to the need for a change in the mainstream curriculum, a change in the attitudes and teaching methods in instruction among all teachers, staff, and administrators if more English language learners are to succeed in the challenging academic content areas. The following section outlines six areas of change necessary for mainstream teachers to incorporate ESL and culturally responsive strategies into their daily teaching:

- *Establish a learning environment that is culturally sensitive and inviting.* An effective teacher of diverse students is the teacher who is sensitive to the students' language and cultural differences and strategize the instruction to take into account these differences. There is a need for increased awareness of all faculty and school staff about the needs of English language learners. The social isolation experienced by many English language learners needs to be addressed. Developing school wide extra curricular activities, such as speaking clubs or multi-cultural centers or peer tutoring or a buddy system, can initiate such a link between native English speaking students and English language learners and provide opportunities for communication and cross-cultural understanding. Classroom teachers need to encourage such interactions and participation and model this kind of interaction by collaborating with other faculty and staff and participating in these activities.

- *Form collaboration between mainstream teachers and ESL/Bilingual teachers.* Mainstream teachers must not only develop curriculum, teaching methods, and techniques to address the specific needs of English language learners, but also collaborate with ESL/Bilingual teachers, guidance counselors, and school staff to establish a collaboration team. Administrators should encourage and initiate and support such a collaboration. Through this collaboration, mainstream teachers can seek information about the students whom they teach, their English language proficiency levels, their home backgrounds, and their home literacy backgrounds. Such a support system at school can also help with the communication between the teacher and the parent(s) and guardians. Bilingual teachers and guidance counselors can be extremely effective in initiating the contact with the student's family where the parents do not speak English. Mainstream teachers should encourage ESL/Bilingual teachers to observe their classes and to become familiar with content textbooks. Also, these teachers should collectively develop a coherent and responsive curriculum during which all parties will influence content objectives and the sequence of instruction. Students' language needs must be identified and resources and materials must be gathered that match up with English language learners' language proficiency levels.

- *Design and deliver lessons with anticipated ESL-related language difficulties in mind.* Mainstream teachers must make conscious efforts to build a language component into their lesson plans. For example, while planning for content teaching, it is often a good idea to plan for anticipated ESL related difficulties, including difficulties with vocabulary, reading and writing tasks, note-taking, following directions, prior cultural, and conceptual knowledge. Once the anticipated difficulties are identified for the lesson, the teacher will look at the lesson in terms of the learner along with the content. This approach will cause the teacher to teach differently. For example, the teacher might realize that students need more visual aids, including maps, pictures, photos, and diagrams to clarify key concepts. A use of visual and audio aids can promote active content learning and language acquisition in general and English language learners in particular. The teacher might want to rephrase questions and lectures on ideas and abstractions using simplifications, examples, repetitions, and demonstrations to get ideas across. Teachers might also want to make sure that students have understood them by making frequent summaries, giving students time to take notes, checking on their comprehension of the textbook reading, taking time to model how to do certain lab work and write a lab report. Before teaching a new lesson, teachers might want to first ask their English language learners to see whether they have already learned something similar to the topic in their native language. They might encourage students to use bilingual dictionaries or glossaries or even ask the librarians to acquire content readings in the students' native language and bilingual dictionaries. English language learners often welcome the idea of having the teacher or native English speaking students simplify key sections of the textbook.

- *Provide culturally sensitive feedback.* In mainstream classrooms, due to the pressure to cover the curriculum and testing and because of the didactic ways of teaching, students are given limited time to respond to teachers' questions or to clarify a point or to ask a question. Scarcella (1990) challenged the traditional teacher talk such as questioning and feedback techniques in the mainstream classroom as being ineffective working with diverse students whose cultural and school experiences might be different from what is expected in American schools. She listed altogether fifteen practical strategies used to enhance classroom talk and cross-cultural understanding. Some key strategies included offering English language learners multiple opportunities and multiple ways of responding to questions, providing students with enough wait time to think through questions, asking varied questions to students with varied language proficiency levels. For example, she suggests asking yes/no and choice questions to students who are at the beginning level of English. She encourages teachers to be consistent with the feedback and to establish tolerance and avoid embarrassing students by spotlighting or putting down students.

- *Encourage and teach transfer skills between languages.* Many English language learners tend to have the mindset that in American schools they are learning everything in English, therefore, what they learned back home is irrelevant. Or they have to give up what they know in their native language in order to learn English. Very often the school reinforces that mindset. Cultural sensitivity also is reflected in the curriculum and instruction. Teachers and administrators should stop viewing diverse students' native language and culture as problems, having a negative impact on students' learning of the new language and content. They should view English language learners' native language and culture as resources to make the learning in the new language and culture more relevant to the students. In teaching concepts or giving prototypical examples or explaining a procedure, it is important to include English language learners' prior knowledge about the concepts and their prototypical examples in the class discussion. In doing so, teachers not only validate these students' knowledge and experiences but also encourage students to hook new information onto what they know already and trigger knowledge and skill transfer. Research in ESL has shown that successful English language learners are often the ones who make constant transfers into English from what they know and the learning strategies used in their native language. All teachers need to use questioning and modeling to teach students how to transfer into English what they know in their native language.

- *Enrich the curriculum and provide English language learners full access to the curriculum.* Very often in schools, hands-on discovery learning or creative activities tend to be assigned more to the honor students. English language learners are either given limited opportunity for such enrichment or their curriculum is watered down or even their textbook is a skeleton-like list of words, stripping all the meat and the excitement, based on the assumption that English language learners cannot handle all this material and they have to learn the basics first. Ironically, rich and contextualized content is exactly what they need most but are often provided with the least. Therefore, mainstream teachers are in a unique position to bridge this gap and provide English language learners full access to the curriculum and to enrich the curriculum. In their exploration of concepts, students use the language in a more contextualized way and seek interactions among themselves and learn academic content through all the senses. It makes learning exciting and real and it also makes a perfect environment for language acquisition where students communicate in a non-threatening way but with meaningful purposes.

CHAPTER 2

LISTENING TO ENGLISH LANGUAGE LEARNERS' STORIES AND ADJUSTING TEACHING TO THEIR BACKGROUNDS AND NEEDS

In the previous chapter we discussed main principles of second language and second culture acquisition for adolescents. In this chapter, we are going to read eight teenager English language learners' stories and to see how their teachers in English, mathematics, science, and social studies classes adjust their teaching to accommodate these learners' backgrounds and needs. These eight students emerged from 60 case studies conducted by graduate students who are content teachers or pre-service teachers across all academic content areas over the past three years. They did the case studies, while taking my graduate level course: Reading and Writing for Diverse Learners. These studies revealed English language learners' real struggles and successes, pains, and joys in their odysseys of second language and second culture acquisition beyond their sheltered ESL class-

Teaching Language and Content to Linguistically and Culturally Diverse Students:
Principles, Ideas, and Materials; pages 19–38.
A Volume in: Language Studies in Education
Copyright © 2004 by Information Age Publishing, Inc.
All rights of reproduction in any form reserved.
ISBN: 1-59311-088-X (paper), 1-59311-089-8 (cloth)

rooms. They also captured successful ESL oriented teaching in various mainstream classes. Each teacher's attempts and efforts at listening and observing these students' language and culture learning and use that information to integrate language and content are commendable. These teachers have de-mystified ESL teaching and demonstrated that ESL teaching is not limited to ESL teachers' job only. Content teachers do have an important role to play in better understanding English language learners and guiding them through academic learning as well (Cummins, 1986, 1994; Genesee, 1993, 1995).

Nargis

Nargis, a 13-year-old girl, came to the US from Bangladesh nine months ago with her aunt and sister. Her parents are still living in Bangladesh and she misses them very much. Nargis loves school. She still remembers she was too excited to go to sleep when her mother told her that she was going to start school the next day when she was six years old. Bengali was her favorite school subject and she enjoys reading and speaking her native language. She is placed in both an ESL class and several 7th grade mainstreamed content classes. In all her ESL and content classes, she is very quiet and reserved in class, living in her own silent world.

Her social studies teacher complained that she was extremely quiet and never raised her hand, and she did not complete her assignment correctly. Half of what she handed in was written in Bengali and the other in English. A closer look of her written work shows that she copied all the questions in English, but her answers to the questions were all written in Bengali. Even when she began to write in English, her English teacher noticed that she never responded to the assignment. For example, the assignment asked her to use figurative language, however, she turned in a writing on how much she missed her family in Bengali.

Nargis is a student still going through her "silent period" (Krashen, 1982). The silent period is one of the characteristics many English language learners shared in their second language acquisition. They may appear silent, passive, and even physically withdrawn. This period can be very short for some students (a few months) and longer for others (a year or two). However, a student who is in silent period does not necessarily mean s/he is not learning anything or not involved in the lesson. Even though s/he is not actively participating, s/he is busy absorbing and processing the new language, observing the world around her or him. In Nargis's case, her trying very hard to do her assignments is a strong indication that she is eager to join in class activities, but her language skills hold her back. As for Nargis's teacher, it is important to read into her silence and recognize her effort by providing her opportunities to break that silence.

Several things that Nargis's social studies teacher and English teacher did made a positive impact on her classroom learning. Nargis's English teacher learned from a bilingual colleague that what Nargis produced was a vivid account of her journey to America and should be built upon for further exploration. Also, from the bilingual colleague, the English teacher learned that Nargis wrote fluently in her native language, a good sign for her second language acquisition and writing. Encouraged by her bilingual colleague, the English teacher began a unit on world folktales. Students not only read folktales from various countries, but also were assigned to write folktales of their own culture. Nargis appeared to be very active in this project. Limited in English, she put her folktale in Bengali first and then asked her Bengali peer to translate it into English. At the presentation, she asked the teacher to allow her to read aloud her folktale in Bengali first and then in English. Though her English was still very limited, the English teacher was delighted to see the joy on her face and her efforts to say something so dearly to her.

Her social studies teacher examined and adjusted his ways of questioning when he called on Nargis to participate. He confessed that before he tended to ask several questions at once. Now dealing with students like Nargis, he used yes or no questions to make sure that she would be able to say something and then build upon that answer gradually. Also, he paired Nargis with her native language speaking peer to help out with her understanding of the assignment. Both Nargis's English and social studies teachers noted the sparks in her eyes when Nargis was able to say a word or two in class and her homework answers shifted quickly from only Bengali to half Bengali and half English to finally English within a semester.

When they were studying Asian culture and history as part of their social studies curriculum, the social studies teacher invited her to share her first hand knowledge about her culture with the class. Nargis happily accepted the task and went out on her way of bringing clothes, souvenirs, and pictures from her home country to class and did a wonderful presentation using Bengali first and then asked her peer to translate it into English. The class was amazed, asking many interesting questions. Even though Nargis could not understand some of the questions, still in the eyes of her classmates, she knew she earned a new respect.

Assar

Assar came to the US from Pakistan with his family two years ago, speaking Urdu only. He progressed quickly and moved from ESL level 1 to level 3. However, after entering high school in the 9th grade, his performance in content classes in comparison did not show the same pace of progression. He liked biology and wanted to make it his major in college. However, biology was the subject that gave him the most difficulty. Assar's biology class was ESL self-contained, the class was taught by a mainstream teacher using the same textbook as their native English speaking peers. The textbook language was filled with jargon and so many complex and abstract "big words" that he had no way of comprehending all of them all at once. Even though he took general science back home in junior high school, still the depth of the subject matter and the amount of biology vocabulary threw him off constantly. Despite that Assar kept good notes of what was going on in class, his notes often did not make any sense when he reviewed them after class due to the teacher's frequent use of abbreviations and sentence fragments. He said that he missed a lot and was unable to make connections between what the teacher discussed in class and what he read in the textbook. Assar worked very hard sometimes without lunch breaks, still, his test scores did not reflect his hard work. In desperation, Assar resorted to his old habit of learning that he used back home: memorizing his textbook. He revealed that he would memorize the textbook section by section.

Assar's difficulty with biology content and language was also shared by many other English language learners, even those who exited ESL and mainstreamed. The reading demands in content classes such as biology can be very challenging for English language learners who have just acquired basic understanding of everyday language. In addition, facing the graduation standards, the amount of subject matter specific vocabulary covered in these classes and in the reading can be overwhelming. Fortunately, Assar's biology teacher quickly learned about his situation and needs. Three things that he did eased Assar's anxiety and helped Assar's biology learning. First, the biology teacher changed his way of board work by giving out complete sentences rather than just phrases or key vocabulary items. He also highlighted key topics and words on the board by putting simplified words or synonyms in the brackets on the side of the new topics and words to ease comprehension. Next, after talking to the chair of the department, the students were given out two sets of textbooks: one, a simplified version with a lower reading level but rich visuals and the other a regular biology textbook. Students could refer back to the simplified version in class quickly to keep up with the lesson, but they can also use the regular version for enrichment and details back home when they have more time to do the reading. Each day the teacher would put on the board the lesson and the corresponding pages of the textbook reading for the day. Finally, with the help of his departmental chair, the teacher gave out copies of biology glossaries in both English and in some of the languages that his students speak at home. Assar revealed that what his biology teacher did helped him and other students like him tremendously. His biology test score improved drastically.

Fatima

Fatima, a 12-year-old girl came to this country from Nicaragua eight months ago with her parents. Due to frequent family moves, she had an interrupted schooling, spending several weeks and even months at a time out of school. Fatima's mother stayed at home taking care of children, while her father worked as a commercial painter of houses. As a 6th grader, while attending ESL classes three periods a day, Fatima spent the rest of her day in an English language arts class. The English teacher had a tutor to work with her on her lessons once a week. In class Fatima sat in the rear of the classroom behind her Spanish speaking friend. It was an arrangement her English teacher made to make sure that her Spanish speaking peer helped with her understanding. Recently, the teacher had doubt about this peer help arrangement, wondering whether they abused this privilege because sometimes they two became too chatty in Spanish, and Fatima did not take risks by speaking English. Even when asked a factual question, Fatima often blushed and said with a thick accent, "I don't remember." Because of all this, she removed Fatima from her peer. Is there any way that the English teacher can get through to her?

To learn about how to work with Fatima, the English teacher went to visit Fatima's ESL class. From the ESL teacher, she learned that Fatima was still in her silent period, struggling with listening and reading comprehension in English. The rule in the ESL classroom was that all students speak in English. Fatima was grouped with a Korean student and an Israeli student playing monopoly, applying the vocabulary they newly learned. The English teacher sat on the side, eavesdropping to see Fatima's performance in the group. The Korean student was going to get some extra money out of the back when the other girls were busy counting their own. Fatima noticed this and said, louder than she usually speaks, "Hey, you are cheating!" Later she said to the Korean student, "No, it is my turn. You just had a turn." The English teacher was pleasantly surprised to see Fatima's correct use of the language, but also be assertive and involved in a real communication. From this observation, she had a different view toward Fatima and ideas for engaging students like Fatima in her own class.

A real breakthrough came when Fatima's tutor used bilingual books to get her open up. The tutor used the anthology *The Adventures of Connie and Diego* (*Las Adenturas de Connie Y Diego*) by Maria Garcia. The book is about third grade reading level with colorful pictures, and it had an English version of the story on one side of the page and Spanish on the other. They took turns reading the Spanish version of the story and then retelling it in English, recording new words learned. After the first few pages, Fatima refused to use the Spanish, saying that that was "cheating." She then focused on only the picture and the English version of the story to do her retelling. The tutor noted "I had not heard so much English come out of this girl's mouth since we met!"

Gina

Gina, a 9th grader who came to the country with her parents and brother from Colombia a year and a half ago, does not want to be American. Reluctant to leave her home country because she had bonded strongly with her peers and friends, Gina claimed that if she could, she would go back to her native land. Gina's negative attitude toward America was also triggered by her brother's quick "Americanization." "He eats fast food." Gina scorned. "He talks back to Mother, and when he pauses in between his sentences, he would say those 'umms,' 'uhhs' . . . We always say what we mean, we don't say 'umms' and 'uhhs' and we don't have the American way of sitting with legs on the table." Gina revealed that when her brother doesn't do his chores, her mother calls him a "lazy American."

To her English teacher's surprise, Gina's attitude was shared by quite a few students in her class when one day their English teacher asked the class a sentence completion question: "I consider myself _____ (American)" after their reading of Conrad Richter's *The Light in the Forest,* a novel about a Native American boy's struggle with his identity. To her surprise, many of her students considered themselves Chinese, Greek, Puerto Rican, Colombian, etc. They did not consider themselves American or Chinese American or Colombian American after being in the country for several years. The English teacher was dismayed. She could not understand why these students were here if they did not like to be American. When she asked them the reason, several students complained about how they were discriminated against by some of their American peers, such as being laughed at during the presentation by their ways of speaking or being shunned from friendship because of their accents and ethnicity. Gina and two other girls talked about how they were harassed verbally by American boys and were not able to talk back and dared not to report. Still others talked about how they had to fight stereotypes and prejudices about who they were on a daily basis.

This open discussion made Gina's English teacher realize the difficulty with acculturation and how marginalized her students were even though they appeared to be well adjusted academically and linguistically. She decided to do something about it. Taking advantage of their next reading, Miller's *Death of A Salesman,* the English teacher conducted a unit on the American Dream. She first assigned the class to write about their journeys of coming over to the US and their dreams and goals. Many of her students noted that they were pretty much told by their parents in a short notice that they would be moving to another country. For many the announcement was made the night before or a week before. This uprooting experience was very dramatic giving no time for the students to be mentally prepared for the new way of life. Separation from friends and family members lead to fear and resentment toward the new culture. Furthermore, some students came only with relatives or siblings, leaving their parents behind, therefore, they had added responsibility and anxiety over the journey. All these mixed feelings were compounded by the initial adjustment to the new culture and the language and demands posed by the new school and the teacher.

Student writing also revealed their family's dreams and goals and reasons for coming over to America. A shared goal among her students was to have the opportunities to achieve in their new culture academically and socially. Many of the students listed their career goals, such as doctor, lawyer, engineer, fashion designer, teacher, etc. Her students' writing gave the English teacher more clues about why these students thought about America differently from what she presumed. Learning about her students' backgrounds and interests helped the English teacher make a decision to include *The House on Mango Street*, by Sandra Cisneros in their unit on the American Dream. Results were phenomenal. Many of her students related their experience to the protagonist's experience in *The House on Mango Street* and they responded by comparing and contrasting the two literature works (*Death of a Salesman* and *The House on Mango Street*) and debated about various issues that they struggled with. The English teacher came to fully realize the impact of the literature works like *The House on Mango Street* when her student's mother came to her at the parent-teacher conference, asking for permission to let her child keep *The House on Mango Street* a few more days so that she could finish reading it.

Finally, with the help of the school guidance counselor, the English teacher arranged several extra-curricular student club presidents and music or sport team captains to come to her class to talk about their activities, inviting students to join and try out. This opened up her students' eyes because many of them did not even know these extra-curricular activities existed or were important part of their school life. As English language learners, they were often told language learning and their grades were their priority; this was especially true to some who came from a culture which valued academic performance only. The English teacher's eyes lit up when a few days later Gina told her that she joined in Spanish club and made some new friends.

Julieta

Julieta, a 10th grader from Argentina came with her family a year ago, was placed in an ESL self-contained social studies class called "World History for Foreigners" and other content classes, while attending three periods of ESL classes during the day. According to Julieta, life back in Argentina is often very trying for Julieta's family. After a failed small business attempt, Julieta's family decided to pull up roots and move to Queens to join her uncle and his family, exploring economic opportunities.

Julieta was determined to learn English. She said, "I want to have command of my English. I want to be able to ask a teacher a question that he is able to understand. I want to be able to answer and express my views in English." Julieta's silent period only lasted for a month. After that she assumed more and more active role in group work and showed a particular interest in a unit on the Ancient Egyptians. However, Julieta's determination to learn was challenged by heavy use of disciplinary specific words and the amount of information covered in her social studies class. Even though she had a dictionary handy, which she called her lifeline, the new words were just too many to look up in the dictionary, such as "settled along the Nile River" "acclaimed," and "at the height of power." In each class, she was exhausted from orchestrating multiple tasks all at once, including listening to the teacher's lecture, checking the dictionary for unknown words, copying notes on the board, and reading the handouts of the documents. Both the textbook and the document handouts were beyond Julieta's language proficiency level. Because of all this, Julieta seldom had time to enjoy the class or participate. Facing the upcoming Regents exam in the world history, both Julieta and her teacher felt the urgency. Her social studies teacher's question was: How to encourage Julieta to learn, but at the same time to make the learning process more manageable and meaningful to her?

One of the avenues that her social studies teacher and Julieta explored was the Internet. Learning that Julieta was fascinated by the web, spending most of her afternoons after school surfing the web at home, they explored several ESL and social studies websites. The social studies teacher made a list for Julieta's website adventure, paralleling the search with the topics covered in the social studies curriculum. The ESL websites got Julieta started with listening and writing exercises, offering instant feedback. The social studies websites provided rich visuals and simpler ways of communication, comparing to their textbook. Also the teacher invited Julieta to communicate with him through e-mail, reporting on what she had found on the Internet and asking questions. Gradually their communication expanded to other members of the class when Julieta paired up with a student from Cambodia and sent e-mail messages to each other, discussing topics that they learned in their social studies class. Inspired by Julieta's desire to learn, the social studies teacher made it part of his daily planning: including a glossary list to cover the key words and phrases that he sensed would be difficult for his English language learners and useful websites for students' exploration. Now he could see more hands shooting up when he asked questions and sparks in Julieta's eyes.

Alex

Alex is a 13-year-old 8th grader, attending a Junior High School. He moved from China with his family four years ago. Due to his schooling back home and some basic English he took back in China, he is faring very well. Alex considers himself a Chinese American, a sign of assimilation that is not often shown in immigrant students who have been living in this country for a short period of time. An American, according to Alex is "someone who lives in this country and takes advantage of all the different things it has to offer." Alex's favorite subject is math. He participates by coming to the board to put his answers and getting hundreds on the tests. He even tutors his classmates during his lunch break. When asked, Alex noted that sometimes even in math words were new and hard to understand. He often got a little confused when he was not sure about the word use in English, even though he knew that he had already learned that mathematics topic back in China. He always had his electronic English-Chinese dictionary out on his desk, constantly punching in words. Once he found out the Chinese equivalents of these words, he understood everything immediately. Alex's parents supported their son's language acquisition and acculturation. They even established a no Chinese rule between 3:00 p.m. to 8:00 p.m. after school from Monday to Friday. The only person in the house to whom they may speak in Chinese was Alex's grandmother. All this motivated Alex to learn and excel. He just tested out ESL program and was really proud of being placed in a mainstream English class.

Alex was doing beautifully in other subject matter classes except in English class. He struggled with the class discussion, a format of learning he was not used to. He could raise his hand to answer some factual questions, but he was shy from answering those questions that did not have right or wrong questions. He revealed to his English teacher, "They can't be right or wrong. Then I don't know what you want me to say." Even though his English teacher explained to him that those questions have to be answered with his feelings or opinions on the topic, still he said that he preferred when the teacher asked more direct questions where there was a right or wrong answer. Alex recalled that teachers in Chinese schools were authority figures, having all the right answers. He did not remember many times that the teacher would ask students questions, and never heard of the question without a right or wrong answer.

Intrigued by his response and troubled by Alex and many of her Asian students' lack of participation, Alex's English teacher decided to read about the educational system and cultural values in mainland China. The two articles that she read were Matalene's article entitled "Contrastive Rhetoric: American Writing Teacher in China" and Carson's article "Becoming Biliterate." She learned that unlike American culture valuing individuality and originality, Chinese culture values collective wisdom and conformity. Children learn from an early age how to behave properly in school and how to respect the teacher as an authority figure. Lectures are a predominant form of instruction and the teacher is the one who has knowledge and passes it on to the students. Questions are not often asked, let alone the questions without right or wrong answers. Even if the teacher asks a question, that is for an evaluative purpose to see whether the student has mastered the content, rather than for the student's feelings and opinions. Therefore, even though Chinese students may have a strong foundation of schooling and get ahead in other subject matter knowledge, they are not prepared for the independent, creative, and critical thinking that American teachers asked for.

Knowing about culturally varied ways of teaching and learning helped Alex's English teacher change her view toward Alex's and other Asian students' inability to respond to her critical thinking questions. She realized a need to raise the issue and compare and contrast different ways of schooling and cultural values. She designed a writing assignment to engage students in writing about appropriate classroom behaviors in American schools and in schools of their native countries or in their previous schooling. This caused students to identify the differences and similarities. Based on their writing, the class had a discussion on the issue. Noticing that many her students really did not know how to answer a question without a right or wrong answer, the English teacher even modeled her ways of thinking, coming up with her views critically, and expressing her feelings openly. The open discussion also got Alex's English teacher to reflect on her ways of questioning. She realized that her wait time for critical thinking questions was the same as factual questions, and she fired a question and expected students to answer it right away. After modeling, she found that even she needed sometime to process the question, organize her thoughts, and find a way to express her views. This discovery led to a change in Alex's teacher's questioning technique. She still asked questions without right or wrong answers, but she would allow the class to first write down what they thought about the question or to pair up to talk about the question and the responses before she demanded an answer. After several weeks, she heard with delight from Alex responding to one of her questions without right or wrong answers.

Andrew

Andrew, a 10th grader, came from Mexico with his family at the age of eight. He went through all the ESL levels and finally tested out of the ESL program and mainstreamed in the beginning of his sophomore year at the high school. Andrew recalled being put into ESL and all the ESL self-contained content classes made him feel like an outcast and prevented him from interacting with mainstream students. Andrew was dying to get out of ESL, however, each time when he took the ESL exit test, his mind "drew a blank," and he failed to pass it, despite the fact he could speak native like English by his middle school year. So testing out of the ESL and being with regular students gave Andrew new-found excitement, confidence, and motivation to learn. Andrew's guidance counselor was informing his mainstream teachers about Andrew's coming, an effort to make his transition from ESL to mainstream classes smoothly.

Andrew's English class was reading *The Lord of the Flies* by William Golding. The English teacher was impressed by his keen sense of understanding and active participation. He revealed that judging by Andrew's speaking and behavior in class he had no idea that Andrew had just exited ESL, if the guidance counselor did not tell him about it. In comparison to

Andrew's fluent oral language, his written language was less fluent, displaying few non-native markers. Most of his mistakes were following a steady stream of thought, being specific, spelling, subject-verb agreement problems, etc. Noticing that these weaknesses were also weaknesses found in many of his immigrant students' writing and the need for preparing them for the English Regents exam in their junior year, the English teacher wondered how he should go about helping his students with their writing.

The English teacher decided to tackle the comparison and contrast essay, a part of the English Regents exam. First, students were given two pieces of literature and read Wylie's Puritan Sonnet and an excerpt from *Ethan Frome* (Table 1).

Then they worked in groups to generate as many similarities and differences as possible on varied literary aspects of the writing on a Venn diagram. Based on their findings, students selected two literary aspects to write about. Afterwards, they came up with an organization plan. Next,

TABLE 1

PURITAN SONNET
Elinor Wylie (1921)

Down to the Puritan marrow of my bones
There's something in this richness that I hate.
I love the look, austere, immaculate,
Of landscapes drawn in pearly monotones.
There's something in my very blood that owns
Bare hills, cold silver on a sky of slate,
A thread of water, churned to milky spate
Streaming through pastures fenced with stones.

I love those skies, thin blue or snowy gray,
Those fields sparse-planted, rendering meager sheaves;
That spring, briefer than apple-blossom's breather,
Summer, so much too beautiful to stay,
Swift autumn, like a bonfire of leaves,
And sleepy winter, like the sleep of death.

From <u>Ethan Frome</u> by Edith Wharton (p. 5, 10)

During the early part of my stay I had been struck by the contrast between the vitality of the climate and the deadness of the community. Day by day, after the December snows were over, a blazing blue sky poured down torrents of light and air on the white landscape, which gave them back in an intenser glitter. One would have supposed that such an atmosphere must quicken the emotions as well as the blood; but it seemed to produce no change except that of retarding still more the sluggish pulse of Starkfield. When I had been there a little longer, an seen this phase of crystal clearness followed by long stretches of sunless cold; when the storms of February had pitched their white tents about the devoted village and the wild cavalry of march winds had charged down to their support; I began to understand why Starkfield emerged from its six months' siege like a starved garrison capitulating without quarter.

About a mile farther, on a road I had never traveled, we came to an orchard of starved apple trees writhing over a hillside among outcroppings of slate that nuzzled up through the snow like animals pushing out their noses to breathe. Beyond the orchard lay a field or two, their boundaries lost under drifts; and above the fields, huddled against the white immensities of land and sky, one of those lonely New England farmhouse that make the landscape lonelier.

TABLE 2

Organizational Pattern One (point by point)
Thesis statement: The speaker in the Puritan Sonnet has the intense and fearless attitude toward the New England winter in contrast to the speaker in Ethan Frome. The attitude was conveyed through the tone of the speaker and the figurative language use.

Paragraph One
A. the tone of the speaker in the Puritan Sonnet: warm and fearless and positive
B. the tone of the speaker in Ethan Frome: cold and depressing and negative

Paragraph Two
A. the figurative language use in the Puritan Sonnet: sky, seasons, water
B. the figurative language use in Ethan Frome: field, community, road

Organizational Pattern Two (all in one/all of the other)
Thesis statement: The speaker in the Puritan Sonnet has the intense and fearless attitude toward the New England winter in contrast to the speaker in Ethan Frome. The attitude was conveyed through the tone of the speaker and the figurative language use.

Paragraph One
A. the tone of the speaker in the Puritan Sonnet: warm and fearless and positive
B. the figurative language use in the Puritan Sonnet: sky, seasons, water

Paragraph Two
A. the tone of the speaker in Ethan Frome: cold and depressing and negative
B. the figurative language use in Ethan Frome: field, community, road

they had to decide on what their purpose of the comparison and contrast was, that was the attitude of the essay. Even though students were quick to compare and contrast two works, they had trouble in understanding that the comparison and contrast essay was more than listing similarities and differences. There were a purpose to persuade and to inform the reader and a coherent organization also. The English teacher helped the students come up with their thesis statement and two organizational patterns as shown in Table 2.

Taking into consideration that many of his students were like Andrew newly exited ESL, he decided to add useful transitional expressions to his lesson. Once the thesis statement and the organizational patterns were on the paper, Andrew's English teacher engaged the class in generating transitional words used for the comparison and contrast. These expressions helped students organize ideas in a coherent way and to add a flow to the essay.

Armed with the framework of the essay and language support, students were able to produce their group comparison and contrast essay. Once the group essay was written, the teacher made multiple copies of the group essays for peer review. Each group would get a different group's essay to read and critique. Students were instructed to make comments and correct errors, pointing at least two positive aspects of the essay and two constructive criticisms. Finally, they put their revised essays on the poster up on the wall around the classroom. The English teacher's face lit up when he saw Andrew was among the peers who were critiquing the use of the subject and verb agreement of one group's essay.

George

George, an 11th grader, came from Haiti three years ago with his mother, brother, and sister. Raised by his grandmother who was a retired teacher back home in Haiti, George had respect for education and learned the importance of discipline and hard work. He revealed that he had a dream to become a lawyer some day. While working at a supermarket after school, George attends ESL classes two periods a day and other periods in mainstream content classes. George likes his ESL class the best. He sits right up front, almost under the nose of his ESL teacher. He is most vocal in that class, talking with the teacher and his peers with all smiles. His hand is up whenever the teacher asks a question. However, in his content classes, such as math (Sequential III) class, George behaves like a different person.

The mathematics teacher asked the students to come to the front of the classroom to write out their homework answers on the board and then to explain how they arrived at these answers. George sat in the back of the room with his head down most of the time, occupied by his work having no interactions with his peers, his teacher, or volunteering any answers. George revealed that he had difficulty with advanced mathematical concepts and was not able to keep up with his homework. As a result, he could not go up to the board to do the homework demonstration. Even if he had an answer, he was embarrassed to talk because of his accent. George recalled that math was one of his favorite subjects when he first came to America. He was good at calculations back in his elementary and middle schools. However, as the content progressed and more and more thinking and language were involved, he gradually fell behind and struggled in class. George was disappointed in himself for letting his mother down. George's mathematics teacher was aware of his silence and poor test scores, wondering what happened to him.

One day after class George approached the mathematics teacher to ask for help. He was totally confused about the concept of functions. While he could understand $f(x) = x^2$, he could not understand $f(x + y) = (x + y)^2$, or $x^2 + y$, or $x^2 + y^2$. George's cry for help was a wake-up call for his mathematics teacher. The mathematics teacher realized that his students had not learned the basic concept of representation. Knowing that the majority of his students were English language learners, he decided to use a language approach to re-teach the concept of functions. The next day in class the mathematics teacher first asked the class what they had learned so far in their ESL classes about the English word order. Students gave him the basic word order: subject + verb + object. Then he asked the students to think about the relationship between the subject and the verb, that is what happens to the verb if the subject is the first person plural like "we" or the subject is the third person singular like "she." Students who were learning about the English syntax and the foreign language had no difficulty in coming up with the sentences like:

> We play basketball in gym everyday.
> She plays basketball in gym everyday.

Why did you change the verb by adding a "s" to its ending in the second sentence? The mathematics teacher asked. Many hands rose, "Because the subject is a third person singular and you have to put a 's' to it." One student responded. "It is one of those English language rules." Another student chimed in. "So, there is a relationship between the two." The mathematics teacher probed. "The verb has to be in an agreement with the subject. In my native language, not only the verb but also the adjective has to agree with the subject." A third student offered his insights. "Then does it seem that the verb form in English is dependent on the subject?" "Sure." The mathematics teacher put a diagram on the board:

S   +   V
Independent   Dependent

"So we call the subject independent variable and the verb a dependent variable." The teacher announced. "What is a variable?" Some student asked. "A variable is an unknown value that can change." The mathematics teacher continued, "Similar to language sentence structure we just discussed, in talking about functions in mathematics, we also talk about the relationship between two variables: one is an independent variable and the other the dependent variable as in the expression." The teacher put the equation on the board:

$$f(x) = x^2$$

"In this expression, x represents an independent variable and $f(x)$ represents a dependent variable. In other words, x like the subject in a sentence can change, and $f(x)$ will follow in agreement with the value of x. Think about the following two examples." The teacher put them on the board:

Celsius = (5/9) Fahrenheit - 32

Distance= time · rate

"How do we use functional expression to represent these two commonly used formulas?" The teacher continued.

$f(x) = (5/9) \, F - 32$

$f(x) = t \cdot r$

"How do we say it in English?" The teacher asked. The class responded: "Function of x equals five-ninth of Fahrenheit and minus 32. Function of x equals time multiplies rate."

"So what is the x?" "'x' represents Celsius temperature and distance." "Very well, these xs are variables. They can be either the temperature value or the distance. So $f(x)$ represents a relationship between the two variables, one depending on the other.

$$f(x) \qquad\qquad\qquad x$$
dependent variable   independent variable

The mathematics teacher knew George had it when he walked over to George and saw the answer in his notebook (see Figure 1).

Secondary English language learners face the increasingly high academic demands across content areas and tough high school graduation standards. The challenge is extremely overwhelming for these students who have not mastered the English language skills needed to meet these academic demands. Teachers of these students also face a tremendous challenge of teaching rigorous content while helping these students develop their language skills at the same time. Several themes of successful teaching illustrated in the above eight cases are:

- Content teachers must become listeners and observers of the changing student body in their classrooms. As illustrated in the above eight

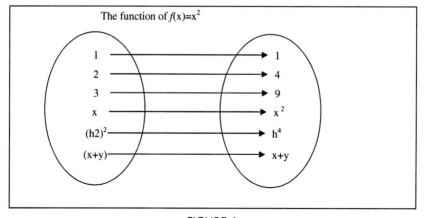

FIGURE 1

cases, English language learners come to our classroom with their own unique experiences, which can be explored and built upon. All the teachers who worked with these eight English language learners as discussed here seek necessary information about their students through ESL/bilingual teachers, other content teachers, and school staff. They also actively seek information from their students, using after class talks, e-mail communication, writing assignments, and tutorial opportunities. They use the knowledge about the students to inform and adjust their teaching as shown in Nargis' case. In the situation where a mismatch is identified as in Alex's case, the teacher is willing to read scholarly journals to find out more about students' prior education and preferred ways of learning. As one of the teacher said, "These students are silently trying hard to be heard, and mainstream teachers must open up their ears to the silent voices of these students."

- Content teachers must make the academic content accessible to all learners including English language learners. Even though all the teachers in the above eight cases face rigorous content curriculum demands, they are still able to make changes to accommodate English language learners' needs. Sometimes these needs can be simplifying difficult academic language by adding a synonym to the key word as shown in Assar's case. Other times the textbook or the reading materials have to be modified and extra resources have to be explored as shown in Julieta's case. Still other times ways of teaching have to be adjusted to these students' needs as shown in Gina's case and George's case. As one of the teachers reflected on her changing ways of teaching:

> You can see for example, the crayfish, for students who may never see crayfish or know crayfish. If a textbook never supplements the picture of crayfish, I, the teacher have to first to define a crayfish: What does it look like? What's the color? . . . So there are certain things that we take for granted, for example, we would say a blue jay and a sparrow, like common things that children would see on the curb when they grow up here. But for these children they may never see these things before since they are new to this country. So you really have to think backwards. If the child never saw the item, let alone the internal structure before, the first thing you have to introduce what it is and how it is and then you can teach biology. (A biology teacher's reflection)

A preservice teacher reflected on her tutorial experience like this:

> (The tutorial) episode really opened my eyes a great deal. Math is usually a subject that most people would think that an ESL student would have the least trouble as far as language is concerned. I found that there was so much terminology in the math book and so many con-

cepts, such as "fair" and random." This clearly demonstrates why content area teachers have to adapt materials in order to address the needs of the ESL student. (A social studies preservice teacher's reflection)

- Content teachers must broaden their areas of competence to include knowledge about language, second language acquisition, and strategies for teaching second language learners and working together with ESL professionals (Genesee, 1993, 1995). Traditionally, secondary education has been often fragmented and departmentalized. Even though many English language learners spend a large amount of time in mainstream content classes, mainstream teachers do not interact or even know about their ESL status or their ESL teachers, and ESL teachers often teach in isolation of the academic demands of the content curriculum. Working with English language learners challenges mainstream teachers to seek support and assistance from ESL/bilingual teachers and to extend their competencies to include some of the skills and practices that are the specialty of ESL teachers, as we saw in Nargis', Fatima's, and George's cases here. George's mathematics teacher in particular demonstrated the best integration of language and content in that he was willing and able to make use of the English language structures that English language learners are familiar with in order to teach complex concepts of functions in mathematics. In recent years both California and New York have adopted teacher certification guidelines that require all teachers to have some training in language, literacy and education in order to work effectively with an increasing number of English language learners in their classrooms. These teachers as shown in the above eight cases can and should serve as models for all mainstream teachers.

- In working with English language learners, mainstream teachers must use more enrichment and elaboration of the content knowledge and provide opportunities for students to collaboratively work with the materials. Extra readings, more student and student interactions, and Internet searches as demonstrated here are both promoting language development, peer interaction, and providing the intellectual challenge. As shown in the above cases, Julieta's social studies teacher invited her to do Internet searches for appropriate materials to learn and communicate, Andrew's English teacher used a series of group work to generate sufficient amount of content knowledge and language assistance to prepare students before writing, and Fatima's tutor and teacher used bilingual literature and group work to get Fatima actively involved in the language learning process. These activities provide the students with ample opportunities and rich contexts for active language use and language and literacy skills development.

- In working with English language learners, mainstream teachers must recognize the powerful impact of culture and attitudes on language and content learning. As shown in Gina's and Alex's cases, an acculturation process is a two-way street, involving second language learners, the outsiders, actively immersing themselves in the new culture and seeking a new identity. Insiders of the target culture actively reach out to accept and understand the differences, withhold their judgment, and introduce their culture to the newcomers. Simply being placed in the new culture cannot guarantee acculturation and positive attitudes toward the new culture. Acculturation needs time and environment to establish, this is especially true for teenagers who left their home country, leaving friends and family members behind for various reasons other than their own wish. Therefore, things that people who grow up in this culture have taken for granted may not be so in working with English language learners, and they may trigger a culture shock as illustrated in Gina's case. Gina's English teacher, instead of demanding a positive attitude, engaged her students in writing and reflecting on their journey of coming over to America. She included literature works that students can identify with and introduced students to the wider school culture. In Alex's case, rather than blaming the student for his lack of expected classroom behavior, the English teacher went out of her way to read about how schooling operates in Chinese culture, trying to understand her student's class participation behavior.
- Mainstream teachers need to have empathy for English language learners and bring students' home culture and background to the class to show the relevance of learning tasks in order to work with these students effectively. Actively seeking students' prior knowledge can be a real challenge for a teacher, especially when the student has limited English language proficiency to express what s/he already knows. One way to find out the student's background is to look at the student's program card to see the ESL/bilingual classes in which s/he has enrolled and to contact the ESL or bilingual teachers or the guidance counselor for background information on the student. Also, for a newcomer, peers who speak the same language or come from the same country can be helpful in getting the background information on the student. In this situation, the student can be allowed to write down background knowledge in his or her native language and then have their peers translate it into English. Insights into the student's background can also be gained through talking with bilingual colleagues who speak the same native language or come from the same country as the student. Finally, a genuine interest in the students and their backgrounds will show to these students

the relevancy of what they are learning with what they have already known or experienced, thus moving these students from the margins to the center of learning.

The following are a few pre-service and in-service mainstream teachers' reflections after working with English language learners:

Reflecting back on my own cross cultural experiences of visiting Croatia and working in a job that involved communicating with people whose native language is not English has helped me to understand the needs of ESL students. I know how frustrating it is when I want to communicate in Croatian but due to the fact of my limited proficiency I am not able to. People might perceive me to be less intelligent but the truth of the matter is that the language is the barrier and not my intelligence. Similarly, in my job and dealing with people from many different countries I have seen the same frustration with these people. This is the same situation that the ESL student is in.—A social studies teacher

This experience has taught me the value of what immigrants go though when they come to our country. I take the language for granted and often find myself at a loss to explain why we use certain words in certain situation—I don't know—we just do is often my explanation. When a young individual comes to the United States and enters our school system as an English Language Learner, the difficulties he faces are enormous. It takes an extremely strong individual to conquer the fear and criticism of learning everything from scratch. As an educator the experience has taught me to be more patient with the student. ELA students will not get "it" on the first try or second try, might not get "it" on the third or fourth try, but after a number of times tasks will begin to sink in, and that is when I know I have accomplished my goal.—An English teacher

I always regretted not speaking another language or spending a prolonged period of time in another country. In the past three semesters working with ESL students I have truly been made aware of what an incredible experience these people have. The small and large successes that they have made are all the more remarkable considering the adjustments they have to make.—An English teacher

I used to interpret silence from the English language learners as a lack of enthusiasm; however, I have come to understand that there can be many reasons for silence. It could mean embarrassment, lack of understanding, discomfort, respect, etc.—A biology teacher

One of my true loves of New York as the place I call home is in its awesome ethnic diversity. I have always admired the bravery of someone who was willing to take a chance on the "American Dream." The ability to grab one's family and brave a long trip to the unknown shores of fate and destiny in search of a better life is, in my estimation, nothing short of true heroism. As we have seen, one of the most difficult transitions to this new life is mastery of language. I have been continuously impressed with the tenacity and desire of some of my ESL students and I praise them for accomplishing goals that I doubt that I myself could reach. I feel I have become infinitely more appreciative of the ESL learners vulnerabilities, needs, and strengths and I will try, with a more experienced set of educational tools, to implement many of the lessons and techniques I have learned this year into my work, next year.—A social studies teacher

CHAPTER 3

ASSESSING AND EVALUATING ELL STUDENTS' IN MAINSTREAM CLASSES

With the Regents exam looming over our heads, the pressure is to create dramatic improvement in all our students' abilities. Still, facing some students do not even speak English fluently, how do you assess their work, let alone prepare them for an exam, such as Regents?—An English teacher

This English teacher's concern is also many other mainstream teachers' concern. Teaching non-native English speaking students, the teacher faces the challenge to assess these students' content knowledge and help them meet the learning standards. Assessment is a double-edged sword. On the one hand, we use assessment to gauge students' academic progress and to inform our own teaching; on the other hand, assessment is more than a self-reflective teaching and learning tool. With almost all states in the US raising high school graduation standards and imposing standardized tests on their students at varied levels of their schooling, assessment is tied to the high school diploma and serves a reward-punishment mechanism to recognize schools and teachers that produced high test scores.

Teaching Language and Content to Linguistically and Culturally Diverse Students:
Principles, Ideas, and Materials; pages 39–65.
A Volume in: Language Studies in Education
Copyright © 2004 by Information Age Publishing, Inc.
All rights of reproduction in any form reserved.
ISBN: 1-59311-088-X (paper), 1-59311-089-8 (cloth)

In this chapter, I discuss assessment strategies used in two contexts of teaching English language learners academic content knowledge. They are: assessing ELL students' content knowledge through daily instruction and preparing English language learners for standardized tests.

ASSESSING ELL STUDENTS' CONTENT KNOWLEDGE THROUGH DAILY INSTRUCTION

When Ashgan came to Ms. G's 9th grade global studies class, she did not speak much English. She sat straightly in her seat everyday with her notebook open and seemingly paid attention to what went on in class. However, from what she was told by the school, Ms. G learned that Ashgan just arrived in the US a month ago from Eygpt and spoke Arabic and French. But she was not given any information about for how far Ashgan was in her global studies, or whether she learned any global studies back in her home country. Also, knowing that Ashgan had almost to zero English language skills, Ms. G wondered where the starting point should be for Ashgan's global studies learning. "How can I tell that she is learning?" "How can I make sure that she understands what I am teaching?" "To be fair to all students, do I grade her equally as others in class?"

Yi Lin has only been in the US for five weeks. She is 15 years old and is placed in the 9th grade biology class. She is from Taiwan and appears to be still in her silent period. She answers almost every question with a headshake. Even when her biology teacher, Tom, asked her if she was Yi, she shook her head but saying "yes." The ESL teacher told Tom that Yi had some English back home in Taiwan, and even though she was not speaking, she might understand more than she appears to be. Despite the ESL teacher's reassurance, Tom still has concerns about her. His question is how can I assess Yi's performance if she does not speak or perform on the test? She performed poorly on the first two tests. On her first test, she wrote nothing but a few Chinese words. On her second test, Yi did not respond to the question "Why photosynthesis is useful?" at all, instead, she wrote the formula of the photosynthesis. "How can I in my good conscience to give her a passing grade with this kind of work?"

Ms. G's and Tom's questions are typical mainstream teachers' questions in working with newcomers from other countries. New students coming to New York City public schools are asked to fill out a Home Language Identification Survey (HLIS). Once the student or the parent indicates on the survey that a language other than English is spoken at home, s/he will take an English proficiency test called the Language Assessment Battery Revised (LABR) to determine whether or not they are entitled to receive bilingual/ ESL services. This test is given out normally in the spring, and all ELL students take the test to evaluate whether they need ESL services and how to place them in a level appropriate ESL class. If the total number of ELL students who speak the same native language reaches 25 or more, then these students are eligible for bilingual education. Their parents have an option to place their children in either bilingual content classes or English only content classes. Currently in New York City public schools, there are seven major bilingual content classes running in varied schools, including Bengali, Chinese, Korean, Haitian Creole, Russian, Spanish, and Urdu. These content classes use students' native language to teach them sciences, mathematics, global histories, and US government and history. Despite these bilingual classes, all students must take ESL classes and take Regents English exam in order to graduate. All ELL students must take the New York State English as a Second Language Achievement Test (NYSESLAT) and achieve a total raw score of 37 on the combined listening and speaking, and 33 on the combined reading and writing sections to meet the exit criteria.

Other than language evaluation, content knowledge evaluation is left to mainstream content teachers. Very often schools are short of bilingual teachers in the language that students speak or the funding to hire a bilingual teacher. In addition, parents would like to place their children in an English-only environment to speed up their second language acquisition. Then if the school has sheltered ESL content area classes, the classes composed of English language learners only, the student will be placed in it. If not, the new student will be placed into mainstreamed content classes mixed with native English speaking students and non-native English speaking students. The new student often attends ESL classes for two or three periods a day, spending the rest of the day in the content classes. Therefore, mainstream content teachers should be aware of the new student's status and be familiar with a few diagnostic tools in order to quickly identify the student's needs and include the student into class learning. Researchers (Collier & Thomas, 1998; Fichtner, et al., 1994; Garcia, 1994; Gonzalez, 1996; Gottlieb, 1999; Hernandez, 1994; Lam, 1993; O'Malley & Pierce, 1996) have argued that assessing beginning ELL students' academic progress should not be based on tests but on ongoing documentation and combined with instruction.

Back to Ashgan's situation, after talking to Ashgan's ESL teacher, Ms. G. decided to do five things. First, she arranged Ashgan to sit close to her desk in order to have frequent observation of her behavior, to give her help when needed, and to make sure that Ashgan followed what went on in class. Seated closely to the teacher, very soon Ashgan would communicate with Ms. G. through signs and facial expressions.

Second, Ms. G. paired Ashgan up with Sue, a peer who spoke French at home and who was also a second language student. Ms. G. figured their native language and Sue's experiential knowledge about second language learning could assure a more personal involvement and assistance. Peer help can be extremely rewarding especially for someone who has gone through all the process. Ms. G would check on the pair during her lesson and learn more insights about Ashgan from Sue. Sue would interrupt her lesson by asking her to clarify something for Ashgan. Ms. G. knew it was time to re-arrange seat for Ashgan when she saw Ashgan become more at ease and talking frequently with Sue in French. This time she placed Ashgan in the middle of the students who did not speak her native language. Ms. G. wanted to create an environment where Ashgan would be pushed forward to learn.

Third, based on her daily observations, Ms. G. adjusted the grading system to accommodate Ashgan's needs. She did not give Ashgan a letter grade in the first two months. From Ashgan's ESL teacher Ms. G learned that it was premature to evaluate Ashgan's progress using the same criteria that she used for the rest of her class. With help of the ESL teacher, she designed a profile chart to document Ashgan's progress. Ashgan received only a "credit/noncredit" grade for the first two marking periods. It was not until November before Ms. G. first noted a breakthrough in Ashgan's oral English and she felt appropriate to begin assessing Ashgan's performance. Ashgan's oral language exploded during the group work. Her notes were complete, she was catching up on her homework, and her test performance showed a remarkable improvement.

Some mainstream content teachers may have concerns over whether it is fair to evaluate a new English language learner differently from the rest of the class. While I respect these teachers' efforts to treat all students equally, I believe that that blind equality can run the risk of not recognizing that all students are unique individuals and may have different needs and backgrounds. Ignoring these backgrounds and needs and forcing everyone to be treated equally can only do a disservice to these students, letting them feeling alienated, inferior, and disengaged. Like siblings in Fu's book (1995), many new immigrants coming to a new culture needs an initial adjustment both academically and socially besides catching up with their language skills. Therefore, instead of giving these students not passing or failures, it is more productive to allow these students time to become familiar with the learning environment and providing opportunities for them to express what they know.

Good assessment and evaluation rather than an end to a student's learning, should be a means which motivates and informs students' learning and teachers' instruction (Wiggins, 1992). With many English language learners mainstreamed into content classes, assessment should be an integral part of instruction and it should be ongoing and achieved through multiple measures.

Back to Yi's case, when Tom, Yi's biology teacher showed Yi's tests to her ESL teacher, to his surprise, the ESL teacher saw something that Tom failed to see. She saw the effort and improvement comparing Yi's first test with her second. She said to Tom that even though Yi did not respond to the question in either of the tests, her writing down of the whole formula of the photosynthesis on her second test should reveal that

1. she knew the question was about photosynthesis,
2. she tried to respond to it by using her knowledge, and
3. she had paid attention in class and kept good notes and read the text-book.

She was telling Tom how big a leap this was for a second language learner. Judging by the improvement and effort, Yi should be given a passing grade. The ESL teacher also advises Tom to use ongoing assessment on a daily basis with Yi. One instructional and assessment strategy is through daily observations. Following the ESL teacher's advice, Tom designed a profile sheet on Yi (Table 3), detailing her second language development.

Tom would go around the room listening to the students' talk during peer work and group work, looking for any signs of understanding, struggling, and participating. Tom soon found out that Yi was actually very active in peer and group work by asking questions from her Chinese peer for clarification and jotting down the notes. Yi did not show much verbally in English, however, observations made Tom see that Yi did involve herself in learning by observing, listening, or following what others were doing. Very soon Tom's profile was filled with details about Yi. He could see exactly where Yi was and how he could adjust his instruction to push Yi forward. Based on his observations, Tom told Yi to show her notes to him in class by marking the part where she did not understand. They have developed a system by Tom walking down the aisle to check for homework and then Yi's notes. By reviewing Yi's notes regularly Tom gained a good understanding of Yi's biology learning and language learning and also got a sense of his own instruction. Once, Tom casually mentioned in class something about guinea pigs. The next day, he walked over to Yi and found a big question mark about that part of the lesson. She did not get it. That alerted Tom to be conscious about some of the cultural references that he made in class.

In his teaching of mitosis, Tom learned from Yi that even though she had copied everything into her notepad she still did not understand the concept, and her electronic translator did not help either. This led to Tom's follow-up lesson using construction paper to demonstrate cells, and the process of mitosis. Students were divided into groups five verbalizing the process using the manipulative. Tom sat in Yi's group and showed Yi step by step. By the end of the lesson, Yi even though was hesitant to verbalize the process, was able to show the correct process involved in mitosis using the manipulative.

However, assessment and evaluation should not stop here. Constant and ongoing assessment should help mainstream teachers adjust their expectations and raise their standards accordingly. Too often mainstream teachers held low expectations for ELL students (Fu, 1995; McKeon, 1994). Language learning like content knowledge learning is not linear, rather it is recursive and has cognitive and language leaps. So an ELL student may not

TABLE 3
Mainstream Classroom Observation Matrix of Beginning ELL Students

	Readiness to learn	Interaction with peers and the teacher	Doing class work
Non-verbal learning behavior	• Student is alert/interested or confused/disoriented/bored • Open the book and the notepad. • Have pens and pencils.	• Nod or smile appropriately during class talks. • Use signs to communicate to peers and to the teacher. • Be able to say simple greetings.	• Follow the directions. • Copy notes.
Verbal behavior	• Write numbers, dates and own name when asked. • Notes are taken, either complete or marked in L1.	• Talk to peers in L1 or in English. • Ask questions from peers. • Ask for help after class or in class when the teacher walks by. • When asked, gives a word answer or Yes/no responses. • Tackle the test or homework in some way either in L1 or in English.	• Frequent use of the dictionary or glossaries to follow the reading or the discussion.
Group work behavior	• Sit close to the group and face the group members. • Get the book or the handout ready for the task. • Readiness to learn	• Pay attention to what goes on in group talks. • Communicate with the group members for clarification and help. • Interaction with peers and the teacher	• Take part in group work by either verbally and non-verbally. • Doing class work

Non-verbal learning behavior	• Student is alert/interested or confused/disoriented/bored • Open the book and the notepad. • Have pens and pencils.	• Nod or smile appropriately during class talks. • Use signs to communicate to peers and to the teacher. • Be able to say simple greetings.	• Follow the directions. • Copy notes.
Verbal behavior	• Write numbers, dates and own name when asked. • Notes are taken, either complete or marked in L1.	• Talk to peers in L1 or in English. • Ask questions from peers. • Ask for help after class or in class when the teacher walks by. • When asked, gives a word answer or Yes/no responses. • Tackle the test or homework in some way either in L1 or in English.	• Frequent use of the dictionary or glossaries to follow the reading or the discussion.
Group work behavior	• Sit close to the group and face the group members. • Get the book or the handout ready for the task.	• Pay attention to what goes on in group talks. • Communicate with the group members for clarification and help.	• Take part in group work by either verbally and non-verbally.

do anything on the first test, a month after, s/he may attempt to answer a lot. Therefore, using classroom observations and daily assessment, a mainstream teacher can gauge ELL students' progress, set up a new goal for them, and push them to catch up with her mainstream peers.

Recognizing that some of his students were not used to participating in class discussions and tending to defer to the teacher as an authority in their schooling back home, Mike, another biology teacher, used varied strategies to constantly train his students to talk about science in class. Mike's lecture was loud and clear. He used wait time when he asked a question. He did not only call on those who raised their hands, but also those who kept silent once he sensed they were ready. For example, knowing that Win Xiang had been in his biology class for almost a year, but still did not speak a word in class, he tried to urge her to join in class discussion.

Teacher:	So another reflex is blinking. Everybody blinks, you blink your eye. It is not voluntary. Reflexes are involuntary. How does blinking protect you? Do you know what *protect* means?
Student 1:	To keep you from harm.
Teacher:	OK, so how does that protect you? How are you doing this with your eye, opening and closing? How is that protection? Win Xiang?
Win Xiang:	(didn't answer)
Teacher:	Want to help her out? (pointed to her neighbor)
Student 3:	Keeping it from [becoming] dry.
Teacher:	Did you hear what she said? (asked Win Xiang again)
Win Xiang:	(nodded her head but still didn't answer verbally).
Teacher:	Did you hear what she said just now? Can you repeat what you said? (asked the whole class)
Student 4:	Keeping it from [becoming] dry.
Teacher:	Can you repeat what he just said? (walked to Win Xiang and asked her for the third time)
Win Xiang:	Keeping it from dry weather [sic].
Teacher:	Good. Can somebody repeat what Win Xiang said loud so that everyone can hear it?
Student 5:	When your eyes are dry you blink to moisten it [sic].
Teacher:	Guys, did you hear that now? It keeps it from drying and keeps dirt from getting into the eye, so it protects it.

Here we see an example of Mike's using several turns to get Win to participate in the class discussion. Two interesting elements in teaching and assessment come out. First, instead of leaving a quiet student alone, Mike held a high expectation of her. That expectation is based on Mike's daily assessment and observations. Sensing that Win had acquired the language power by now, he nudged Win to articulate her understanding orally. Second, Mike demonstrated that good assessment is an integral part of teaching. By using elicited responses from other students first to set up a non-threatening environment, Mike prompted Win to speak up in the end. This incident turned out to be a turning point for Win. After that incident she participated frequently in class.

Several strategies used by above teachers to assess ELL students' content knowledge can be summarized by the following seven guidelines:

1. Conduct ongoing classroom observations to document ELL students' learning behaviors and academic performance.
2. Allow ELL students to sit close to you or sit with students who speak their native language and allow ELL students to use their preferred language to demonstrate their understanding.
3. Establish a profile chart of ELL students, especially those who are at emerging stage of second language learning in order to gauge their non-verbal signs of learning.
4. Use multiple assessment strategies rather than relying on the test results alone to get a holistic view of ELL students' performance.
5. Use visual oriented and hands-on assessment strategies to measure comprehension and understanding.
6. Constantly revise your expectations of ELL students and adjust your assessment accordingly.
7. Redesign and modify your assessment methods and directions to provide ELL students with a chance to respond.

For intermediate or advanced ELL students or students who just exited from the ESL program and mainstreamed into content classes, there is also a need to assess their language and literacy skills and use the findings to help mainstream teachers tailor their instruction according to these students' needs. Very often these students have already developed basic communication skills and appear to be fluent in oral English. However, that oral fluency may disguise problems of the written English and mislead the teacher into believing that these students should be equally fluent and proficient with reading and writing skills.

In comparison to other literacy skills, reading skills, specifically, are often hidden and difficult to evaluate. Students with reading difficulties can go unnoticed for quite a long time. Therefore, there is a need for the mainstream teacher to learn some basic evaluation techniques used to evaluate reading comprehension and behavior in order to identify students' reading needs and abilities. One informative and easy to use tool is the miscue analysis, (Goodman, Watson, & Burke, 1987). The miscue analysis involves the teacher first assigning a student to read aloud a reading passage, while taking notes on the text to mark the student's miscues, such as repetitions, substitutions, pause, omissions, mispronunciations, self-corrections, etc. After the read-aloud, the teacher asks the student to retell the story or summarize what has read. Then the teacher analyzes the transcript of the read-aloud and the retelling and groups the miscues into several categories to see the pattern, the quantity, and the impact of the miscues. Three commonly used categories include

1. semantic acceptability (whether the miscues fit with the meaning),
2. syntactic appropriateness (whether the miscues interrupt the sentence flow), and
3. graphical resemblance (whether the miscues match the actual words or phrases in some way).

The following are two examples of such an analysis done by English teachers:

There were only hills and valleys of water around me now. When I was in a valley I **could** see nothing
       (pause)   coo
and when the canoe **rose out** of it, only the ocean stretching away of away.
         (pause) rollz ou   (pause)
Night **fell** and I drank from the basket. The water cooled my **throat.**
    fall   dero
The sea was black and there was no **difference** between it **and** the sky. The waves made no **sound**
Da   different   (omit)   soun
among **themselves,** only **faint noises** as they went under the canoe or struck against it. Sometimes the
      themself   faded noise   (pause)
noises seemed angry and at **other** times like people laughing. I was not hungry because of my fear.
noise seem   another
The first star made me feel less afraid. It came out low in the sky and it was in front of me, **toward** the
                                                               estoward
east. **Other stars** began to appear all around, but it was this one I kept my gaze open. It was in the
      another star
figure that we **call a serpent,** a star **which** shone green and **which** I knew. Now and then it was hidden
         called spart   whi   whi
by **mist,** yet it always came out brightly again. Without this star I would have been lost, for the waves
   mis
never **changed.** They came always from the same direction and in a manner that **kept** pushing me away
      change   (omit)   kep
from the place I wanted to reach. For this reason the canoe made a path in the black water like a snake.
    (pause)   (pause)
But somehow I **kept** moving **toward** the star **which** shone in the east.
        kep   estoward   whi
Excerpt from Island of the Blue Dolphins by S. O'Dell

Analysis
There are altogether 26 miscues in a short reading of about 250 words. Maria, a 8th grader, made an average of one miscue every ten words, a closer examination of these miscues shows that the majority of these miscues are second language pronunciation problems. Maria's native language is Spanish and I can see some native language influences here such as her difficulty in pronouncing the /th/ sound, and omissions of certain sounds in words ending with "t" "s" and "d". However, Maria's retelling shows that she has achieved basic understanding of the text. Her miscues at the semantic level such as "faded noise" "called spart" "rollz out of" do not seem to distract her from getting an overall meaning. At first I thought she might not understand the word "serpent" but she told me that she got the idea in the end because of the phrase "the black water like a snake."

When I look at Maria's writing, she has trouble with certain word endings, such as verb –ed ending and the third person singular. This points to the need for her to practice on these forms of language both orally and in writing. Also, Maria's use of the context clues to understand the word "serpent" excites me, and maybe I can structure something for her and the whole class to learn how to use contextual clues in reading.

FIGURE 2

It is a miracle that New **York** works at all. The whole thing is **implausible**. Every time the residents
                Yerk   impossible
brush their teeth, millions of gallons of water must be drawn from the Catskills and the hills of

Westchester. When a young man in Manhattan writes a letter to his girl in **Brooklyn**, the love message
Wetchester   Brookleen
gets blown to her **through a pneumatic** tube-pfft-just like that. The **subterranean** system of telephone
                thoughts (pause) poomatic (omit)   (pause) subferranean
cables, power lines, steam pipes, gas mains and sewer pipes is reason enough to **abandon** the island to
                                                        abondon
the gods and the weevils. Every time an incision is made in the pavement, the noisy **surgeons** expose
                      (pause)   (pause) surginias
ganglia that are tangled beyond belief. By rights New York should have destroyed itself long ago, from
gang
panic or fire or **rioting** or failure of some **vital** supply line in its circulatory system or from some deep
                (pause) reeoting   veetal
labyrinthine short **circuit**. Long ago the city should have **experienced** an **insoluble** traffic snarl at some
laboratory   cirweet   experience   (pause) insollable
impossible bottleneck. It should have **perished** of hunger when food lines failed for a few days. It
                                  perish
should have been wiped out by a **plague starting** in its slums of **carried in** by ships' rats. It should have
                                plagoo staring   carrying it
been **overwhelmed** by the sea that licks at it **on** every side. The workers in its myriad cells should have
     overwhelm   in
succumbed to **nerve**, from the fearful pall of smoke-fog that drifts over every few days from Jersey,
                nervez
blotting out all light at noon and leaving the high **offices** suspended, men **groping** and **depressed**, and the
blooting   office   grouping   depreesed
sense of the world's end. It should have been **touched** in the **head** by the August heat and gone off its
                              touch   hear
rocker. Excerpt from <u>Here is New York</u> by E. B. White

Analysis
There are 30 miscues in this read-aloud by Richard, a 11th grader whose native language is Spanish. After
reviewing the transcript and Richard's retelling, I realized that he did not understand the reading. There
are some native language influences such as pronouncing the words with an –ed ending. But most
dominant miscues he made were semantic miscues, such as "grouping" for "groping", "reeoting" for
"rioting", "insollable" for "insoluble", and "impossible" for "implausible." These miscues prevented him
from understanding the story. Richard's retelling was very sketchy, an indication of a failure to
comprehend the story. Before this exercise, I thought Richard could handle a reading material like this
one, since he had been in the U.S. for more than five years and was mainstreamed in his middle school.
However, the finding of the miscue analysis has made me think again. Richard revealed that he had
trouble with big words and with what he called "woofy" language or figurative language use. I wonder whether
the problem here is due to use of big words or figurative language use or both.

This miscue analysis is a wake-up call for me to see where my students are at in their reading abilities. I
am thinking about re-examining the reading materials that I use with this class in general and Richard in
particular. Richard's reflection on his own reading process made me wonder whether this is a prevalent
problem for other students. I plan to give Richard another miscue analysis using a reading material that is
descriptive. I also plan to investigate my other ELL learners on this.

FIGURE 3

The analysis can offer the teacher an in-depth knowledge about the student's reading behavior and patterns of that behavior, for example, the reader frequently mispronounces certain words or has trouble with certain sentence structure. Periodic use of the miscue analysis can monitor students' reading skill development and give the teacher an idea whether the reading material is appropriate for the reader and strategize ways to assist the student with reading accordingly. Table 4 is a literacy assessment matrix detailing assessment strategies for mainstream teachers to use to evaluate

TABLE 4
Literacy Assessment Matrix of Intermediate or Advanced ELL Students

Skills Assessed	Assessment Strategies	Identifiable Behaviors and Indications
Listening/ Speaking skills	• Class observations • Questions and answers • Group/pair work Presentations	• Greetings/leave taking and small talks with peers and the teacher. • Understanding of specific cultural references and disciplinary specific terms in class discussions. • Requesting information and assistance. • Use of language to describe, explain, and express. • Participation in group/pair work, class discussions and presentations. • Understanding oral instructions, demonstrations, and explanations.
Reading skills	• Miscue Analysis • Retelling • Reading journals/logs • Vocabulary • Reading surveys	• Sound-word association, accuracy, and pattern. • Pronunciation of words. • Speed of reading and pauses during the reading. • Understanding of the reading passage. • Repetition of the word or phrase during the reading. • Substitutions of the original words or phrases during the reading. • Attempts at making meaning and corrections made during the reading and retelling. • Quantity and quality of writing to respond to reading. • Questions asked and comments made during the reading or after reading. • Reading interests and preferences.

Category	Methods	Focus
Writing skills	• Journals/logs • Writing conferences • Writing assignments • Error analysis • Writing surveys	• Quantity and quality of writing. • Talking about one's own writing process and understanding of the writing assignment. • Problems found in coherence, organization, ideas, and format. • Error patterns made in sentence structure, word order, tenses, pronouns, agreement, etc. • Number of errors. • Vocabulary use, variety, and misuses. • Writing interests and preferences.
Learning/ Test-taking skills	• Examining the notes • Reviewing the test • Observations • Self-reflections	• Notes completion, use of visuals and graphics, selective note-taking, and organization of the notes. • Understanding the test directions and questions. • Highlights, marks, and poses questions on the reading handouts. • Frequency of the dictionary use and other learning resources. • Asking for help and for clarifications from the teacher and peers. • Pre-viewing and reviewing the lessons and the assigned readings. • Self-reflection on and regulation of one's learning, strengths and weaknesses and progresses and learning goals. • Use of language and conceptual knowledge transfers from L1 to L2.

TABLE 5

	The Cause of the American Revolution
I.	French and Indian War:
	• Fought between the _____ and the _____ in North America and ended in 1763. The _____ won the war and took complete control of North America.
	• _____
	• In order to pay off their massive debts, the British began to place heavy _____ on the _____.
II.	Sugar Act:
	• Placed heavy _____ on _____ which was being sold in the colonies.
	• _____

intermediate or advanced English language learners' language and literacy skills.

Chamot and O'Malley (1994) emphasized the importance of cultivating effective learning skills and outlined major learning skills across academic disciplines for students in general, ELL students in particular. Among these, note-taking skills, though appear simple and straightforward, can be overwhelming for an ELL student in that the learner has to juggle multiple tasks, such as listening, reading, and writing all at once to make notes. In addition, effective note-taking involves students not just copying what is on the board but drawing a meaningful roadmap that identifies key points and summaries crucial information. Organization and consistency of the notes are two indicators of effective note-taking. Mainstream teachers should check students' notes and model effective note-taking strategies rather than assume that ELL students can take notes. Brian, a middle school social studies teacher uses a systematic approach to teaching his students what and how to take notes. In the beginning of the semester, after finding out that his ELL students had very limited and incomplete notes, Brian provided a handout for them each day before class that outlines the key information but with a few blanks for his ELL students to fill out. By the end of the lesson, he would quickly go over the notes as a whole class, identifying effective note-taking strategies and checking for understanding. As the semester went on, blanks in Brian's handout became bigger and longer and finally his ELL students would no longer need Brian's handout to take notes. Table 5 is a sample handout that Brian used with his ELL students.

PREPARING ENGLISH LANGUAGE LEARNERS FOR STANDARDIZED TESTS

With a nationwide implementation of the new learning standards and standardized tests in recent years, all students including those who are not English proficient, must take these tests in order to meet the learning standards and graduation requirements. While native English speaking students struggle to meet the high graduation standards, ELL students have double jeopardy in that they have to perform in academic content areas using the new language in which they are not fluent. In the past, schools and programs tended to negotiate this dilemma by excluding ELL students from these types of tests or gave them a simpler version such as RCT used in New York State. However, this approach created a new problem of equity and access when the standardized tests results were often tied to the type of high school diplomas that the student earned and the results would determine the student's future academic career. As a result, ELL students were often placed in low track classes and were shut off from the challenging curriculum and rich resources, which were reserved for Regents' classes only.

Recently, the New York City Board of Education required that all students who entered 9th grade in September 1996 or thereafter, no matter whether they are ELLs or non-ELLs, must pass five Regents exams including English, Math, Science, Global History/Geography, and US History/Government in order to graduate with a diploma. However, an inclusion of ELL students in this assessment and evaluation process does not guarantee equity. An inclusion of ELL students in standardized tests without a modification of the tests or accommodation procedures produces problematic results. It is not surprising to find that ELL students have not performed as well as their native English speaking peers in these content assessments. For example, an examination of the recent Regents biology, English, and global history results in New York City public high schools indicate that ELL students' passing rate was only about half of the English proficient students' passing rate (2003). Why is that? An obvious reason is that ELL students' English proficiency is prohibiting them from performing on these tests. Although the standardized tests claim to test students' content knowledge, it is often difficult if not impossible to assess content knowledge without some understanding of the language used to describe, explain, argue, and express that content knowledge. A closer examination of these tests shows that these tests are designed for students who are not only native or fluent English speaking but who also share common cultural experiences. However, for ELL students who have different cultural experiences than mainstream students and than the cultural experiences that the test makers have in mind, cultural biases along with language difficulties interfere with the assessment of the content which intended to test, thus produce invalid results (Butler & Stevens, 2001; McKeon, 1994; Mohan, 1982).

Tables 6 through 8 and Figure 4 are samples of standardized test studies done by a group of mainstream teachers in my Language, Literacy, and Culture in Education course in Fall 2002. Cultural bias here refers to a test question that "requires special cultural knowledge that is available only to particular cultural groups" (Mohan, 1982, p. 135). According to Mohan, it is important to separate content knowledge and cultural and language

TABLE 6

Question 51 on Regent's Living Environment Jan. 2002
The Pine Barrens is a government-protected environment located on the eastern end of Long Island. A proposal has been made to allow a shopping mall to be built in the middle of the Pine Barrens. Although the developer has promised jobs for people in the surrounding communities, some community members oppose the building of the mall due to the negative effects it would have on this fragile ecosystem. Identify two negative effects this mall would most likely have on the Pine Barrens.

Analysis
The above question uses shopping malls as a key argument for the negative impact on the Pine Barren, an ecosystem located on Long Island. However, for an ESL student who has been in this country for a short time or lives in an area without shopping malls, this question might pose difficulty in understanding, let alone to write a short answer to identify the two negative effects. (by a science teacher)

TABLE 7

Regents U.S. History and Government: June 2002
Question 45. The aging of the baby boom generation will most likely result in
    (1) an increase in Social Security spending
    (2) a decrease in health care costs
    (3) a decrease in infant mortality in the United States
    (4) a balanced federal budget

Analysis
The correct choice is (1), but an ESL student would have to know that the "baby boom generation" refers to people born between 1945 and 1955, following World War II. Do students learn this term in school, or is it a cultural feature of society, like knowledge of rainfall in Washington State? "Baby boomers" is a term in current usage in American society, and is not a historical term, which an American student could only learn about from a textbook. Therefore, this question may contain a subtle cultural bias against non-native English speaking students, who would not know the meaning of the term, unless they had learned about it from a textbook. (by a social studies teacher)

TABLE 8

Regents English Task I: Listening Passage, August 1999
My favorite piece of communications technology is disgustingly low-tech. I don't have call-waiting. I passed on Caller ID. I wouldn't own a cellular phone, a mobile phone, or even a cordless phone. I don't have or want a pager, and a car fax is definitely not in my future.... Now I'm Mr. Multi Media. I'm online, on the 'Net, and on the ball, sort of. I enjoy an occasional e-mail as much as the next guy. In fact, I'm so forward-thinking, I own a CD drive, though, in truth, I probably give it more of a workout with products by Mozart than by Microsoft...

5. The speaker implies that the advantage of his CD drive is its capacity to:
    1) speed communication
    2) provide entertainment
    3) store information
    4) simplify research

Analysis
The listening material incorporates many cultural references about technological advances in communication. It contains words and phrases that can be considered slang, such as "low-tech," "call-waiting," "Caller ID," and "CD drive." For ELL students who are new to this culture, they may not have time to gain insight into this American high tech popular culture. In addition, some Western cultural references, such as a mention of Mozart, assuming that students should have already known who Mozart is. On this vein, I must point out some of the multiple choice questions following the listening depend on the student's understanding their specific cultural references in order to be answered correctly. Not knowing these cultural references may cause a student to lose valuable points off the test. (by an English teacher)

Question # 37 on Regents U.S. Government in August 2000

The main obstacle to solving the problem shown in the cartoon was the
1)   failure of Congress to respond to public opinion
2)   Government's inability to fund social programs
3)   In efficiency of the Government's tax-collection
4)   demands of a variety of special interest groups

Analysis
All the people from box 1-5 are gathered together in box 6. An arm is holding out a mug with a $ sign on it, obviously asking these people for money. But, who is this person? Anyone who has lived in America and is familiar with this country's history and government will easily identify this arm as being the arm of "Uncle Sam"- also known as the U.S. government. So, the government is reaching out for money known for taxes from the people. A foreign-born student will not be able to interpret the symbolism of the arm reaching out.

American-born students have also been exposed to American History in the making through television, through the news, through newspapers, and through discussions of current events in school as part of their social studies and language arts classes. For example, they may be familiar with certain Supreme Court cases, certain laws that have been enacted, and the election process in this country, because of their exposure at an earlier age. Also, American-born students have read literature that relates to the history of this country. For instance, Huckleberry Finn is a book read by almost every American student and it familiarizes everyone with the era of slavery. Such books and even movies (for example, "Gone with the Wind," "Birth of a Nation," "Glory," "Pocahontas," etc. When a student enters junior year of high school, he/she takes a course in American History. During the first semester of the senior year, a student will take U.S. Government. These two courses are designed to inform students about American History as well as government. They have also had civics instruction in lower grades.

For an ELL student, who has not acculturated not received education in this country, this test question has put them in a disadvantage. Therefore, it is a culturally biased question. (by a social studies teacher)

FIGURE 4

knowledge in testing and evaluation in order to achieve validity. "Language tests should test language, and content tests should test content" (Mohan, 1986, p. 122). The intertwining of the content knowledge, cultural knowledge, and language knowledge on the standardized test can put ELL students at a disadvantage.

Although some of the language difficulties can be reduced by allowing the student to use dictionaries or to take extra time, students who have the previous education with different content objectives and instructive methods need more than a dictionary to pass these tests. For example, some Asian and European students come from an educational system where multiple choice questions were not used in the tests. They may have difficulty in approaching this type of standardized tests. They may be apprehensive about guessing between the choices unlike their native English speaking peers who have been trained to do so through their schooling. Also, language and reading challenge built into the questions comparable to the students' respective grade level cannot be overcome simply by using a dictionary or by sitting there for a longer time. Mohan (1982) compared and contrasted the levels of inference demanded in reading tests, including semantic inference, made by drawing a conclusion from the reader's world knowledge and factual inference made by drawing a conclusion from the reading material. In testing ELL students' content knowledge, if the demand for semantic inference is too great, then the test is for cultural knowledge rather than for content knowledge. Dong (1999a, 1999b) called for the reform on essay tests on college undergraduate students. She questioned the problematic use of agree/disagree essay format and its implication for ELL students' writing performance. Cited from the research literature and surveys from students from diverse language, cultural, and educational backgrounds, she argued for cross-cultural understanding in test design and test grading. Tables 9 through 14 are samples of such test items which pose tremendous language difficulties for ELL students. These language difficulties can be characterized as an over-complex sentence structure, switching back and forth between literal language and figurative language, confusing test directions, and use of uncommon vocabulary.

Butler and Stevens (2001) proposed several accommodations for English language learners in taking standardized tests like Regents exams. They include text modification strategies, such as assessing students' content knowledge in their native language, rephrasing the text questions to reduce linguistic complexity, providing cultural notes and glossaries, simplifying test directions, and reducing cultural bias. Moreover, ESL/bilingual teachers or personnel should be invited to the standardized tests such as the Regent's exams for assistance and support.

Several multilingual versions of the New York State Regents tests in content areas such as biology, global studies, US history and government, etc. have been developed for ELL students, including Chinese, Haitian Creole, Korean, Russian, and Spanish. However, what about the students whose native languages are different? They also recommended several administrative strategies to offer ELL support, including providing extra time, allowing the students to use bilingual dictionaries, and explaining the directions orally or in students' native language. These accommodation strategies are not the solutions to the problem.

Despite the above strategies used to accommodate ELL students' needs, more has to be done when the standardized testing involve a large number of ELL students. Reform in standardized testing is needed at three levels.

TABLE 9

Question 8 on Regent's Biology in January 2000
One immediate cause of a decrease in the rate of photosynthesis is a reduction in the availability of
_____

   1. carbon dioxide
   2. carbon monoxide
   3. hydrogen
   4. nitrogen

Analysis
The wording of the question could present a problem to non-native English speakers who may not be familiar with this typical scientific writing like the sentence above. The sentence is filled with big words, such as immediate, decrease, reduction, and availability, which make the reading difficult. In addition, students may be lost in the middle of the reading, since the subject of the sentence is so remote from the verb and the blank. Actually, the sentence does not have to be this complex in order to convey information. To help the students, I rewrote the question, and it could read, "If there is less_____, the rate of photosynthesis will be less." (by a science teacher)

First, with a significant number of students being ELL students in public schools in states such as New York, California, Texas, and Florida, an involvement of ESL/Bilingual professionals in the high-stakes test design and review for cultural bias and language accessibility are necessary. Norm procedures have to make sure to include ELL students. Is it fair to use a universal test to evaluate all students, including ELL students? Can a test designed to evaluate students from one culture be used to evaluate students from different cultures? If not, then we need to think about designing a different version of the test using modified language and reduced cultural bias for ELL students. Also, the answer and the rubric used in these tests have to be re-examined to see whether they are appropriate for ELL students. For example, can we judge an ELL student's response based solely on what we consider to be appropriate as shown in some social studies test items? Consider Tables 10 and 15.

Second, to prepare ELL students for the standardized tests like Regents, a general awareness toward language and cultural factors in content tests

TABLE 10

Question #33 on Regent's U.S. Government and History: August 2000
Question 33: Why Truman decided to drop the atomic bomb on Japan?
   1) to end the war while limiting American lives
   2) to punish the Japanese people by destroying their country
   3) increase Japan's potential as a future aggressor
   4) divert forces to fight Germany

Analysis
The correct answer is (1) to end the war while limiting American lives, but a student from Japan may choose (2) to punish the Japanese people by destroying their country. The student's answer is legitimate because that is how he/she learned the history of his/her country. (by a social studies teacher)

TABLE 11

Reading comprehension passage on Regent's English August 2002

Then Dad had a watch, which kept almost perfect time. He used to have me sit on his lap and show me this timepiece. He told me about what a wonderful thing this watch was, and he taught me to tell time by it. I learned how a man measured time before I knew what time was. Time was something to me, when I was a child, like wind and water. *Time was flowing and eternal, like an invisible river. We could divide it into seconds, minutes, hours, days, weeks, months and years, but that didn't bring us any closer to it. There were yesterdays, and time was with us now, and there would be tomorrows.* (an excerpt from Jesse Stuart's "Child's Time and Clock Time")

Reading comprehension Question:
As describe [here], the author viewed time as being
1. unfriendly
2. exact
3. abstract
4. perfect

Analysis
The passage begins in a regular, narrative voice and then it shifts to prose, talking philosophically and metaphorically about the writer's perception of time as shown in italics. For ELL students who may be familiar with descriptive and narrative writing, they may be confused by the change of the writing style. They may have difficulty in understanding this part of the abstract writing about time, thus unable to answer the question. (by an English teacher)

---

among mainstream teachers is necessary. With more and more ELL students coming into our classrooms for content specific education and with learning the language being part of learning the academic content, this awareness is especially crucial for the mainstream teachers to integrate language into their specific academic content instruction. Language awareness should be built into daily lesson planning and classroom assessment if the teacher deals with ELL students on a daily basis. I believe that planning on cultural notes, ESL anticipated difficulties, and language objectives in lesson designs will force the teacher to step back and think in the shoes of an ELL student. Once specific language and cultural difficulties for ELL students are articulated, the mainstream teachers are on their way to

TABLE 12

Critical Lens Statement in Regent's English August 2002
"If the literature we are reading does not wake us, why then do we read it? A literary work must be an ice-axe to break the sea frozen inside us." By Franz Kafka adapted

Analysis
The guidelines for this "Critical Lens" asks students to "provide a valid interpretation" of the quote. Could ESL learners be expected to infer and draw their own conclusions based on the quote? Could they be expected to have read two works that they have thoroughly concluded to "wake us"? In addition, the L2 learner could misconstrue the wording of the quote. To "wake", according to the English language means to waken. To get up from a sleep, even. ESL learners may have a hard time determining that the word should not be taken literally, rather figuratively. (by an English teacher)

TABLE 13

Regent's U.S. History and Government: June 2002
Question 3. The lack of a national executive and judiciary under the Articles of Confederation suggests that the founders of the American republic
    (1) risked tyranny for the sake of effective national government
    (2) copied the British constitution
    (3) prized national unity above the sovereignty of the state
    (4) feared a strong central government

Analysis:
The correct answer is choice (4). This question contains several difficult words: tyranny, sake, prized and sovereignty. The word "prized" is used to mean "favored" or "valued," and may not be the obvious meaning to a student who thinks a "prize" is something you win when you enter a contest. Tyranny and sovereignty are technical words used in social studies, but they can be difficult to understand. The word "sake" is not any easy word for ESL students and the phrase, "risked tyranny for the sake of effective national government" is itself extremely difficult, when it means, "wanted an effective national government, even though it might lead to tyranny." (by a social studies teacher)

TABLE 14

Regent's Global Studies: January 1999
Question 16
"North Americans are always among us, even when they ignore us or turn their back on us. Their shadow covers the whole hemisphere. It is the shadow of a giant." By Octavio Paz
Which attitude is being summarized by this Latin American writer?
    1. admiration for United States technology and wealth
    2. desire for American culture values and traditions
    3. resentment of United States economic and political influence
    4. envy of American democratic institutions

Analysis
For ELL students who are not from Latin countries or who are not familiar with the U.S. history with Latin American countries, this excerpt may confuse them from comprehending what the writer is trying to say. Use of prose instead of straightforward expository writing to make a point in a global history test adds difficulty to ELL students' comprehension. (by a social studies teacher)

TABLE 15

Regent's Global Studies: January 1999
Question 16
"North Americans are always among us, even when they ignore us or turn their back on us. Their shadow covers the whole hemisphere. It is the shadow of a giant." By Octavio Paz
Which attitude is being summarized by this Latin American writer?
    1. admiration for United States technology and wealth
    2. desire for American culture values and traditions
    3. resentment of United States economic and political influence
    4. envy of American democratic institutions

Analysis
For ELL students who are not from Latin countries or who are not familiar with the U.S. history with Latin American countries, this excerpt may confuse them from comprehending what the writer is trying to say. Use of prose instead of straightforward expository writing to make a point in a global history test adds difficulty to ELL students' comprehension. (by a social studies teacher)

reduce the difficulties and assist ELL students' learning. This awareness also helps mainstream content teachers to view the standardized tests from a set of different eyes. Tables 16-18 are examples of the above elements (cultural notes, ESL anticipated difficulties, and language objectives) prepared in lesson plans developed by mainstream teachers in my Language, Literacy, and Culture in Education course.

Third, more efforts have to be made to better evaluate ELL students. Research has shown great promise in using performance assessment techniques. Performance assessment, unlike standardized tests, evaluates students' learning in contexts by assigning students to perform specific tasks that require them to weave different knowledge sets and skills into a meaningful and coherent whole and by engaging students in reflecting on their authentic work that reflects their efforts, progress, and achievement over time (Khattri, Kahe, & Reeve, 1995; Paulson, Paulson, & Meyer, 1991; Wig-

TABLE 16

Subject: English
Students: 10th grade diverse students
Topic: Langston Hughes poem "Harlem"

Curricular Objectives:
Students will recognize the importance of diversity and reflect on their American dreams and the American dream Hughes talks about.
Students will understand Hughes' metaphorical use of language and use that language to write a poem about their American dreams.

Language Objectives:
The students will develop their expressive vocabulary, such as adjectives to describe their American dreams.
The students will be familiarized with the questioning technique that Hughes uses here to engage the reader.

ESL Anticipated Difficulties:
In Langston Hughes' poem, "Dream Deferred," certain words may be unfamiliar to the ESL student. A glossary is prepared (see below). In addition, a pre-activity, using a drawing of a raisin as a response to the poem recognizes the difficulty that an ELL student may have in understanding the symbolic use of raisin in this poem. Also, the creative use of six questions by Hughes in this poem should be examined for sentence structure and functions.

Cultural Notes:
This lesson is specifically geared toward the multicultural classroom of today and is especially fitting after the recent tragic events (9/11). The ESL students may not be familiar with the term "American Dream"-though that dream is what has brought them here; therefore, this term will be discussed in class. Students should be encouraged to share their stories of coming to America. Also, the importance and impact of Martin Luther King Jr. as a leader of the Civil Rights Movement during the 1960s may need to be introduced.

Glossary:
Deferred: delayed, postponed
Raisin: dried grape
Fester: rot, stale
Stink: smell bad
Crust and sugar over: sugar forming a hard surface
Sags: hangs down
Explode: blow up

TABLE 17

Subject: Social Studies
Students: Middle School 7th graders
Topic: The Preamble to the U.S. Constitution

Curricular Objectives:
Students will gain an understanding and an appreciation of the purposes of government as established over 200 years ago by internalizing the meaning behind the Preamble to the U.S. Constitution.

Language Objectives:
Students will comprehend a difficult government document through the use of provided glossary terms and interaction with a partner.
Students will rewrite the Preamble into an easier text for the class to understand.
Students will practice skills of reading, writing, speaking, and listening to accomplish this task.

ESL Anticipated Difficulties:
The text of the Preamble is somewhat difficult to comprehend, especially for second language learners. This is the reason I have provided a glossary of difficult terms. However, by "rewriting" this difficult document into language the whole class can understand, I hope to reduce the anxiety an ESL student would have in future interpretations of other difficult texts. Also, class dictionaries are encouraged to use for support. I will also use pair work to promote interaction and easy the reading difficulty.

Cultural Notes:
Students should be familiar with some idea of the laws which governments write and dictate. As part of the "do now", I will ask students if they are familiar with the written laws from their native country. That prior knowledge will lead into a discussion regarding the U.S. Constitution. If the student's country has laws written by different people and for different purposes, then it is a good idea to use that prior knowledge to compare and contrast that prior knowledge with what we will be learning.

The Preamble to the U.S. Constitution
We the People of the United States, in Order to form a more perfect Union, establish Justice, ensure domestic Tranquility, provide for the common defense, promote the general Welfare, and secure the blessings of Liberty to ourselves and our Posterity I do ordain and establish this Constitution for the United States of America.

<u>Glossary:</u>
<u>Union:</u> the United States of America are often called the Union.
<u>Establish:</u> to set up
<u>Justice:</u> the law, fairness
<u>Ensure:</u> to make something certain; to assure or guarantee it
<u>Domestic:</u> within or relating to one's country
<u>Tranquility:</u> calmness, peace
<u>Common:</u> The people; the community
<u>Defense:</u> the armed forces of a country.
<u>Promote:</u> to publicize
<u>General:</u> relating to, involving or applying to all
<u>Welfare:</u> the health, comfort, happiness of a person or a group, etc.
<u>Secure:</u> free from danger; feeling safety
<u>Blessings:</u> a cause of happiness, relief or comfort
<u>Liberty:</u> freedom
<u>Posterity:</u> future generations
<u>Ordain:</u> to arrange
Constitution: written rules and laws

TABLE 18

Subject: Earth Science
Students: 9th grade diverse students
Topic: Temperature field diagrams

Curricular Objectives:
Students will be able to:
Identify isotherm intervals on a map.
Construct temperature field diagrams.
Analyze temperature field diagrams in terms of gradient, profile and the location of the heat source

Language Objectives: Students will be able to:
Understand the scientific terms used to describe temperature fields.

ESL Anticipated Difficulties:
The anticipated language difficulty probably will be the scientific terminology, such as isotherm and gradient. The concepts of an Isotherm map should not be difficult for the students to understand once they understand that the term Isotherm means lines that connect the same temperature in a field. How do you get this across to the ESL learner? Most importantly I will break down the words by root and describe each one, like:

-Isotherm- *Iso* means equal and *therm* means heat therefore, Isotherm is a line drawn on a weather map connecting points having the same mean temperature.
-Gradient- A rate of change in certain variable factors, as pressure, temperature, inclination, etc.

Cultural Notes:
Meteorologists all over the world study weather and temperature changes. The idea of temperature should be familiar to most students. It may be extremely helpful to explain that the United States use Fahrenheit instead of Celsius. In order to activate students' prior cultural knowledge, probing questions about weather, temperature, and their home country can give the teacher an understanding of what knowledge these students have already obtained. If the students have learned something related to temperature fields, they can be encouraged to draw the fields or verbalize these concepts in their native language to enhance knowledge transfer.

gins, 1992). Performance assessment focuses on the process and the purpose of learning. It also goes beyond the knowledge telling and the passive learning model and enables the teacher to teach and assess creatively and students learn and demonstrate their learning actively.

In working with English language learners, performance assessment is especially enticing in that it offers a comprehensive view of these students' language learning and academic learning in context. Therefore, the teacher can trace students' progress and identify their strengths and weaknesses on an ongoing basis. Standardized tests are often used as an after-the-fact one shot device unable to accurately evaluate the performance of the learner when the learner's language skills are still developing. In the late 1990s, some high schools in New York City adopted the Regents Biology Variance Curriculum, which used a thematic approach to biology learning and teaching and focused on the conceptual development and inquiry in learning biology. Both native and non-native English speaking students in the selected New York City high schools were required to compile biology portfolios that included four research and creative biology projects and to complete two in-class free response essays during the school year besides taking the Regents biology exam by the end of the year. Students' final course grade was a combination of the three, the portfolio, the free response essays, and the Regents Biology Test. This curriculum, according to both the science chairs and the teachers, though still very limited, was better than the previous curriculum in that it offered more chances and an on-going process for students, especially non-native English speaking students, to succeed rather than to rely on the Regents biology exam alone.

The four biology projects included a science museum visit reflection, a month long journal documentation of a scientific experiment, an interview with a local scientist with reflection, and a reader response to a scientific journal article. These projects tapped into students' rich families and cultural backgrounds and engaged students in a unique and meaningful way. Rather than being an object of assessment, students were active participants in these tasks, conducting scientific experiments, seeking and interviewing scientists, visiting museums for discoveries, and reading for enrichment. The four projects offered rich opportunities to observe students in a broader context where students were doing science, reflecting on one's learning, conducting scientific inquiries, and making connections between biology learned in school and biology in real life. These performance assessment strategies should be included as part of the formal assessment. The following are some excerpts from these students' projects:

> My visit to the American Museum of Natural History in Manhattan last Friday was a big adventure for me. Since coming to over to America I have not had a chance to tour Manhattan myself. My father got me a subway map and I marked the place on the map before I left home. It took me an hour and a half by train to get there. There were a lot of exhibits in the museum. I chose "Ocean Life" because I liked the ocean most. The exhibit was on the first floor. Once I walked into the entrance of the exhibit, I was in the middle of the ocean world. The introduction gave me an idea of what a fish was: an aquatic vertebrate animal, usually possessing gills in the adult stage and having limbs in the forms of fins. I was fascinated to learn that unlike other commonly recognized groups of animals, the fish is a heterogeneous assemblage of groups that cannot be recognized by any defining trait. So the word fish can refer to an individual fish or a group of fish. The exhibit was divided into four sections. They were: diversity and evolution, anatomy, breathing, reproduction of the fish . . . I was glad that I learned about the use of the word *fish*. The most interesting thing I found is the fish's external fertilization and development. The exhibit said that a single cod could produce about three million eggs. What happens to these three million eggs once they are produced? Do other fish eat them before they are fertilized? What is the birth rate for these eggs? I have taken a lot of notes and am thinking to investigate the fish in my fish tank at home.—By a Bangladeshi student

I interviewed my father an Albanian doctor specialized in cardiology. He has been working for 30 years in my country. However, because of the war, we had to leave our country and move to the US last year. Now he is no longer a doctor, but I still have immense respect for him. When I asked my father about his career, he told that he graduated from the University of Medicine of Tirana, Albania. After the medical school, he worked as a country doctor for two years and then was employed as a cardiologist at Berat Hospital. He has published a lot of scientific articles and many books. He also worked as an adjunct professor at University of Medicine and a member of Albanian Cardiology Association. He was honored with the highest award: Doctor of Medical Science for his achievement. When I asked what was the most difficult time in his career as a doctor, my father told me that was the time when he was a country doctor, a doctor away from the big city that he didn't have enough experience and sometimes he didn't have the necessary medication for the patients. Also being far away from other doctors made his work very difficult. At the end of this investigation I asked myself if I wanted to enter this career. My early childhood dream has been to be a doctor. Raised in a family where my father is a doctor and looking to him and admiring him for what he was doing, I always wonder what else can I be better than being a doctor. After finishing this interview, I found that I learned a lot from my father and knew more about why I wanted to be a doctor.—By an Albanian student

Day 12

The plant, Accent Carmine Impatiens, in the shoebox in the corner of my room is almost dying due to lack of light. The unborn baby flower is dead. Some of the leaves are already fallen apart. I could see the difference now between the second plant and this one. The second plant at the window with sunlight is still green and healthy. Most of its leaves are green and its branches are growing taller. I give both plants water. The second plant looks very nice and the leaves are wide like yesterday's leaves. By now I could answer my own questions between the two plants that I experimented . . . (An excerpt from a Korean student's journal on an experiment on two identical plants one receiving the sunlight and other without light.)

I recently read an interesting article named "The cell from hell: Pfiesteria strikes again—in the Chesapeake Bay" written by Mary Hager and Larry Reibstein and published in *NewsWeek*. After reading the article I learned that from the beginning of organisms on earth, there has been a struggle between these organisms for food. Many of these organisms used to change their homes and stay out of trouble in order to survive. As we learned in our biology class, often strong organisms survive and weak ones die. Most recently, scientists discovered a micro-organism in water called Pfiesteria. Even though it is a tiny organism, it has an unusual survival ability. It can reproduce rapidly and it kills hundreds and thousands of fish. This organism was first discovered by a botanist, Dr. Joann Brukholder in 1991. However, there has no research done to investigate the impact of Pfiesteria on humans. Some scientists even wonder whether fish killed was because of Pfiesteria or the polluted water. I like this article because writers give us different points of views about Pfiesteria. It shows that in biology we are constantly learning new things and finding the unknown. My question is why they named this organism Pfiesteria? What are some of the ways that the scientists can investigate the real cause for the fish's death? As I live close to the East River I know there are many things to consider in order to be certain that Pfiesteria is the killer. I would like to keep reading about this topic and find out more about it. (by a Columbian student)

CHAPTER 4

TAPPING INTO ENGLISH LANGUAGE LEARNERS' PRIOR KNOWLEDGE

TAPPING INTO ENGLISH LANGUAGE LEARNERS' PRIOR KNOWLEDGE IN SCIENCE INSTRUCTION

English language learners have prior knowledge about the world that they come from either through their life experiences or their home school learning. For these students to embark the new knowledge, it is natural to begin with what they know (Allen-Sommerville, 1996; Banks & Banks, 1997). This identifying or activating students' prior knowledge is crucial because English language learners are more likely than their native peers to approach the new knowledge with apprehension. Daunted by the task of learning the new language and the new content knowledge, they often focus on what they don't know and what they lack in the subject matter knowledge. Therefore, they first need to be convinced that they might have some knowledge on a given topic, they have something to offer, and the learning task is not an impossible one. A few ideas below illustrate what

Teaching Language and Content to Linguistically and Culturally Diverse Students:
Principles, Ideas, and Materials; pages 67–95.
A Volume in: Language Studies in Education
Copyright © 2004 by Information Age Publishing, Inc.
All rights of reproduction in any form reserved.
ISBN: 1-59311-088-X (paper), 1-59311-089-8 (cloth)

biology teachers can do to tap the new knowledge into English language learners' prior knowledge in their teaching of sciences.

HOME SCIENCE LEARNING SURVEY

English language learners are new to American culture and the English language, however, they are not new to reading and writing in their native language. Many of them have already had some schooling, if not equivalent to American grade levels. Therefore, a science teacher must become aware of their reading and writing habits back home. A questionnaire on their reading and writing habits can reveal a lot more information on what

TABLE 19

1. A good science reader is a learner who
    a.   reads fast
    b.   memorizes what s/he reads
    c.   understands all the words
    d.   always makes guesses
    e.   does other things (Please explain.)   _____

2. Do you like reading about science in your native language? Why?
    _____

3. Do you like learning science in your school back home? Why?

4. What did you learn in science before coming to America?
    a. plants
    b. animals
    c. chemistry
    e. physical science
    f. other (Please explain.) _____

5. How did you learn science back home?
    a. Reading and memorizing the textbook
    b. listening and memorizing the teacher's lecture
    d. taking the test
    e. writing science papers
    f. doing science projects
    f. other (Please explain.) _____

6. How do you read the science textbook in English?
    a. translate the reading into my native language
    b. look up in a dictionary for every new word (my native language dictionary)
    c. read more slowly and memorize each word
    d. read aloud to practice my pronunciation
    e. ask my friend from my country for help with reading
    f. do other things (Please explain.) _____

7. How is it different in class between your learning back home and learning here in the U.S.?

8. What is most difficult for you to learn biology in English?

they have been doing, why they do what they do, and the differences in their reading and writing lives in comparison to American teenagers. If the students are newcomers, the questionnaire can be translated into their languages with the help of a bilingual teacher or bilingual student. By surveying students on their home learning, the teacher has not only learned what s/he can capitalize and address later but also set the tone for a positive classroom learning environment where students' home culture and background are appreciated. Sample questions are in Table 19.

HOME COUNTRY BIOMES

English language learners are experts of their own country. A biology teacher can set the stage of the unit on ecology, for example, by asking the students to identify their country first and then show the deserts, mountains, forests, grasslands, oceans, rivers, etc., on the map. For newcomers, a bilingual map or a map brought by the student can be used for the purpose. Or the teacher can group students who come from the same country or cultural background together for the task. Working with the whole class, the teacher can ask students to describe their country, identify those biomes that they know, and compare and contrast the biomes in their

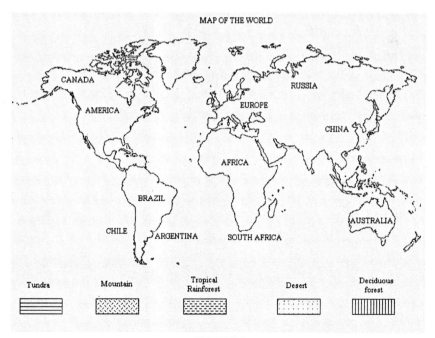

FIGURE 5

country with those of the US (see Figure 5). Based on what class has come up with, the teacher then introduces the new concepts and the readings on biomes and ecosystems.

HOME CULTURE FOOD CHAIN

Before going into the topic on food chain, a biology teacher can ask English language learners to draw a food chain based on a favorite home meal that they like or used to have in their country. For example, a Chinese student likes to eat Chinese dumplings (Figure 6). The dumplings are made of flour, vegetables such as cabbage, and pork or beef. Pork comes from the pig which eats vegetables, and beef from the cow which eats grass. Thus, the food chain is structured with humans on the top, pig and cow on the second level, and vegetables and grass at the bottom. Based on what class has come up with, the teacher then can proceed to talk about the topic on food chain.

EXOTIC HABITATS

In this activity, the biology teacher asks students to brainstorm the plants and animals that they know (Keating, 1997) to use students' home cultural knowledge as a starting point of instruction. English language learners can begin with their home town or city and use the legends to work their way

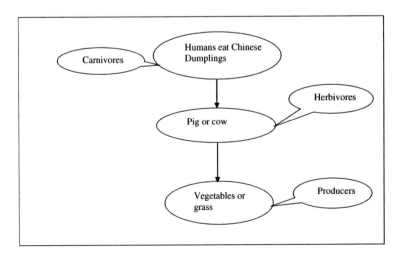

FIGURE 6

TABLE 20

Animals	Country	Habitat
Panda	China	Southwest mountains in China
Water buffalo	Turkey	Grassland in Black Sea
The Ferruginous Duck	Poland	Wet low land
llama	Peru	South American mountains

through the map. Or students can draw their own map and give information in both English and their native language. Students who come from the same cultural backgrounds form groups of three or five and are supposed to come up with a chart filled information as much as possible on their animals and plants. As a whole class, the teacher can lead the class to compare the charts between groups and countries for similarities and differences and ask questions about geographic location and characteristics features of the habitats of these plants and animals (Table 20).

Further questions can ask students to describe what they have come up with as follows:

- What does this animal eat?
- Where does this animal live?
- What does this animal fear most?
- Who is this animal's friend?
- How does this animal get its food?

IMMIGRANT POPULATION GROWTH PATTERNS

English language learners' families and communities are rich sources for learning about population growth and for the teacher to get to know students' family backgrounds (Brouse, 1990). Many topics in science can be easily connected to students' home culture and family history. For example, in talking about population growth patterns, students can actively seek information from their parents or elders in the community, thus involve family in the learning. By doing so, immigrant students' parents will feel their culture and history are an important a part of their children's education, thus enhance both students' self-concept and school and family relationship. Very often teachers believe that immigrant parents cannot help their children with homework due to their lack of English proficiency. However, these teachers do not realize that these parents have a lot of offer to their children's education. Harris Stone and Stephen Collins (1973, p. 68) designed an activity using students' interviews and information cards to find out (see Table 21).

TABLE 21

Population Survey		
Family of Carlos		
1. Age of mother ___ Age of the youngest child ___ Age of the oldest child ___		
Age of father ___ Age of the youngest child ___ Age of the oldest child ___		
2. Would another child crowd the home? Yes___ No ___		
3. Number of children in the family. _____		
4. More children expected? Yes ___ No ___ How many? ____		

a.   The average childbearing age of the people in your culture
b.   People's feelings about how large their families should be.
c.   Their feelings about what is a "crowded" condition.

TAPPING INTO ENGLISH LANGUAGE LEARNERS' PRIOR KNOWLEDGE IN MATHEMATICS INSTRUCTION

Culturally Varied Ways of Learning Mathematics

We often hear people say that mathematics is a universal language. It is typically expected that students, no matter what their native language is, will have little language problem with learning mathematics in English because numbers speak the same. This folk knowledge, however, has to be re-examined when we work with students whose native language is not English. While some mathematical symbols are universal across cultures, others are quite different. The procedures used to solve mathematical problems can be complex or even contradictory across languages. One example is the culturally varied ways of solving division problems. A colleague told me a story about a mathematics teacher's frustration with a boy from Colombia who just couldn't do it even after several individualized lessons. Out of desperation, the teacher asked the boy, "Can you just follow what I am doing step by step?" The boy said, "if you just let me do it my way." The boy began showing the teacher his way and came up with the correct answer. At that moment, the teacher's mind clicked. She turned around asking the whole class, "Can you show me the different ways of doing this problem?" In a few minutes, the teacher got three more different ways. Dawe (1986) and Philipp (1996) emphasized an increased attention on the part of the teacher to students' culturally varied procedures of

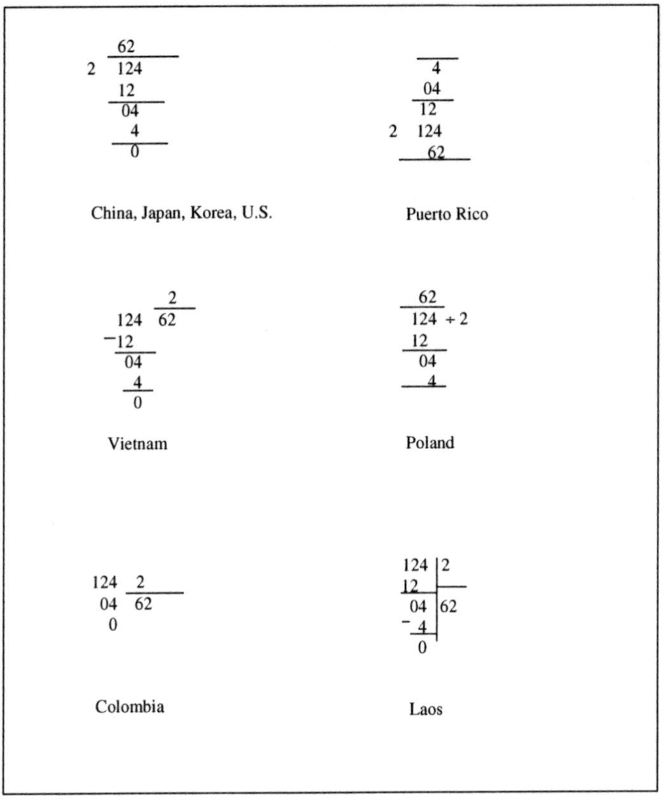

```
        62
   2 ‾124‾‾                               ‾4‾‾
     12                                    04
    ‾04‾                                  ‾12‾
      4                             2   124
    ‾0‾                                   62

   China, Japan, Korea, U.S.            Puerto Rico


              2                           62
    124  ‾62‾‾                        124 + 2
   −12                                 12
   ‾04‾                                ‾04‾
     4                                   4
   ‾0

     Vietnam                            Poland


                                      124 │2
   124  2                             12  │‾‾‾
   04  ‾62‾‾                          ‾04‾│62
    0                                 − 4 │
                                      ‾0‾

    Colombia                           Laos
```

FIGURE 7

doing mathematics, such as algorithms. Figure 7 shows different ways of solving division problems across cultures.

Another culturally varied way of learning mathematics is done through a critical examination of the number formation and words used to describe these numbers across languages. The English system of numeration is based on grouping by tens and powers of ten with language endings such as -teen and -ty as tens (Figure 8).

In other languages, number description is different, thus revealing different patterns in the expression. By exploring these differences, both native and non-native English speakers will gain a new appreciation for a creative way that people throughout the world express themselves in words for a number. Also, by exploring mathematics for patterns and meaning trains students the ability of logical thinking skills. Finally, an activity like this gives English language learners an opportunity to shine. Figures 9 and 10 are examples of such an analysis.

Number	English	Number	English	Number	English
1	one	11	eleven		
2	two	12	twelve (2+10)	20	twenty (2·10)
3	three	13	thirteen (3+10)	30	thirty (3·10)
4	four	14	fourteen (4+10)	40	forty (4·10)
5	five	15	fifteen (5+10)	50	fifty (5·10)
6	six	16	sixteen (6+10)	60	sixty (6·10)
7	seven	17	seventeen (7+10)	70	seventy (7·10)
8	eight	18	eighteen (8+10)	80	eighty (8·10)
9	nine	19	nineteen (9+10)	90	ninety (9·10)
10	ten				

FIGURE 8

Number	French	Number	French	Number	French
1	un	11	onze (1+10)		
2	deux	12	douze (2+10)	20	vingt
3	trois	13	treize (3+10)	30	trente (3·10)
4	quatre	14	quatorze(4+10)	40	quarante (4·10)
5	cinque	15	qunize (5+10)	50	cinquante (5·10)
6	six	16	seize (6+10)	60	soixante (6·10)
7	sept	17	dix-sept(10+7)	70	soixante-dix (6·10+10)
8	huit	18	dix-huit (10+8)	80	quatre-vingt (4·20)
9	neuf	19	dix-neuf (10+9)	90	quatre-vingt-dix
10	dix				(4·20+10)

FIGURE 9

Number	Chinese	Number	Chinese		Number	Chinese	
1	一	11	十一	(10+1)			
2	二	12	十二	(10+2)	20	二十	(2x10)
3	三	13	十三	(10+3)	30	三十	(3x10)
4	四	14	十四	(10+4)	40	四十	(4x10)
5	五	15	十五	(10+5)	50	五十	(5x10)
6	六	16	十六	(10+6)	60	六十	(5x10)
7	七	17	十七	(10+7)	70	七十	(7x10)
8	八	18	十八	(10+8)	80	八十	(8x10)
9	九	19	十九	(10+9)	90	九十	(9x10)
10	十				100	一百	(1x100)

FIGURE 10

Historical Inquiry of Cross-Cultural Mathematics

One area of multicultural education is to use linguistically and culturally diverse students' own culture and history as a context for learning (Banks, 1993; Zaslavsky, 1991, 1999) by including non-Western knowledge and perspectives in the curriculum and instruction. In mathematics, a teacher can use a history inquiry approach to exposing students to non-Western culture's mathematical achievements, or ethno-mathematics. This not only corrects the misconception that Western cultures are mathematically

---

Chinese Kou Ku Xuan: Pythagorean Theorem

The earliest extant Chinese text on astronomy and mathematics, the Chou Pei, is notable for a diagrammatic demonstration of the Pythagorean (or kou ku) theorem. Needham's translation of the relevant passage is illustrated by the figure below, drawn from the original text. The passage reads:

Let us cut a rectangle (diagonally), and make the width 3 (units) wide, and the length 4 (units) long. The diagonal between the (two) corners will then be 5 (units) long. Now, after drawing a square on this diagonal, circumscribe it by half-rectangles like that which has been left outside, so as to form a (square) plate. Thus the (four) outer half-rectangles, of width 3, length 4 and diagonal 5, together make two rectangles (of area 24); then (when this is subtracted from the square plate of area 49) the remainder is of area 25. This process is called 'piling up the rectangles'. (Needham, 1959, pp. 22-3)

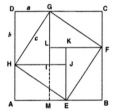

In terms of the figure above, the larger square ABCD has side $3 + 4 = 7$ and thus area 49. If, from this large square, four triangles (AHE, BEF, CFG and DGH), making together two rectangles each of area $3 \times 4 = 12$, are removed, this leaves the smaller square HEFG. And implicitly,

$$(3 + 4)^2 - 2(3 \times 4) = 3^2 + 4^2 = 5^2$$

The extension of this 'proof' to a general case was achieved in different ways by Chao Chung Ching and Liu Hui, two commentators living in the third century AD. In modern notation, Chao's extension may be stated thus: if the shorter (kou) and longer (ku) sides of one of the rectangles are a and b respectively, and its diagonal (shian) is c, then the above reasoning would produce

$$c^2 = (b-a)^2 + 2ab \quad = \text{square IJKL} + \text{rect DGIH} + \text{rect CFLG}$$
$$= \text{square AMIH} + \text{square MBFL}$$
$$= a^2 + b^2$$

An alternative explanation is based on the identity

$$(a + b)^2 \quad = a^2 + 2ab + b^2$$
$$c^2 = (a + b)^2 - 2ab = a^2 + b^2$$
$$= \text{square ABCD} - 4 \text{ ? DGH}$$

(from the <u>Crest of the Peacock</u> Joseph, G. G. pp. 180-181, Princeton University Press, 1991)

FIGURE 11

advanced or superior, but also helps English language learners relate to the subject matter knowledge by validating and embracing the mathematical contributions made by their cultures. Students can be invited to do a group project on such a historical inquiry by asking non-native speaking students about how some of the mathematical principles and terms were derived in their cultures and varied ways of solving problems. The following are examples of cross-cultural mathematics (Figures 11-13).

Native American Perceptions of Geometry

The Power of the Circle

You have noticed that everything an Indian does is in a circle, and that is because the Power of the World always works in circles, and everything tries to be round. In the old days when we were a strong and happy people, all our power came to us from the sacred hoop of the nation, and so long as the hoop was unbroken, the people flourished. The flowering tree was the living center of the hoop, and the circle of the four quarters nourished it. The east gave peace and light, the south gave warmth, the west gave rain, and the north with its cold and mighty wind gave strength and endurance. This knowledge came to us from the outer world with our religion.

Everything the Power of the World does is done in a circle. The sky is round, and I have heard that the earth is round like a ball, and so are all the stars. The wind, in its greatest power, whirls. Birds make their nests in circles, for theirs is the same religion as ours. The sun comes forth and goes down again in a circle. The moon does the same, and both are round. Even the seasons form a great circle in their changing, and always come back again to where they were. The life of a man is a circle from childhood to childhood, and so it is in everything where power moves. Our tepees were round like the nests of birds, and these were always set in a circle, the nation's hoop, a nest of many nests, where the Great Spirit meant for us to hatch our children. (from *Black Elk Speaks*, told by John G. Neihardt, 1998, pp. 194-196)

African Counts

Counting by 10s by people from Africa, such as Zulu people, was based on the use of finger counting, making signs with fingers for each number. Finger counting became such a popular tradition that people used their fingers as a handy calculator (Zaslavsky, 1999). As a result, the meaning of the numbers from one to ten in the Zulu language presents strong visual images associated with finger counting (Figure 14).

Home Learning Experience with Mathematics

Many second language learners encountering a new learning environment and learning tasks in English tend to think that what they learned

Arabic Algebra

The word *al-jabr* appears frequently in Arab mathematical texts that followed al-Khwarizmi's influential *Hisab al-jabr w'al-muqabala,* written in the first half of the ninth century. There were two meanings associated with *al-jabr.* The more common was 'restoration', as applied to the operation of adding equal terms to both sides of an equation so as to remove negative quantities, or to 'restore' a quantity which is subtracted from one side by adding it to the other. Thus an operation on the equation $2x + 5 = 8 - 3x$ which led to $5x + 5 = 8$ would be an illustration of *al-jabr.* There was also another, less common: multiplying both sides of an equation by a certain number to fractions. Thus if both sides of the equation $(9/4)x + 1/8 = 3 + (5/8)x$ were multiplied by 8 to give the new equation $18x + 1 = 24 + 15x,$ *this too* would be an instance of *al-jabr.* The common meaning of al-muqabala is the 'reduction' of positive quantities in an equation by subtracting equal quantities from both sides. So for the two equations above, applying *al-muqabala* would give

$$5x + 5 = 8$$
$$5x + 5 - 5 = 8-5$$
$$5x = 3$$

and

$$18x + 1 = 24 + 15x$$
$$18x - 15x + 1 - 1 = 24- 1 + 15x - 15x$$
$$3x = 23$$

The words *al-jabr* and *al-muqabala,* linked by *wa,* meaning 'and', came to be used for any algebraic operation, and eventually for the subject itself. Since the algebra of the time was almost wholly confined to the solution of equations, the phrase meant exactly that.

(from the <u>Crest of the Peacock</u> Joseph, G. G. pp. 324, Princeton University Press, 1991)

FIGURE 12

Russian Peasant Algorithm

Multiply 225 by 17
Solution

→	225	17
	112	34
	56	68
	28	136
	14	272
→	7	544
→	3	1088
→	1	2176

$$17+544+1088+2176=3825$$

This method, known in the West as the 'Russian peasant method', works by expressing the multiplicand, 225, as the sum of powers of 2:

$$225=1(2^0) + 0(2^1) + 0(2^2) + 0(2^3) + 0(2^4) + 1(2^5) + 1(2^6) + 1(2^7)$$

Adding the results of multiplying each of these components by 17 gives the answer.

(from the <u>Crest of the Peacock</u> by Joseph, G. G. pp. 65, Princeton University Press, 1991)

FIGURE 13

Number	Zulu word	Meaning
1	nye	State of being alone
2	bili	Raise a separate finger
3	thathu	To take
4	ne	To join
5	hlanu	All the fingers united
6	isithupa	Take the right thumb
7	isikhombisa	Point with the forefinger of right hand
8	isihiyagalombili	Leave out two fingers
9	isihiyagalunye	Leave out one finger
10	ishumi	Cause to stand

(from Africa Counts by Claudia Zasklavsky, pp. 47, Lawrence Hill Books, 1999)

FIGURE 14

TABLE 22

Math Survey

I have learned math for _____ years.

	Agree	Disagree
I am good at math.	_____	_____
I did well in math in my native country.	_____	_____
Math is my favorite subject back home.	_____	_____
I believe math will be useful in my future.	_____	_____
My parents push me to learn math.	_____	_____
Math is difficult to learn.	_____	_____
Learning math in English is difficult for me.	_____	_____

In my native country, I learned math through (check all the relevant answers)
_____memorizing math rules and formulas
_____practicing problems over and over again
_____asking for help from someone who is good at math
_____taking notes from the teacher
_____reading the math textbook
_____going over a math workbook
_____working with my peers or classmates on math problems
_____Other (please explain)

My math teacher back home taught us math by (check all the relevant answers)
_____explaining the rules and formulas
_____demonstrating how to solve a problem
_____assigning us to do many exercises every day
_____asking us to memorize the rules and formulas
_____teaching us how to think
_____grouping us into study groups to work on math problems
_____other (please explain)

Is there any difference in the writing of mathematical expressions or in ways of solving problems in math you learned back home compared with math you learn here in the U.S.?

How different is the way of teaching by your math teacher back home compared with your math teacher here?

What is the most important factor influencing how well you do in math here in the U.S.?

What is your biggest problem in learning math now?

back home in their native country is useless. They have to abandon what they have learned in their native language in order to learn English. However, it is not true. Cognitive second language learning theory argues that certain cognitive abilities are shared cross-language and can aid students' learning in a second language (Cummins, 1984, 1986). In learning mathematics, even though the vocabulary sounds and looks different at first glance, however, it might not be that different if the students use cognitive learning strategies to connect actively the mathematical concepts and ideas expressed in English with those in their native language. In doing so, students make active transfers of knowledge between languages and English words once they are linked with certain concepts in their native language become easier to learn. Therefore, knowledge about English language learners' mathematics learning back home in their native country is important for a mathematics teacher to seek actively. Table 22 is a sample survey about these learners' previous mathematics learning.

TAPPING INTO ENGLISH LANGUAGE LEARNERS' PRIOR KNOWLEDGE IN ENGLISH LANGUAGE ARTS INSTRUCTION

Story of Journey to America

Every English language learner brings to the classroom a deep reservoir of experiences that the English teacher can exploit (Dong, 1998, 2002). These stories could be about escaping from a war, joining long separated parents, pursuing a better life, etc. By providing opportunities for these students to tell their stories orally or in writing in English, the English teacher motivates these students to communicate to the class, generates a sense of belonging, and acknowledges that these students have led an unique life. Another benefit of these stories is that the reader or the audience of the stories will gain a new understanding of their peers and of cultures other than their own. Even though these students might talk about the difficulties of adjusting to the new culture and learning the new language and revealing a sense of frustration and homesickness, the sharing of these experiences and feelings provides these students with some sense of acceptance, understanding, and validation of what they have been going through. For the students who are new to this culture, these stories drawn from their own interests and experiences can serve as an icebreaker and a confidence booster for them. In addition, these stories are usually received with enthusiasm by classmates. Here are few stories told by English language learners:

I arrived in America on August 16, 1999. When I first came to the USA, I had a hard time to live in the USA. I am sure my parents had much harder time than I had. I didn't know how to speak English. In order to assimilate myself into the new culture I chose to embark on a high school football career. Playing football changed my whole life in my new country. Since I had cultural and language barriers, playing football with new American friends was not as easy as I thought it would be. I faced new and unfamiliar challenges including four hours of practice daily after school that made me exhausted. I had to study twice as hard as American students to close my language gap. Sleeping was kept minimum. I fought with tiredness every night. I tried hard to make the team. I knew it is a tough sport, that's one of the reasons I tried out for it. When I made the team I felt so excited and happy that I earned a spot to play on the team with my friends. Sometimes I had a hard time understanding what the Coaches were saying and what my friends were laughing and talking about. Over the years, I have improved my listening and speaking English skills day by day. Football also allowed me to meet many new friends who became my best friends. I had a lot of fun with my teammates and coaches during the 2 seasons I played. I received a lot of help from my teachers, coaches, parents and friends. Although I had really hard time in America at the beginning I learned a lot from my challenges. I will keep working hard the best as I can.—A Korean 12th grader

Coming to the US is something very important for the people in my country (Dominican Republic) especially for people in the place that I used to live in. People down there where I used to live in are very poor. They think that by coming to the US they are going to have a better future. But not all are fortunate enough to come to the US, and my family and I are lucky ones to come here. My grandmother came to the US first. I really don't know how she did. Then she brought her 11 children. My father was one of the last children who came to the US After five years, my father was able to bring us to the US, my mother, my sister, my brothers, and me. When I came to the US, I was 8 and I started going to school in PS 108 in the 3rd grade, and then went to IS 302. I am going to be able to go to university and be the best that I can be.— A Dominican 9th grader

It was difficult to me for adapt to this country because first I didn't know how to speak English and it was hard. I do not have a lot of friends because people here don't speak the language I speak. When I came to school for the first time, I felt very bad because I didn't understand what the teacher was teaching. Fortunately, the teacher asked to all the class if someone spoke Spanish so they could translate for me. I became a friend with the girl who helped me to learn English, and through her I met other people. But I never gonna forget my country Colombia because my family and all my friends are still there.—A Colombian 9th grader

Here in America the school is different from my country. In Colombia, we stay in one room all the day and we have the same teacher for all classes or sometimes we have different teacher but we stay in the same room . . . Another difference is that the teacher in my country speaks Spanish and teaches in Spanish. But here many teachers can speak Spanish but they don't teach in Spanish. The textbooks we use here for social studies talk about America and Colombia, not like the textbooks we had back in Colombia, it was all about Colombia . . . I really like better in Colombia because I was born there and I can't adapt the life in America. I am not saying that I don't like this country because I really do. But the thing is that in Colombia I have all my family, my friends, and I miss them. But my parents are there and I have to be here with they, and my parents say that you can have a better life, and better education, and a good job.—A Colombian 11th grader

When I first came to this country from Bangladesh, I felt alone. I didn't know anyone in this country. I feel like I was stuck on an island with my family. I couldn't speak English. All I did was sleep for two months in home and watch TV. So after a couple of months I went to school. I felt like I didn't go to school but I went a different world where no one knew me. I could not talk with them or communicate with them because all of them spoke was English. Some kids made fun of me because the way I wore my clothes. They thought wasn't cool. A lot of teachers didn't understand me, even my ESL teacher couldn't understand me . . . I started to learn English and I started to communicate with other people. After one year, I spoke more English. I was able to say what my problem was. So that was three years ago. Now I speak English. But the way I pronounce things, it's not American. It's British way. I have to learn more English when I go to ESL. I think I am going to succeed and I feel like I am going to graduate from high school.—A Bangladeshi 10th grader

Going to a new school in a new country was very difficult for me and I was scared to attend school. In the beginning I believed that the only language spoken at school was English. My first days of school were tormenting. When I first arrived to a classroom, I found myself lost in a place which I didn't belong. As I sat next to other students, I heard them talk and play, but I couldn't be part of that. I remember my first teacher. She was from Cuba. She used to help me so much with my English. Sometimes when other students bothered me, she was there to defend me. Learning English was very difficult. At the beginning it was a total frustration. Each day of school I was learning new words.—A Cuban 9th grader

Home Language and Literacy Survey

Knowing about English language learners' home culture and language as well as their journeys to America is the first step towards culturally responsive teaching. Many English language learners who come to American high schools are already literate in their native language and have received an education back home. Even if some students have an interrupted schooling owing to wars, their knowledge about their native language and their educational experiences back home can be used as a resource in teaching. Research studies have found that educational and literacy learning expectations and experiences are culturally varied (Ballard & Clanchy, 1991; Holyoak & Piper, 1997; Kaplan, 1988; Matalene, 1985; Purves, 1986). Students from different cultures often hold different expectations and have varied literacy experiences. Those expectations and experiences are often a mismatch with what the teacher expects and what a student who has grown up in America. These mismatches could lead to clashes and frustration on both sides and result in students' poor performance. Therefore, investigating these students' previous educational and literacy experiences becomes important in order to provide culturally responsive teaching. In an English class, the teacher can either ask the students individually for such information or survey them to see their preferred ways of learning and the cultural norms which existed in their past educational experiences. This information gained from such an inquiry can raise the teacher's consciousness of his or her ways of teaching and detect possible mismatches in teaching and learning between the teacher and the student. The following is an example of a survey of students' previous writing experiences:

- What is your native language?
- When and how did you learn to write in your native language?
- What writing assignments do you remember that your teacher back home assigned to you?
- How did your teacher back home go about teaching you how to write in your native language?
- What are the differences between writing in English and writing in your native language?
- Do you write in your native language now? If so, what do you write about and to whom?

By focusing on differences as well as similarities in the language, culture, educational system, and reading and writing experiences, an English teacher can guide these students to write reflectively and critically about their prior life or school experiences. Writing something that these students have knowledge about while others may not stimulates motivation and creates a genuine purpose for communication. In addition, students' writing like this can further inform the teacher of the areas of difficulties and possible mismatches in teaching and learning to tailor his or her instruction to these students' needs (Shen, 1989). An example of such a writing survey is in Table 23.

Below are the responses from both high school and college students when asked to write about the differences between writing in English and writing in their native language:

TABLE 23

Writing Survey

Your Name:
Your Native Language:
Language that you can write:
When did you learn to write in English?
Where did you learn to write in English?

Under each statement, check the blank that you think fits you best.
a. I am good at reading in English.   Agree__   Disagree__

b. I am good at writing in English.   Agree__   Disagree__

c. What kinds of writing did you do in your school back home?
___stories   ___journals   ___research papers
___essays   ___poems   ___letters
___no writing at all   ___other (please specify)

d. How did your teacher teach you how to write back home?
__brainstorming ideas   ___class discussing on the topic
__writing an outline   ___asking for more drafts
__providing a model of good writing   ___revising my papers
__correcting and commenting on my writing   ___using peer responses
__reading famous writers' works as models   ___lecturing on how to organize
__memorizing good phrases and words   ___teaching grammar and words
Other (Please specify) _____

e. How frequently did you write for school back home? (write down the number of times you wrote for
school work)
__1~2 times a week   ___3 more times a week
__1~2 times a month   ___3 more times a month
__Other (Please specify)

Mark the following expectations that apply to you.
f. I expect my writing to be corrected word by word by my English teacher.
___Yes   ___No

g. To me, copying words from the text without saying where they are from is acceptable
___Yes   ___No

h. I like to have my friends or my classmates read what I have written in English.
___Yes   ___No

i. I use the following sources when I write in English:
___a native language dictionary   ___a grammar book
___a writing manual   ___an English dictionary
___a bilingual dictionary   ___a thesaurus
___other (Please specify)

Bengali vs. English

One difference is that here in English when we write a paragraph, we have a
main idea. And for that main idea, we have to give details to support the
main idea. The details have to be so clear that everybody can understand
[them]. But in my country [Bangladesh], my culture, sometimes, we were
not encouraged to give details, we just gave some hints. And nobody had any
problem understanding these hints.

Chinese vs. English

In China there is no I. There is "we." The word "I" is used as a bad word like "individual." This is disrespectful to the government in China. To be selfish is very bad in China.

My Chinese teachers helped me know how they wrote by explaining the words they chose and ideas they wrote about. We can copy their words and this is a way of learning flow to write.

I must memorize beautiful phrases and sentences included in dictionaries hoping that I may use them in future writing assignments. I must quote others writing and turn to other essays for help and reference and turn to handouts containing famous quotes for reference in writing.

I consider it important to memorize sentences to write better. If the English teacher required me to write a long English essay, I would turn to famous sayings and sentences derived from famous writers and essays on the same topic. I would imitate what other people say and use their sentences in my essays. I would use famous sayings, proverbs, and quotable phrases quite often, just as I use them very often in writing Chinese essays, for I consider they are essential in writing Chinese and English essays.

Greek vs. English

I found that American system of writing an essay is very different from the system in my country. In Greek, if we write an essay, we don't write it in five paragraphs. You can use as many paragraphs as you can. Also, you don't have to give details and examples. One important criterion in distinguishing a good essay from a bad essay is by your use of vocabulary. The more complex words and long sentences you use, the better the essay.

Japanese vs. English

In Japan we are modest and polite. What we call old fashion way. We are trained to appreciate our feelings and the writers intention of writing not directly. We try to use what we call "guessing skill. " Write as not directly as we can and read as not directly as we can.

All the teacher here wanted was example, example, example, concrete, concrete, and concrete. I can't understand why the reader must be told everything. Why must we be so obvious in English writing?

Korean vs. English

I began to write in my native language, Korean, when I was nine year old. I had to write my diary as homework almost every day. I am still writing diaries.

I write about the most important thing that happened to me, my feelings about the school and my friends, and my dreams. It helps me learn to write in English too.

In Korea, the teacher encouraged us to use the wise man's sayings, such as what Confucius says. By doing that, the teacher would understand me. But here I feel very confused about how specific the examples have to be. For example, once I wrote about a very influential Korean Ancient philosophy called nihilism. I am a believer of that philosophy. But my teacher did not know it. I sense that it is not only that the meaning is lost in translation but also Americans do not believe in that. Words like that make my writing very strange to the reader. But I don't know how to make my writing clear to American readers. Also, here when I write in English, I have to give specific examples. I feel very confused about how specific the examples have to be.

Urdu vs. English

Back in Pakistan, my teacher would assign us to copy directly from the textbook using loose-leaf paper. This helped me with writing. I am still using this method when I have trouble understanding the reading or have difficulty in getting started with a writing task in English.

My teachers always read good essays from my classmates in front of the class I also like to read my classmates' work because it can help me to find the differences between theirs and mine. I can absorb their merit in order to improve my own writing. My teachers were used to teaching us writing this way.

Polish vs. English

There are a lot of things different between the two languages, English and Polish. Sometimes when I write, I like to write it in a general way not specific . . . In Polish, when we wrote papers, we didn't have to give statistics or write sentences specific, such as what happened first, and then the next, and giving examples. We were supposed to just give clues rather than being specific.

When I was in the 7th and 8th grades in Poland, my teacher gave us a lot of books to read; and based on the reading, she was preparing topics for the assignments. . . . She gave us a lot of freedom in our writing. Our assignment could have different forms of our choice: it could be a letter, a monologue, a dialogue, defending one's position. We had to write what the author's point was, who the main characters were, how can we compare them with our lives and our experiences, and what our personal opinion was about the book.

Russian vs. English

In Russian, we usually have a very big introduction and a big conclusion. For example, if we are supposed to write about computer use in modern life, we are supposed to start like this "Mathematics was greatly appreciated by our great leaders, now it is used more in the technology such as computers." We can give a personal example, but not much because the teacher does not value that much of it. We are supposed to give a political and historical background. In the conclusion, we kind of finalize the result. I should prove the advantages of the use of the computer by saying yes, by the examples that I give in this composition, I have proven the idea that I said in the beginning.

When I came to the United States, I learned a new word "brainstorm." In Russia, I have never thought before writing and never made a list of things to write about. I just sat down, took a pen and paper and started to write. It was never me who wrote, it was my pen. In Russia, students do write a lot. In my middle school years, we used to write compositions for 10-15 pages. I had one great teacher. She did not give us any unusual techniques, but she explained to each and every student any mistakes he or she made, and told us how to write better. She gave us such nice topics that everyone wanted to write. The teacher told us: "You think you are students? No! You are writers!"

Spanish vs. English

Writing in Spanish, we focus more on the introduction. The introduction is much longer. We were told to write long introductions. But here they asked us for a short introduction but more details in the body.

The most satisfying school assignment that I can remember was when I had to do a research project in my high school back home. The project was about some of the pre-Inca cultures in my country. In the field research I had to go to some ruins in the mountains with my fellow students. The trip was fun and the ruins were a nice place to visit with a lot of tourists around. In my group I had to be the leader because I was the one with more background knowledge about the subject. At the end our research paper was about 40 pages long, full of graphs and pictures.

When I was more proficient in Spanish, we started to read the famous authors like Miguel de Cervantes and other famous Spanish novelists. They influenced me a lot in my style of writing. I fell in love with the way how they used the written word in their novels. Since then, I started to use complex sentence structures in Spanish with a great many fancy words. Thanks to them, I gained a vast knowledge of the Spanish vocabulary.

Multicultural Literature
Reading & Discussion

The rationales for using multicultural literature with English language learners are many. Second language acquisition theory (Krashen, 1982) has suggested meaningful, comprehensible, and relevant input can reduce second language learners' anxiety and promote language acquisition. Many English language learners are insiders of their home cultures and they have an intimate experiential knowledge about their culture and rich resources to draw on for in-depth reflection. While they may be at loss when reading canonical literature, however, they can be at ease when reading literature about their people and culture because they have the cultural background knowledge; thus, these students can relate to the stories and the characters in the text easily. This relevance is the first step toward making literary transactions in literature reading (Rosenblatt, 1978). They easily identify with the sadness, difficulties, and feelings of alienation engendered by moving from their native country to the new country, especially in reading immigrant literature, the literature about people living between cultures. They can share the sense of displacement and feelings of confusion and tensions between their native language and the new language and between their home culture and the new culture. When these students read a text that contains content with which they are familiar, the reading becomes easier and enjoyable. They can focus on the language issues, such as grammar and vocabulary. They can have a deeper discussion on the concepts and themes (Genesee, 1995). Finally, being able to relate to the situations portrayed, English language learners often feel empowered, even validated by reading such literature. It shows to them that they are not alone in their experiences and feelings and that their situations are worthy of exploration. If a class is heterogeneous, it is often a good idea to pick and choose a text written about the student's culture. Students should be encouraged to research literature about their native culture and use their selection for self-sponsored reading. The following is an excerpt of a class discussion on a topic about which many non-native English speaking students have a lot to say:

(Negi, the protagonist in *When I Was Puerto Rican*, is thrown into an English speaking class to learn English.)

> Teacher: I believe bilingual education is appropriate.
> Karen: I remember when I came to the US, and I was put into a bilingual class and there were Chinese kids in there who had to listen to the Spanish and English instruction. They never taught in Chinese.
> Jessica: If Negi takes bilingual classes, she'll learn at her level and she'll learn both languages. She'll have more of an advantage because if they put her in an all English class, she won't know nothing.
> Joel: They should put kids in an all English speaking class.
> Teacher: Why?
> Joel: Because when I came to this country, they put me into an English class, but they put my brother into a bilingual

class. I learned English within about three months. He still
doesn't know very much English. [Reaction from other
students—"wow"]

Evelin: But if you put a kid that doesn 't know English into an
English class, he'll just sit there lost.

Vicky: But if he sits there quiet, he can observe and learn.

Adam: Couldn't they have a separate place to learn English?

Jonathan: Yeah—It's called school! [Laughter]

Vicky: How would you feel if you were Negi?

Jessica: Uncomfortable. It would be so hard.

Appendix B is a list of such readings by ethnic backgrounds and language proficiency levels.

Cross-Cultural Writing

Cross-cultural writing is a writing exercise that the students research and share information about their own cultural history or literature (Barillas, 2000; Freeman and Freeman, 1994; Herrell, 2000). Such a writing assignment can be paired up with a social studies unit or center around a literature theme for critical and creative writing. Students can be asked to interview their family members and elders in their community for insights about the topic. Doing these studies not only promotes non-native English speakers' active participation, but also gives them a sense of pride in investigating and writing about their own cultural history and literature. In doing so, these students are no longer marginalized but moved into the center of the learning. Their creative and critical work adds to our understanding of major literary issues and fills a gap of cross-cultural understanding. The following is a sample of a few high school English language learners' writing about gods in their own cultures before learning the unit on Greek mythology.

God of Fish

My God is the God of fish, specifically fish that live off the coast of Dubrovinick. His name is Walla Walla Ding Dong, Walla for short. The people of Dubrovinick pray to a 30-foot statue of this God that is located in the center of the town. He provides the locals with enough fish to make smelly shoes out of it (it's considered good luck). Once a year they hold a great smelly festival, it drives the tourists right out of the town. It helps in the mating rituals of the towns people because the smell of the fish distracts the women from the awful stench of the men. So the great and powerful Walla provides food, shoes and babies for the people of Dubrovinick.

My Mexican God

My God is Chongo. Chongo is the God of Dance. On special occasions, the people of Colombia dance to celebrate and honor all that Chongo has bestowed upon them. On one very special play in particular, Chongo and his beautiful wife Iagorka dance to cleanse the world of all its evils. Chongo's special power is his dance, when Chongo dances, the people of Columbia are filled with hope, strength, and pride. When his beautiful wife Iagorka joins him in the dance, the world becomes one with peace, soothing, beautiful in all its happy tranquility.

After reading "A Celebration of Grandfathers" by Rudolfo Anaya (1998), students can be asked to write about their grandparents. The following are students' essays on their grandparents:

My grandmother is a very important figure in my life. My grandfather died about seven years ago, so I did not really get to meet him, since he was suffering from a terrible illness. When my parents tell me stories about him all I hear is about how much of a good and decent man he was. I know my grandmother loved him very much because every time I talk about him her face expression becomes sad.

I have always looked up to my grandmother because of various things. She is very old and lives in Dominican Republic and ever time she comes to New York, she leaves with a cold. I have always loved my grandmother because she has always sacrificed her health and discomfort to come visit her grandchildren. If she only knew how her visits have always pleased my family deeply.

My grandmother is a very happy person. She can light up a room when she enters because of her cuteness and happiness. I have always appreciated the way she took time to cook for her family. It did not matter how tough the circumstances were because when she was here there was always a cooked dinner on the table. I hope that when I have children I can cook for them as good as she has cooked for me. One thing I have learned from her is that happiness makes life worth living.

TAPPING INTO ENGLISH LANGUAGE LEARNERS' PRIOR KNOWLEDGE IN SOCIAL STUDIES INSTRUCTION

One of the goals of social studies instruction is to lead students to see multiple points of views of events, people, cultures, and phenomena. For example, global studies, which is studied for two school years in grades 9 and 10, is a course about understanding and respecting our global society and culture differences. With a class of students who come from diverse language, culture, and educational backgrounds, the mixing lends itself nicely for cross-cultural comparisons and the examining of different points of views. Even though non-native English speaking students may not have studied about American culture, they are "experts" of their own culture and have an insider's point of view of what they do know best, their own culture. Also, in their everyday lives, they have already faced the kinds of issues studied in social studies and have developed sets of values and beliefs about individuals, groups, communities, societies, rights and responsibilities, etc. Their life experience and previous schooling have shaped the way they conceptualize human behavior. All this background knowledge that the students bring into the social studies classroom should be acknowledged, embraced, and used to teach social studies (Olmedo, 1993, 1996). Diversity in our classrooms represents opportunities for expanding ideas, for learning about language, and for cultural exchanges among students. When we think of second language learners, we tend to first think of their lack of English proficiency. Seldom do we realize that a culturally and linguistically diverse classroom is a natural resource, and few realize the educational benefits that can be attained through understanding how diversity can enhance the learning experience, particularly the teacher who is striving to develop a global perspective. The following are a few ideas that purposefully investigate these learners' prior knowledge and the possibilities of using this knowledge in a social studies classroom.

Multicultural and Multilingual Map Study

One way of getting English language learners familiarized with the concepts of maps is to ask students to bring a variety of maps to the class, such as a street map, a subway map, a map for tourists, maps of their native country, the map of the world, physical maps, political maps, a map in English, a map in their native language, etc. Let the class examine these maps to see what each presents, is used for, and what they share in common and how they differ. Compare maps with each other in their symbols, verbal descriptions or legends to see their functions and meaning. If the students bring in a map in their native language, let them share with the class their map and compare that with an English map to see the differences. Assign students to make maps of the world in groups. For the students who are new to the country, a bilingual map of their own country or a translation of the map of their country into English should be acceptable. Ask the class to pay closer attention to the location, scale, and elevation, latitude and longitude, and legends. Finally, compare various maps of the world to show different perspectives of how people view themselves and the world. For example, a map that places America in the center of the world can be compared with a map that places Asia in the center of the world.

Family and Home Cultural History Interviews

Non-native English speaking students can enrich the discussion of a social studies class by conducting their own family and home cultural interviews (Olmedo, 1993; Short, 1994b, 1997, 1999). With a class of students from all over the world, a social studies teacher can put students into contact with the best source of global studies learning—natives of the culture. For students who have recently arrived in the US, a social studies teacher can capitalize on the student's interest and curiosity about the new culture by surveying them about their initial impressions and similarities and differences in climate, geographic location, educational system, ways of life comparing the old culture and the new one, etc. Many English language learners have in an extended family living with grandparents and relatives who can play an important role in contextualizing for students' understanding of the social studies concepts. By using examples from these students' family histories or cultural investigations, the teacher can find a new way of introducing social studies topics that are relevant and meaningful for the students.

Grouped together according to their culture or individually, students can be assigned to conduct an interview with their family members, relatives, and community leaders from their culture to describe their journeys to America. More information can be gathered on the family and cultural history, including major historical events or wars fought in their native countries, the political and economic systems, important historical figures, basic values and beliefs of the family and the culture on certain issues, such as responsibilities, rights, interpersonal relationships, authority, etc. Sample interview questions are as follows:

Family and Cultural History Interview Questions:
1. What is the climate and geographical location of your country?
2. What is a typical family like in your culture (the number of people in family, who runs the family, responsibilities of the family members, relationships between parents and children, grandparents and grandchildren, and among siblings, family rituals and activities)?
3. What are the differences in their living, work, play, and people's views toward them in comparing city people and country people, elder people and young people, women and men in your culture?
4. What is the school like in your country? What is a typical day for a high school student? What did you learn in your social studies back in your country? What is the relationship between the teacher and the student back in your native country?
5. What kind of the government is there in your country? Who are the most important leaders? How did they come to power? How much and what do they control?

6. What was your country like at the time before you came to the US? (the political and economical situations, major events, and people's ways of living)
7. What do people value most in your culture? What did people talk most about back then when you were in your country and now?
8. What are the most important historical events or wars fought in your country that you can remember? Describe them in detail. Who are the heroes or heroines in your culture? Why?
9. What are some of the important dates marked in the calendar back in your country? Why?
10. Did the world political and economic events affect your family or your country? In what way?

Cultural History Study

An extension of the interview is a cultural history study. Barillas (2000), Freeman & Freeman (1994), and Herrell (2000) discussed the benefits of engaging students into researching and investigating their family and cultural history. By capitalizing on English language learners' family and cultural history, the social studies teacher sends the message that these students' and their family's voices are valued and are an important part of learning history. These studies not only parallel with social studies goals, especially in global studies, but also develop students' language skills by listening, speaking, reading, and writing. Students can either work in groups or individually to examine historical events from both their family members' perspective and from the perspective of a social studies textbook. Students will first brainstorm important questions to be used in the interviews with their family members, read the textbook, or even do a library or an Internet search. Then, they will conduct their interviews with their elders, grandparents, uncles, aunts, parents, etc. and document their results focusing on the personal and historical events before they were born. Once the interviews and the search are completed, students will draw a timeline to illustrate their findings. They will write up timeline details of interest and present all these to the class. The following is an example of the product of such a study.

Figure 15 and Table 24 are examples of the product of such a study.

Theme-Based Social Studies Instruction

Traditional global studies or world history is often taught either using a chronological approach, going through the timeline or a geographic

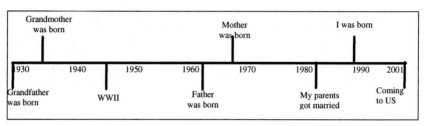

FIGURE 15

TABLE 24

Points of Interests:
1928: My maternal grandfather was born in El Paso, Mexico. That was the year of the assassination of Obregon, the great man. As a self-made and multi-talented man and a former president, Obregon was loved by the whole nation. His death threw the country into chaos.
1934: My maternal grandmother was born in El Paso, Mexico. That was the year when Lazaro Cardenas took power and succeeded Calles to become the youngest president of Mexico. The new president took a series of steps to reform the Constitution and to help the poor resolve the agrarian problem. He divided large farmland into small lands and gave them to farmers. He also controlled foreign oil.
1962: My father was born in a family of farmers. He had five brothers and three sisters. He often told me that his childhood years were spent on the farm most of the time, helping out his father and uncles. He proudly told me that he was a good farmer like his father and he enjoyed all kinds of farm work. He also told me that those years after he was born were good years, a high point of Mexican economy. Under the ruling of Diaz Ordaz, Mexico became an economic power in Central America. President Ordaz also was the first president who reached out to our neighboring nations and built a friendly relationship with them.
1966: My mother was born in a doctor's family. Her father worked as a country doctor in the rural area and her mother stayed home taking care of three children. My mother told me with excitement that she got to know my father through one of the visits to her father's country doctor's office.
1982: My parents were married. My mother was at the time a student at a nursing school and my father a technician, working at a local farming equipment company.
1987: I was born. I am the youngest of four children. I have two sisters and one brother. My brother now attends Hunter College, my elder sister is a senior and my other sister is a junior in High School.
2001: My family and I came over to America to find a better life.

approach, focusing on one region of the world at one time. If students have not received previous social studies instruction in this country or have had social studies instruction back in their native country but with different focuses and approaches, then they may have missed important topics and issues. This is especially true with the cumulative nature of social studies curriculum and testing structure. Furthermore, with an emphasis on

Western civilization and history with a strong Euro-centric point of view presented in a US global studies curriculum, students from non-western cultures might be at a disadvantage of comprehending and understanding certain historical developments, events, and concepts. A cross-cultural approach which organizes around concepts or themes within a chronological or geographical approach appeals to non-native English speaking students.

Many concepts or themes such as justice, prejudice, immigration, violence, revolution, etc. are broad and basic enough for everyone to have some prior experience or knowledge that the social studies teacher can build on. Also, concepts or themes like these invite cross-cultural and past and present comparisons and contrasts, which naturally focus on the interrelationships between cultures, provoke multiple perspectives, and deepen students' critical understanding of significant events and concepts. For example, in a unit on Confucius, the teacher should discuss the theme of age and prestige and how being an elder is perceived in different cultures. Students can easily understand this concept from their personal and cultural experiences. This understanding then can be extended to cross-cultural comparisons comparing and contrasting different cultures, such as Chinese culture and American culture or Mexican culture and Polish culture. These cross-cultural comparisons can then become the starting point for the unit to learn how the elderly were venerated as unique sources of knowledge and wisdom in Chinese culture, and how to honor one's parents, composed one of Confucian principles *Xiao*. Reilly's (1997) *The West and the World: A History of Civilization from the Ancient World to 1700* had a thematically organized world history which can be used along with other chronologically or regionally organized social studies textbooks. Table 25 an example of such comparison and contrast using Confucius philosophical ideas of age and elderly.

TABLE 25

	Word	**Chinese meaning**	**English meaning**
Meaning	Elder	older in age and wise in knowledge	pertaining to old age
		Proverbs: The older the better.	Having lived or existed for a long time.
Use		"elder" is often paired with other words used as compound words to mean the high social status and power: elder teacher, elder learner, elder worker, etc.	

Cross-Cultural Name Investigation

Second language researchers have suggested that non-native English speaking students learn a second language when they have opportunities to use the language in interaction with their peers and the teacher and when they are active in their own learning (Freeman & Freeman, 1994; Lightbown & Spada, 1993). One way of involving second language learners is to do a cross-cultural name investigation by inviting students to research the meanings of their names, the background information on how they got their names, how people from different cultures name their children, what similarities and differences in gender, social, cultural, educational, economical backgrounds between cross-cultural naming rituals and classifications, etc. The activity can begin with the teacher asking students to write his or her name down in both English and in their native language and letting students show to the class how to pronounce their names properly. The next step involves the students explaining the meaning, the ritual, such as the sequence of the first and the last name, and the way they were named by filling out a name table. This investigation can be a cross-cultural learning experience for a social studies teacher too, since many teachers find some non-Western names hard to pronounce, let alone to know the significance behind it. Results from the investigation can easily lead to a discussion by students sharing their findings about their names, metaphorical meanings behind their names, and cultural insights. All this promotes verbal interaction and boosts second language learners' self-esteem, and provides the teacher with valuable information on the students, which can be used later in social studies instruction to make historical and anthropological concepts closer to the students. Table 26 shows Yee's (1999) global name table for organizing the findings in writing.

TABLE 26

Global Name Table				
Student Name	Country/Culture	Language	Meaning	Pronunciation

CHAPTER 5

TEACHING DISCIPLINARY SPECIFIC VOCABULARY TO ENGLISH LANGUAGE LEARNERS

TEACHING SCIENTIFIC VOCABULARY TO ENGLISH LANGUAGE LEARNERS

Elaborated Semantic Webbing

This is a brainstorm activity that invites students to generate as many words or phrases as possible associated with a given word or a concept. This allows students to relate their own experience and prior knowledge with the new words and develop associative thinking skills. The words or phrases generated by the class form a web centered around the key vocabulary item or the concept. The web can draw a picture how the surrounding words relate to the key word or the concept under study. An expansion of

Teaching Language and Content to Linguistically and Culturally Diverse Students:
Principles, Ideas, and Materials; pages 97–124.
A Volume in: Language Studies in Education
Copyright © 2004 by Information Age Publishing, Inc.
All rights of reproduction in any form reserved.
ISBN: 1-59311-088-X (paper), 1-59311-089-8 (cloth)

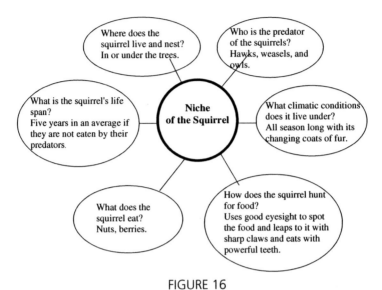

FIGURE 16

the web is to put the surrounding words into sentences or questions to demonstrate how the ideas are expanded into sentences, which can be written either in a question form or a statement form. So English language learners can see how the words are constructed into sentences. When the ideas run out, the teacher can guide students to group their associations into categories and sub-categories to clarify and organize the existing web as in Figure 16.

Concept Probing before Definition

With a large size of biology specific vocabulary required in the curriculum, many biology teachers are likely to give out short definitions of each vocabulary item during the lesson. This kind of defining and memorizing the new words runs the risk of losing the sight of teaching new concepts, especially when many biological terms are not concept explicit. Definitions alone cannot convey the meanings adequately. One way to focus on concepts rather than isolated words is to talk about meaning of the new words without mentioning the word itself or integrating the new concept into the familiar ones or experiences to make their relationship clear (Bernhardt, et al., 1996). In addition, gestures, body language, as well as rich visuals and hands-on experiences will all serve the purpose of introducing the concept, which will lead to better understanding and retention. For example, in introducing the concept of adaptation, the teacher shows the class of a series of pictures of animals, such as giraffe, hawk, duck, cactus, armadillo, polar bear, and ermine living in different habitats, and asks the students to think how the animals adapt to their ecosystems.

Classroom Talk on Adaptation

Teacher: Take a look at this picture. What is this?

Student 1: A polar bear.

Teacher: Do you know any bears besides polar bears?

Student 2: Black bears.

Teacher: Where do black bears live?

Student 2: In the jungle.

Teacher: Where do polar bears live?

Student 3: In a very cold place.

Student 4: In the Arctic.

Teacher: Right, in the arctic. Why are the different kinds of bears found in different parts of the world? Why aren't all bears found in the same place of the world?

Student 5: Because the weather is not the same.

Teacher: Why is that?

Student 5: Polar bears can only live in the cold place.

Teacher: How so?

Student 6: Because look at the picture here, the ice and the snow.

Student 7: Black bears cannot survive in that cold.

Teacher: What does a polar bear do to survive the cold?

Student 8: They have fur, white fur. Black bears do not have that thick fur and their fur is black.

Teacher: Interesting, how come a polar bear's fur is white?

Student 1: They have to hide to blend in?

Teacher: You are saying that they use the white fur to defend themselves?

Student 9: The white color is also transparent the sunlight to keep them warm.

Teacher: OK, so the polar bear's fur and the color of the fur are for some special adaptation purposes. Let's look at this picture. What is going on here?

Student 10: The duck is swimming in the river.

Teacher: What kind of environment does a duck live in?

Student 11: It's warm and close to the water.

Student 12: Ducks have fur too.

Teacher: Is that fur?

Student 8: I don't think so. How can it have fur if it lives in warm climate?

Student 9: I know what it calls.

Student 13: It's feather not fur.

Teacher: Why does it have feather?

Student 13: Feather helps it move, swim.
Teacher: What does the fur function?
Student 14: Fur keeps bears warm.
Teacher: So why ducks have feather and polar bears have fur?
Student 1: Because they have different functions.
Student 13: I know, because they have to adapt to their environments.

In the above example, the biology teacher used rich visuals and simple exploratory questions to introduce the concept of adaptation first before teaching the word definition. During the discussion, when the student had trouble with the words "feather" and "fur" instead of dismissing it as a language issue, he let the students explore the words before he asked them to focus on the function of the feather and the fur, thus pushed students to actively think about the word use rather than the definition. Once the students worked through the meaning of feather and fur and adaptation, which was the topic of the day, they worked as a group to make a table of the animals on the pictures and their adaptive features in the environment as shown in Table 27.

Matching Synonyms/Antonyms

Unlike native English speaking students, non-native English speaking students often have limited oral English vocabulary for everyday use when they go into a science class. However, science classroom discussions often require students to have at least daily communication skills and basic communication vocabulary in order for the teacher to explain or describe new

TABLE 27

Animal	Adaptation	Function	Ecosystem
Giraffe	A long neck	Function	Grassland and forest
Cactus	Spike leaves	To store water and protect itself from predators	desert
Hawk	A sharp beak, large eyes	To hunt for food	Forest
Duck	Large feet and a wide mouth	To swim and to catch fish	Water
Armadillo	Hard shells	To protect itself from other animals	Desert
Ermine	Changing color of the fur and a long tail	To defend itself	grassland
Polar bear	White fur	To keep warm	Arctic

TABLE 28

Temperate deciduous forest
Each fall, this biome **blazes** with color as maples, oaks, and birches drop over million leaves on every acre of rich forest soil. These trees are called **deciduous** trees because they lose their leaves each year. By dropping leaves, deciduous trees **protect** their **tender** tissues **from** the **oncoming** winter. Still, this biome is a **temperate** place--it rarely gets too hot or too cold. Winter snows soon turn to spring rains as birds **migrate** here from the tropics. Through the summer, the birds eat insects and **raise** new **babies**. Then they return south as the **lovely** rain of fall leaves begin once more. From <u>Our natural homes</u> by S. B. Collard III. 1996.

Match the following words with their synonyms:

a. Deciduous
b. Tender
c. Temperate
d. Oncoming
e. Lovely
f. Blaze
g. protect...from
h. raise babies
i. migrate

k. travel
l. delightful
m. keep...from
n. falling leaves
o. soft
p. mild, moderate
q. shine brightly
r. approaching, near
s. grow up babies

concepts. Without the basic communication vocabulary, English language learners often not only are short of words in expressing themselves but also have a hard time in understanding the biological terms and concepts. Therefore, a conscious effort has to be made by the teacher to constantly expand the words learned with the words unknown and teach everyday vocabulary as necessary. During my research at one high school, a biology teacher established a routine of putting a synonym in parenthesis on the side of any new word she introduced to class on the board. Another strategy is to assign reading with an exercise requiring students to use synonyms or antonyms as shown in Table 28.

Word Building Using Prefixes and Suffixes

Researchers in science education have voiced concerns about the sheer size of specialized vocabulary to be acquired by high school students in biology (Anderson, 1991; Gibbs & Lawson, 1992; Leonard & Penick, 1993; Lumpe & Beck, 1996). Close to 1,000 specialized words have to be learned in a high school biology textbook making biology very hard for native English speaking students, and doubly difficult for non-native English speaking students. Therefore, science teachers need to develop ways of teaching vocabulary effectively. Many words in biology have prefixes or suffixes which can be generalized and learned effectively using knowledge of word formation (Vizmuller-Zocco, 1987). For example, biotic factors vs.

TABLE 29

a. a green plant that produces its own food	_____
b. a person teaches	_____
c. an organism that breaks down dead organisms and their wastes	_____
d. an organism that prey other organisms for food	_____
e. an organism that consumes other organisms	_____
f. an organism that eats dead animals	_____
g. a person who drives	_____
h. a person who follows	_____

Come up with five words that begins with bio- (life) to see how they are related.
Biotic   Biomes Biomass   biosphere   symbiosis

abiotic factors, heterotrophy vs. monotrophy. In the following, a word game is illustrated using ecological word formations. Put the students in groups of five and give each group a list of word prefixes and suffixes and words to be matched up to form new words. The group finishes first correctly wins. Table 29 shows eight words that end with the -er (a person or thing that does the things) and possible combinations followed by bio—.

Multilingual Science Glossary

Monolingual dictionaries often do not include scientific words and the glossary in the back of the biology textbook are written based on the assumption that the reader is a native English speaker and has already had a working vocabulary to begin with. Therefore, the definition of a word is likely to be above the English language learners' language proficiency or vocabulary size. For students who are newcomers, the beginning phase of biology learning can be overwhelmingly difficulties if the teacher insists on English only in teaching vocabulary and concepts. At this stage, the teacher should focus on facilitating transfer of the students' content knowledge in their native language to English. Dong (2002) argued that

> even though English language learners may not know the English word for photosynthesis, they may have already had the concept established in their native language. So once the subject matter teacher identifies what students know and helps them to make the connection between what they are learning now and what they have already known, content specific concept learning speeds up because students only need to learn a new way of saying the old concept. (p. 42)

A multilingual glossary helps the students make the connection to the new biological term with something they might have already known in their native language. Students' native language in this context assists the knowledge transfer, eases language difficulty, and builds confidence. Also with

English	Biome	Mitosis	Photosynthesis
Bengali	বায়োম	মাইটোসিস	ফটোসিনথেসিস
Chinese	生物群落	有絲分裂	光合作用
Haitian Creole	biyòm	mitoz	fotosentèz
Korean	생물군락	유사분열	광합성
Polish	biome	mitoza	fotosynteza
Russian	биом	митоз	фотосинтез
Spanish	bioma	mitosis	fotosintesis

FIGURE 17

modified English definitions of words adjusted to these students' level of English proficiency and placed side by side with the definitions in their native language, students' second language acquisition will catch up. Figure 17 is a multilingual ecology glossary. Bilingual glossaries are available in school ESL/bilingual departments and district offices.

TEACHING MATHEMATICAL VOCABULARY TO ENGLISH LANGUAGE LEARNERS

Everyday Words and Mathematical Words

The language of mathematics is unique in its ways of generating, thinking, and communicating abstractions and generalizations using symbols and rules. Although certain aspects of mathematics such as numbers, signs, and rules are universal across languages, however, the words, usage, and sentences used to describe, represent, and express them are varied from language to language and from culture to culture. Whereas $1 + 1 = 2$ may be universally understood, the English expression "one pluses one equals two" is not. Also, the process of arriving at the answer is not universally the same. These expressions and ways of learning and communicating mathematics become essential to the learning of secondary school mathematics and even math educators (Esty, 1992; Miura, 2001) consider it important to integrate language into mathematics content knowledge learning to enable students to understand complex mathematics concepts. For example, the vocabulary taught in secondary level mathematics classrooms is far more abstract, condensed, and removed from real life. It can often confuse a native English speaking student, let alone a non-native English speaking student. Furthermore, second language learners may need to learn everyday English words and phrases used to express mathematical concepts that many native language speakers have already acquired or used in the mathematics classroom. Figure 18 is a list of such vocabulary.

Even though contextual information often plays an important role in learning the meaning of these words, still, a lack of basic everyday vocabulary can put English language learners at a disadvantage.

Multilingual Mathematics Glossary

If mathematics teachers treat learning mathematics as learning another language, they will find creative ways of teaching mathematical terminol-

Everyday words	Mathematical Words
Add, plus, sum, more, increased, combined	+
Subtract, minus, remainder, less, decreased, discount, difference, exceed,	-
Multiply, by, times, product,	x
Divide, average, per, cancel, mean, ratio, quotient, rate, proportion,	÷
Some	a positive real number
None	zero
Hardly	close to zero
Least, lowest	the smallest number in a set of numbers
Equal to,	=
Greatest	the largest number in a set of numbers
Common (factor, multiple)	shared
Like (terms)	same expression
Positive,	a number bigger than 0
Negative,	a number smaller than 0
Whole (number)	a number bigger than 0
Simplest form	a number can be only divided by 1 or itself
Prime (number)	a whole number with two whole number factors
Phrases	
times as much	multiply
more than	plus, add
decreased by	subtract
increased by	add
separate ...into...	two numbers whose sum is...
percent of	multiply
exceed by	subtract

FIGURE 18

ogy to ensure comprehension and application of the new concepts before doing any arithmetic calculations. Researchers in bilingual education and second language acquisition have found that students' native language plays a more active role in reading and concept learning in their second language learning (Durgunoglus, 1997; Gonzales & Schallert, 1999). For non-native English speaking students, some may have already advanced in their mathematics learning, learning the new concepts is just learning another way of communicating their mathematical ideas. For others who might not have had the exposure to the new concept or idea, then they need to learn both the concepts and the ways of communicating using these concepts. For both groups of non-native English speaking students, learning mathematical vocabulary in their native language enables them to make immediate associations between the language and the concept, thus promoting comprehension and understanding. Figure 19 is a sample glossary in Arabic, Bengali, Chinese, Haitian Creole, Korean, Polish, Russian, and Spanish. Bilingual glossaries can be formed in ESL/bilingual departments of the school and school district offices.

Mathematical Language and English Swapping

Mathematics teachers are aware that the difficulties in learning are likely to be related to mathematical language learning. The expression of concepts, such as sequence, order, and rules rely on carefully structured and condensed language, reflective of deductive and logical thinking (Esty,

English	asymmetrical	bisect	coefficient
Arabic	لا متناظر	ينصف	المعامل
Bengali	অসমতিনম	বিখন্ডন	সহগ
Chinese	非對稱	等分	係數
Haitian Creole	relasyon	bisekte	koefisyan
Korean	비대칭의	이등분하다	계수
Polish	asymetryczny	przecinać	współczynnik
Russian	асимметричный	делить пополам	коэффициент
Spanish	asimétrica	bisecar	coeficiente

FIGURE 19

Fill in the blanks with appropriate expressions.

Statements	Algebra
A number x plus 3	_____
_____	x-3
A number x less 7	_____
_____	x+12
A number twice as much as x	_____
_____	x-2
The sum of a number y and 0.25	_____
_____	2x+3
A number decreased by 15	_____
_____	2-x
Wen's age (x) 5 years from now	_____
_____	5x-10
Number of minutes in x hours	_____
_____	10(2x)
Interest on x dollars for 1 year at 5%	_____
_____	x/8
Three is seven more than a number x	3=x+7
The sum of two consecutive integers	x + (x+1)
	x (x+2) (when x is an even integer)
The ratio of two consecutive odd integers	_____ (when n is an odd integer)

FIGURE 20

1992). Students, especially non-native English speaking students with a low level of English proficiency, often have trouble with comprehending and using mathematical language, such as statements used to express mathematical meaning. Also some English language learners who have had a strong mathematics background in their native language tend to short circuit mathematical language learning, considering it less important than doing the actual calculations. Therefore, an explicit teaching of language is as important as the manipulation of mathematical symbols and numbers. An exercise requires translation methods in which students are asked to translate a statement into an algebraic expression or vice versa as in Figure 20.

Graffiti Mathematics

Many non-native English speaking students find copying class notes becomes a tremendous task. Even though they may recognize mathematics symbols used by the teacher and put on the board, the meaning behind these symbols is either lost in their notes or is not completely documented. Therefore, visual presentations of certain mathematical concepts will help students understand both language and the concept. Assigning students to create visual representations also enable the students to get over the lan-

Congruence: congru≡ence	Perpendicular: Perpen⊥icular
Factoral: factor!al	Absolute value: abso | x | ute value
Exponent: expo∧e∧t	Sum: Σum or ∫um
Slope: s∠ope	Root: √oot

FIGURE 21

guage barrier and get the mathematics concept across. An idea of mathematics graffiti can be used as a way to engage students into visually associating mathematical symbols with their meanings as shown in Figure 21.

Vocabulary Diagrams

Visual presentation is crucial for English language learners who can benefit from concrete and graphic medium rather than verbal language alone. Some students may be more attuned to spatial learning, and a map or a diagram can send them out on the quest of word exploration. Even though using shapes and spaces has become a regular part of mathematics instruction, these shapes and diagrams can be used to teach mathematical vocabulary, too. Vocabulary diagrams are especially effective in enhancing students' understanding of the relationships between concepts.

Venn Diagram

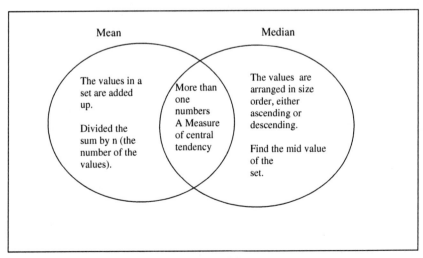

FIGURE 22

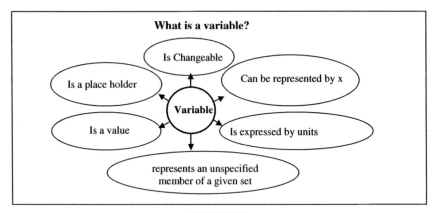

FIGURE 23

Concept Attribute Map

Toumasis (1995) demonstrated a concept worksheet that he experimented in his class to help his students understand and verbalize their understanding of important mathematical concepts. Concept attribute mapping works best for concepts that students have trouble with or similar concepts. By not only learning about the definition of the concept, but also by visually demonstrating their understanding of the concept through attribute mapping and illustrating these attributes using examples and non-examples, students gained a deeper understanding of the concept learned and communicate their understanding both visually and verbally. This sends the message to the students the importance of concept learning and very often the process of doing all this leads to a rich discussion (Figures 23 and 24).

Example:

Temperature is a variable.
It can be represented by *x.*
It is changeable.
It can be measured in degrees.
It is expressed by different degrees in a range of temperature from winter to summer.

Non-example:

12 is not a variable
It is unchangeable.

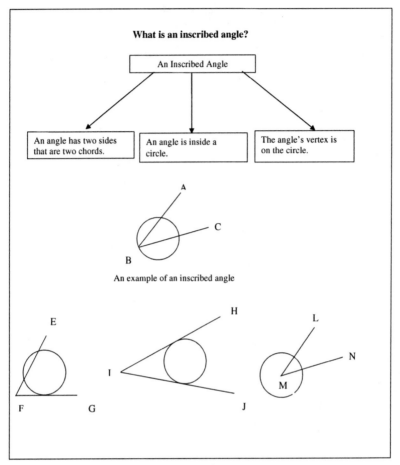

FIGURE 24

Word Building Using Prefixes and Suffixes

Second Language acquisition involves the learner actively exploring new language, comparing and contrasting the new language their native language, and seeking some patterns or making sense of it. Vocabulary learning works similarly. According to Chomsky (1959), a well known mathematician and linguist, language learners are born with a mind that creatively constructs the language learned rather than only passively receive what is taught. This creative construction also shows its power in second language acquisition. Therefore, mainstream teachers need to assist students with their innate creative language construction in teaching

TABLE 30

1	2	3	4	5
monomial	bisect	trilingual	quadrangle	quintuplets
monocycle	binomial	trinomial	quadrant	quintuplet
monodic	bisector	triangle	quart	pentagon
	biconditional		quadrilateral	
	binary operation		quartiles	

dia-: through
diagonal
diameter
diagram

Trans-: across, change
Transformation
translation
transversal

Equi-: same
Equivalent
Equilateral

mathematical vocabulary. With many mathematical terms coming from either Latin or Greek roots, one way of learning these terms is through instruction on word formation. McIntosh (1994) illustrated ways that she invited her students to find patterns in word roots in their learning of geometry vocabulary (Table 30).

TEACHING VOCABULARY IN LITERATURE TO ENGLISH LANGUAGE LEARNERS

Human Tableau

Kinesthetic learning has a unique place in teaching vocabulary in the English class. Creating a human tableau by asking students to use their bodies, facial expressions, and gestures to represent a significant concept, scene, or moment in the story helps English language learners to enter into the experience of the story and explore the deeper meaning of the words in tangible and concrete ways. For example, students can create a mural of love as Shabanu might have in mind vs. a mural of love as her father might have in mind in Staple's (1991) *Shabanu: Daughter of the Wind*, or an image of womanhood Annie John might imagine in Kincaid's (1997) *Annie John*; or Linda's image of freedom at Willy's funeral in Miller's (1976) *Death of a Salesman*. Once the mural is on display, the teacher can ask the audience to guess the meaning behind the tableau and write down possible images, insights, feelings and use a word list or ideas generated by the class to further the exploration of the key concept or vocabulary under study.

Character Physicalization

One method in second language instruction which has proven effective, especially in the beginning stage of second language learning, is called Total Physical Response (TPR, Asher, 1977; Krashen & Terrell, 1983). According to second language research, second language learners, like first language learners, begin language acquisition with listening and conducting physical movements before verbal responses. Demanding verbal responses immediately or frequently will result in anxiety and will restrict language acquisition in the early stage. TPR requires the students to act out some of the verbal responses physically without uttering a word. By asking students to engage in physical movements, the teacher can enhance students' understanding of words and concepts and create a close connection between the student and the character that they have portrayed (Pirie, 1995). Physicalization can focus on the character's body movements, facial expressions, or gestures. For example, in Steinbeck's *Of Mice and Men*, students can be asked to act out the beginning scene of Lennie's and George's stop at the river on their way to the ranch following the contrastive descriptions below:

Lennie	*George*
Restless eyes,	walked heavily with sloping shoulders,
walked quickly,	dragging his feet, his arms hung loosely,
took off his hat	drank from the surface of the green pool,
wiped the sweat-band with his forefinger	drank with long gulps,
and snapped the moisture off,	snorting into the water like a horse,
leaned over and shook George by the	knelt beside the pool
shoulder,	and drank from his hand with quick scoops,
dabbled his big paw in the water and	he threw a scoop of water into his face
wiggled his fingers	and rubbed it about with his hand, under his chin
so the water arose in little splashes,	and around the back of his neck.

Word Pictures

Vocabulary proves to be one of the biggest hurdles in second language acquisition. Normally a typical native speaker's actively used vocabulary is beyond 100,000 words (Adelson-Goldstein, 1998). Nagy and Anderson

(1984) estimated that high school student should know about 45,000 words by graduation. In order to increase non-native English speakers' vocabulary size in limited amount of time so that they can read authentic texts and deal with content an explicit vocabulary teaching and learning is necessary. Research in both first language and second language acquisition has shown that purposefully learning vocabulary can be effective (Duin & Graves, 1987). Word pictures, such as drawings and cartoons, give students a means of engaging visually with the new word and using the visual language to represent meaning. Students can be asked to either simply illustrate a newly learned word or a phrase or to create a series of pictures to tell a story using given vocabulary. Students can also collect cartoon strips or newspaper or magazine pictures for them to use in their word pictures. In addition, students can write down the collocations, grammatical features, word formation information, and pronunciation aids to gain a full understanding of the word use rather than isolated word definitions. The teacher can display these word pictures on the wall and require students to use them in their writing. This will increase exposure and retention. Figures 25 and 26 are two sample word pictures created by students.

	Sporadic adj. Happening irregularly	
New York City had a sporadic rain pattern last year.	Synonym: Unpredictable Irregular Uncommon	Antonym: predictable regular common

FIGURE 25

	Perplexed adj. Confused, worried	
The student was perplexed when he did not understand the questions on the exam.	Synonym: Puzzled Bewildered Confounded	Antonym: clear certain understanding

FIGURE 26

Writer's Word Palette

A word palette is a log keeping track of language learners' acquisition of vocabulary. It is a valuable tool in language learning in that they initiate the learner's responsibility for their own learning by setting up a record of word learning and building a system to review the words learned. Also, it gives the learners freedom to pick and choose words to learn. Designed appropriately, they should be used as part of a writer's notebook to document ideas and useful expressions to lead students to reading and writing (Noden, 1999). The palette can be grouped by themes, such as words about feelings and relationships; or they can be grouped grammatically, such as vivid adjectives or powerful verbs. They can also be grouped by literary techniques, such as characters' moods, physical descriptions, setting, intriguing dialogues, etc. Rather than simply finding a definition of the word unknown in their reading, a word palette should include the following:

- Noting the context where the new word appeared: (copy down the sentence)
- Guessing the word meaning using contextual clues
- Highlighting the surrounding words (collocation and grammatical elements)
- Finding a dictionary definition (for beginners the definition can be bilingual too)
- Marking the pronunciation of the word (stress, vowels)
- Making a sentence of your own using the new word.

Dictionaries and Thesauri

Teachers who work with non-native English speakers in class often find these students busily searching the words that block their understanding in a bilingual dictionary or an electronic translator. Although students are familiar with these bilingual language tools, they may not be familiar with other rich resources available in English. Very often bilingual dictionaries may not accurately depict the word meaning and use. Once an English teacher asked her English language learners to look up in their bilingual dictionaries for the word "hot" to her surprise, she found out that some of their bilingual dictionaries mis-defined the word meaning, comparing to the definition in an English monolingual dictionary. As students progress in second language learning, teachers of these students should introduce them to English language resources and teach them how to use these resources. Also, teachers of English language learners should include some of these resources in their own class library to encourage these learners to use these resources. The following is a list of ESL oriented language resources:

The BBI dictionary of English word combinations. (1997). Amsterdam: John Benjamins Publishing Company.
Cambridge dictionary of American English. (1999). Cambridge University Press. It has both hard copy and a CD Rom version with audio recordings of the words pronounced and features to make your own notes to every entry.
Longman essential activator. (2000). UK: Longman.
The Newbury House dictionary on American English (1996). Boston, MA: Heinle & Heinle Publishers.
Makkai, A. (1987). *A dictionary of American idioms.* New York: Barron's.
Spears, R. A. (1994). *NTC's dictionary of phrasal verbs and other idiomatic verbal phrases.* Lincolnwood, IL: National Textbook Company.
The American Heritage thesaurus for Learners of English. (2002). MA: Houghton Mifflin Company

Sensory Imagery

This is a strategy that encourages students to create an image in their minds to support the understanding of concepts and to develop students' ability to use visual imagination to construct meaning and get students actively involved in the reading. An imagery exercise asking students to draw or write down any pictures coming to mind, especially in the beginning of the reading or during their reading, can serve as a comprehension check to see whether the students have difficulty with the reading. One particular imagery prompt is a star diagram to engage students in writing or drawing all the sensory words that they can come up with after an initial reading (Collie & Slater, 1999). It can also be simply a question and answer sheet to ask students to pay more attention to their senses. Below is a list of questions using varied perspectives for an imagery exercise.

Using the first person description	Using the third person description
What can you hear?	What does it sound like?
What can you see?	What does it look like?
What can you feel?	What does it feel like?
What can you taste?	What does it taste like?
What can you smell?	What does it smell like?

Connotation and Collocation

Second language vocabulary learning involves not only learning individual words but also fixed chunks of words or phrases and learning to use them appropriately (Bahns, 1993; Howarth, 1998). Collocation, the combination of words, and connotation, the attitude the words or phrases convey, are often culture bound and are the most difficult parts of second language vocabulary acquisition (Stubbs, 1995). The way of using these chunks of words or phrases tends to distinguish a non-native speaker from a native speaker and marks the student's writing or speaking of less idiomatic and with a foreign accent. Many English teachers routinely conduct vocabulary instruction and quizzes in their classrooms. However, in dealing with English language learners, this routine vocabulary instruction needs to be expanded to teaching the collocation and connotation aspects of vocabulary use. Research in second language acquisition has shown that attention should be paid to the interrelationship between the words in vocabulary teaching in order to increase the power for the students to use the new words appropriately. For students whose native language is not English, learning about how the words are used in combination with other words is crucial because they might not have sufficient exposure to natural language use and their native language might have different sets of collocations or connotations from those of English words. Table 31 is an example of cross language collocations and connotations in comparison to English.

Metaphorical Ways of Thinking

An important part of learning a new language is to learn the new ways of thinking and representing the world (Douglass, 1987; Kaplan, 1966; Pugh, Hicks, & Davis, 1997). These ways of thinking and representing the world are shaped by a conventional conceptual framework, or metaphors people use. The metaphors we use everyday, such as "Tennis is not my cup of tea," create meaning and enhance mutual understanding. Metaphors are not just for poets or writers, they are for everyone. As Lakoff and Johnson (1980) argued that "Our ordinary conceptual system, in terms of which we

Collocation of other languages	English
Open a joke (Chinese)	tell a joke
Say lie (Chinese)	tell lie
Drive a bookshop (Polish)	run a bookshop
Make attention to (French)	pay attention to
Finish a conflict (German)	resolve a conflict

Cross Language Connotation Examples

Word	Chinese	English
Fat	positive or neutral	negative connotation
Privacy	negative connotation	positive connotation

TABLE 31

An apple a day keeps the doctor away.
You are the apple of my eye.
One rotten apple spoils the bunch.
Don't mix apples and oranges.
The apple doesn't fall far from the tree.
Baseball and apple pie are American.
We live in the Big Apple.

FIGURE 27

both think and act, is fundamentally metaphorical in nature" (p. 3). Unlike native English speaking students who have already acquired culturally oriented metaphorical thinking, non-native English speaking students have to learn this thinking starting from scratch in order to communicate effectively. Vocabulary instruction should extend beyond individual words, and metaphor teaching in the English classroom should go beyond the poetic use and include the conventional use. This way English language learners learn not only the language and the rhetorical device but also the culturally oriented concepts behind metaphors (Figure 27).

TEACHING SOCIAL STUDIES VOCABULARY TO ENGLISH LANGUAGE LEARNERS

Concept Exploration Through Senses

Pictures, realias, drawings, photos, and any visual symbols or images allow the students to make connections between visual images and concepts taught. Preferably, a social studies teacher compiles a collection of visuals, including pictures, realias, drawings and photos, and matches these visuals with the key concepts to be learned. A picture is worth a thousand words. A slide show of Egptian pyramids or pictures of the French Reigns can help with the concepts and the themes under study and increase comprehension. The following is an example of the use of modeled artifacts to engage a class of English language learners who are placed in groups and asked to respond to this assignment.

It was 1974 and you were in the Chinese city of Xian. You were an archaeologist who was called upon to analyze something that was discovered here.

Students are given the least amount of information about the fragments. They work together in answering the questions for 20 minutes.

TABLE 32

What is this object? Describe the object using five senses.
   a. What do you feel when you touch it?
   b. What shape does this object look like?
   c. What was the color, texture, and weight of the object?
   d. What is the object made for? stone, wood, or other materials?

How old is this object?
   a. Are there any marks on the object telling you about the age of the object?
   b. What does the surface look like?
   c. Can you guess the age of the object?

Where was it made?
   a. at home
   b. in factory
   c. handmade

What does this object tell us anything about the history and the people who use it?
a. Who might use it?
a. What was their culture like?
b. What would they use it for?

What is the value of this object?
Cheap
Expensive
Valuable

Is there anything we use today similar to this object? If so, what is it?

What does this object remind you of?

After which the class comes together again and go over some key questions. When the students' curiosity has reached a peak, the teacher will put the pieces together like a puzzle and present the model soldier as a whole. The students will then review their answers to the questions in Table 32 and talk about their understanding of the concept "artifacts."

Concept Visualization

Concept visuals using icons and pictures to represent concepts are powerful and revealing in achieving holistic understanding of complex and abstract concepts. Many terms used in social studies classes center around key concepts of *liberty* and *democracy* upon which this country is based. A thorough understanding these terms should involve not just memorization of the definitions but an engagement of students' visual, audio, and verbal skills and a participatory approach to learning how these concepts are used. Figures 28 and 29 are examples of student generated visual and verbal representations of dictatorship and election.

Dictatorship n.
Having complete power in the
hands of one person

Under Hitler's dictatorship in
WWII, people in Germany had no
freedom or democracy at all.

Synonym:	Antonym:
Domineering	modest
Oppressor	oppressed
Autocrat	democrat

FIGURE 28

Election v.
To select by voting

Students elected her as their
student union president.

Synonym:	Antonym:
Choose	force
Vote	appoint

FIGURE 29

Concept Physicalization

Many social studies concepts and terminology may be difficult to define, especially when the students have limited vocabulary to begin with. In second language learning, an approach called Total Physical Response (TPR), developed by Asher in 1982, aimed to use body movements and facial expressions to communicate. The teacher acts as a commander of a play, while the students respond the teacher's command by conveying meaning through physical movements. Research has shown that using this kind of bodily/kinesthetic intelligence can help the learner to learn the concept through active participating in constructing the meaning making process. For example, based on the given handout of a cartoon or a picture depicting imperialism or slavery or colonialism, students in groups of three can make a human sculpture of the cartoon or the picture. Then the group presents the sculpture to the class and has both the audience and the creators of the sculpture talk about what is going on in this sculpture by the teacher asking open-ended questions, such as why they position themselves in certain ways, what the relationship was among the people involved in the sculpture, the feelings provoked through doing or viewing this, and what concept was conveyed through this sculpture. Afterwards, the teacher can ask the students to come up with their narrative descriptions of what they just saw and the new understanding of the concept.

Realias for Symbolism

Realias are items collected from home or school for demonstration to be used to strengthen the relationship between words and meaning. Certain realias embody symbolic political behavior and cultural and historical values that can be used to expose English language learners to a deeper understanding of a historical or political phenomenon (Cline, 1996). First, a social studies teacher needs to demonstrate what a symbol mean using realias, such as a heart, a flag, a graduation cap, etc. Students can also be encouraged to bring items from home to let the class guess their symbolic meaning, such as a Chinese writing brush, a turban, a saki dress, etc. When a link between the realias and their symbolic meaning is established, the class can begin to see how certain realias have symbolic political meaning in this culture. The following is a list of a few realias and their symbolic representations of law and justice in US history:

Realias	*Symbolic Representations*
Handcuffs	police
Bible	church
The Statue of Liberty	Immigration
Teddy Bear	Theadore Rooselvelt
Ford automobile	Mass production
Fire fighter's helmet	FDNY-heroes
Yellow ribbons	wishing troops in Iraq to come back safe and sound

Group Mime Game

In order to help students understand social studies concepts, such as trade, trade imbalance, imports, exports, etc., a social studies teacher can ask her students to first write on an index card three items of what they wear, carry, and use, and then note where these items were made (for example, My T-shirt is made in China. It's an import item). Then the teacher picks the students whose items are made in different countries, such as China, Japan, Mexico, to come to the front of the class. These students are told to hold the larger poster with their representative countries and stand in a circle to symbolize the globe. They are all interconnected by a rope. At the same time, a student at the board will locate these countries on the map on the board. Afterwards, the teacher gives out another index card to each student in the circle and asks them to give examples of catastrophes. For example, earthquakes will occur in Japan, drought in Mexico, a war in Iraq, and political turmoil in China. Once everything is set, the teacher announces some kind of the catastrophe, for example, an earthquake has struck Japan, then the student whose country is mentioned will pull on the rope to show how the countries in the globe feels the pull. Each country will take turns to express how they feel using the body gestures or facial expressions. The audience will also comment on what they have seen. In the meantime, the student at the board will jot down all these reactions on the board. Finally, the teacher asks the class to discuss how the global economy works from this experience.

Semantic Differential Scale

With a multicultural and multilingual student body, different ways of seeing the world should be used to teach a concept. Using a semantic differential scale as in Table 33 can ease the anxiety of speaking and capture students' perceptions of the concepts or themes under study. A use of the semantic scale can also identify students' beliefs and attitudes that a class discussion or a formal writing assignment cannot (Zevin, 1993). For English language learners, a semantic scale or a checklist can help them

TABLE 33

Privacy is something…							
good	—	—	—	—	—	—	—	bad
closed	—	—	—	—	—	—	—	open
personal	—	—	—	—	—	—	—	public
self-owned	—	—	—	—	—	—	—	shared by others
secret	—	—	—	—	—	—	—	everyone knows

Being independent means…

Getting married	_____	reaching to certain age	_____
Pay your own bills	_____	leaving home	_____
Taking care of your parents	_____	holding a job	_____
Making your own decisions	_____	purchasing a house and a car	_____
Having children	_____	having the right to vote	_____

see the varied meaning behind the word which they may not have access to otherwise. Once they have responded to the scale, the teacher can then ask questions about their responses or group students into groups to further discuss the concepts under study.

Concept Maps

A concept map goes beyond the word web by categorizing the related concepts generated and sorting them into some kind of logical orders. Also, the teacher can ask the students to elaborate their map by expanding the words into phrases or sentences. In working with students who came from countries, which operate under different political systems, a concept map can be a valuable tool to identify differences and relationships. In addition, certain social studies topics, such as social structures under the Old Regime in France and check and balance reflected in the US government can all be turned into graphics to help students organize varied information without losing sight of the major concept. Figure 30 is a concept map of the social structure of France.

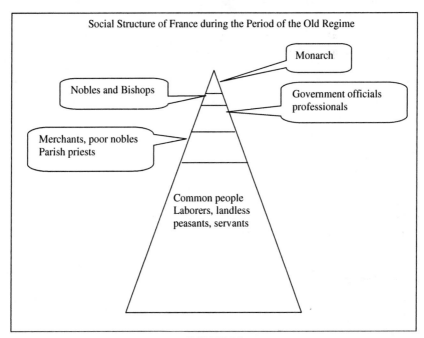

FIGURE 30

Historian's Word Journal

Effective learning occurs in social studies when students do history rather than learn history. A historian constantly observes, documents, reflects, and finds a way to describe what has happened. Keeping an historian's word journal is a way to add excitement to language and history learning. Many English language learners find it difficult to express their knowledge and ideas in both written and spoken English. This is especially true when their limited vocabulary prohibits the articulation of their intelligence. Keeping an historian's word journal over time can help generate ideas and also develop an independent learning habit. The word journal will have three parts: identifying the new word, predicting the meaning of the word, and finding the meaning of the new word. Students can copy down the whole sentence or the paragraph where the new word has found. Then they will guess from the contextual clues of the meaning of the word. Finally they will consult a dictionary to find out the meaning and compare and contrast the dictionary meaning with what they predicted to see any parallels. Each day the teacher might ask the class for a new word that they learned and encourage students to exchange their word journal with each other to learn more words. Sample historian's word journal instructions are like this:

- Divide the page in half with the words on the left side and their meanings and illustrations on the right.
- Organize the words according to the topic or theme, such as civilization, French Revolution, Industrial Revolution, etc.

When doing the journal, write more than just a word's meaning. Include visual illustrations, translations or pronunciation of the word too. While keeping the journal, ask the following questions:

- Is it a noun, verb, or adverb, etc.?
- Have you include the whole sentence to show the context where this word is used?
- Give an example in your own words to show how the word is used.
- Is there any information about how the word is pronounced?
- How is the word related to other words you know on this topic?

Class Vocabulary Calendar

Many teenagers learning a second language need frequent evaluations and reinforcement from their peers or teacher to keep their confidence high and provide them with a sense of accomplishment and success.

TABLE 34
Month of October: The Slave Trade and European Imperialism

	Monday	Tuesday	Weds.	Thursday	Friday
Week 1	• Slave: to work for people without being paid • During the Civil War, many slaves from the south escaped to the north of the U.S.	• Con-vert.to: change • Our school converted the trailor into our ESL class-room.	• Famine: no food and hun-gry • I heard from my dad that a famine occurred in the year when I was born because of a poor har-vest.	• Expand: become larger • Our ESL teacher told us that the number of students in our school has expanded in recent years.	• Desirable: good, valuable • Europe-ans saw African lands as desirable markets to use for their own purpose.

Vocabulary learning for English language learners can be tedious and boring when the progress is slow and new words are too many to learn. A social studies teacher should facilitate students vocabulary learning by organizing a vocabulary calendar (Allen & Marquez, 1998) in the beginning of the year, or the semester, or each month and putting the calendar on the wall to show students' progress and to remind them of using these words. The teacher can use poster calendars either weekly or monthly, or s/he can make their own calendars on the poster. Words in the vocabulary calendar have to be selected by the students rather than the teacher. In the beginning, students may jot down a word learned in class or in their reading and vote for a word to be put on the calendar. Once the word is in, the students have to compose a sentence and note any interesting features about the word. They are encouraged to use dictionary definitions, their own descriptions or their native language translations to describe the word. Gradually, they can move to using English to explain the word learned. Once a month, the teacher can design a jeopardy game to check on class' progress on the words learned. For the words with most difficulty, the teacher can also ask students to illustrate the words and compose a story or a dialogue based on these words. A sample weekly social studies calendar is as in Table 34.

Tracing the Word Family through Prefixes and Suffixes

With a large number of disciplinary specific words used in the social studies class, knowledge about the basic word formation is a useful tool to increase English language learners' vocabulary and to enable students to learn words independently. One way is guessing the word meaning from the prefix or the suffix. Research in second language acquisition and learning has suggested that knowledge about word formation, and the meaning potentials, can facilitate the acquisition of words and use of words (Day, Omura, & Hiramutsu, 1991; Hancin-Bhatt & Nagy 1994). For example, comparing Spanish speaking students with Korean speaking students, Spanish speaking students have an advantage of guessing English words using Spanish cognates either subconsciously or consciously. Since many social studies terms share common Graeco-Latin prefixes and suffixes, by teaching students, especially language learners whose native languages are not alphabetic, the social studies teacher can create a general language awareness and make learning these long and complex words meaningful and manageable. Below is a sample of a few commonly used social studies words.

Prefix:
- ex-(out) as in exile, extermination camp, excommunicate
- pre-(before) as in prehistoric, predestination
- mono-(one) as in monotheism, monopoly

Suffix:
- -crat (to rule) as in democrat, aristocrat, autocrat
- -ment (state) as in government, management,
- -graphy (map) as in geography, topography,

CHAPTER 6

SECOND LANGUAGE READING INSTRUCTION IN MAINSTREAM CLASSES

SECOND LANGUAGE READING INSTRUCTION IN SCIENCE CLASSES

Parallel Reading

One hurdle in English language learners' science learning is reading the textbook. For example, the biology textbook is often very decontextualized, and far more advanced than these learners' English language proficiency levels. One method for assisting these students' content reading is to provide students with different versions of a text, which are tailored to different levels of English proficiency. These versions can be selected and adapted from juvenile literature or they can be written by native English speaking students or even the teacher. After reading one version of the text, students can be given a different version of that text for comparison and for reinforcing the understanding of the key concepts. Many juvenile literature works and newspaper articles lend themselves into good candidates for such a selection. Using this kind of extensive reading drawn from

Teaching Language and Content to Linguistically and Culturally Diverse Students:
Principles, Ideas, and Materials; pages 125–165.
A Volume in: Language Studies in Education
Copyright © 2004 by Information Age Publishing, Inc.
All rights of reproduction in any form reserved.
ISBN: 1-59311-088-X (paper), 1-59311-089-8 (cloth)

such a rich reservoir of language use and expressions over time, students will develop their vocabulary and language skills as well as their scientific conceptual knowledge. Different groups or individuals in class can be given different versions of the text to read, and they come as a group to establish as many parallels as possible on a given topic or theme. New vocabulary terms will be explained in the passage and offered a pronunciation guide. Finally, using juvenile literature can expose beginning English language learners to a different genre of reading, that is story telling, which has proven to be beneficial to students' overall language growth (Borasi & Brown, 1985). In the following there is a demonstration of the different readings on the topic of the food chain.

Original Text

In all but a few small ecosystems, the autotrophs are plants and other photo-synthetic organisms. They trap energy from sunlight and use it for the synthesis of sugars and starch. These substances can be changed to other organic compounds that are needed by the plant, or they can be broken down for energy. Heterotrophs can only use the chemical energy stored in organic compounds for their life processes. These organic nutrients must be obtained from the bodies of other organisms—either plants or animals. Because autotrophs are the only organisms in an ecosystem that can produce organic compounds (food) from inorganic compounds, they are called producers. Since heterotrophs must obtain nutrients from other organisms, they are called consumers.

Within an ecosystem, there is a pathway of energy flow that always begins with the producers. Energy stored in organic nutrients synthesized by the producers is transferred to consumers when the plants are eaten. Herbivores are the primary consumers, or first order consumers. The carnivores that feed on the plant-eating animals are secondary consumers, or second-order consumers. For example, mice feed on plants and are first-level consumers. The snake that eats the mice is a second-level consumer, while the hawk that eats the snake is a third-level consumer. Since many consumers have a varied diet, they may be second-, third-, or higher level consumers, depending on their prey. Each of these feeding relationships forms a food chain, a series of organisms through which food energy is passed. Feeding relationships in an ecosystem are never just simple food chains. There are many types of organisms at each feeding level, and there are always many food chains in an ecosystem. These food chains are connected at different points, forming a food web. (from *Biology: The Study of Life* by Schraer & Stoltze, Prentice-Hall, 1995, p. 828)

Simplified Version

Living things depend on each other for energy. Most of the energy in an ecosystem comes from the sun. The energy moves from the sun to organisms within an ecosystem. There are two main groups of organisms in ecosystems: producers and consumers. Producers take in energy from the environment. The tree is a producer. Most producers take in energy from the sun. All of the other organisms in an ecosystem are consumers. Consumers, like the bird get energy from other organisms. Some consumers get energy by breaking down dead organisms and wastes. This type of consumers is called decomposers. For example, when the tree loses its leaves, they are broken down by decomposers, such as bacteria in the soil.

Energy flows from producers to consumers in an ecosystem. The path of energy between producers and consumers in an ecosystem is called a food chain. What might happen if a change in the environment killed the tree? An important food source would be lost. The flow of energy in that ecosystem would change. Many organisms would die without other sources of food.

There are many food chains in an ecosystem. These food chains are all connected to one another. In fact, the organisms in an ecosystem may be a part of more than one food chain. All food chains in an ecosystem taken together are called a food web. As food web is called a web because the many different paths of energy in an ecosystem are like a web of many food chains. The loss of the tree in the food chain will affect not only the organisms in that food chain but also the organisms in other food chains in the ecosystem. The loss of the tree will affect the whole food web. (from *Essentials of Biology*, by Joseph Pignatiello, et al. 1998, Holt, Rinehart and Winston, pp. 171.)

Story telling

There was an old lady who lived near a pond. She was scientist and enjoyed using a microscope. With her microscope she could see tiny things. One day she went to the pond and filled a jar with the water from the pond. She brought it back home and put a sample of it under the microscope. This is what she saw: algae converts sunlight to energy.

The next day she went back to the pond and found a fish. The fish ate the algae. She catches the fish and brings it home. Accidentally, she leaves a lid to the bucket off and her dog eats the fish. The dog choked on the fish and died in the yard. Flies and birds picked on his remains. The rest of the dog's body decomposed and became fertilizer for the plants in the back yard. The old lady was sad, but as a scientist, she understood all of this was part of the food chain.

Poem

In a wild forest a baby plant once said
"When mommy plant will be my turn to die?"
"When it's your time to die, there's no place to go
but this cycle of life you should know.

Of the beasts that eat meat,
You should not have fear, but beware
Of the plant-eating herbivores,
Such as cows, mice, horses, and deer.
We as autotrophs, can form our own good,
But to eat other animals we believe is quite wide.
These are the carnivores, eagles, and lions,
They sit on the top of this food chain
Without ever trying.
Even these animals have fear too
Because they die, return to the earth and
Become food for me and you.

Jigsaw Reading

Part of English language learners' reading difficulty results in the demands on the quantity of reading. A science teacher can divide a reading passage into manageable chunks to enhance students' reading comprehension, interaction, and an effective use of class time (Colosi & Zales, 1998). Each student is given one part to read, and another student is given another part to read. Afterwards, students form groups of three or four with each member having just read a different part of the text. The choice of the number of group members depends on the number of parts of the text. For example, if there are three parts of the reading, then students form groups of three. They are then asked to retell what they read to the group. Since each student is reading a different part of the whole reading, an information gap is created so that every student has something to say or listen. The telling and listening has a real meaning for piecing together the whole passage. Students ask for meaning and therefore listening and speaking skills are also practiced in the process. This created a natural interaction between each other, and in the end students complete the whole story as a group. Finally the teacher reads the whole passage to check for students' understanding.

Putting Scrambled Sentences Together

This activity trains students to be active readers to make sense and place an order of series of sentences on a given topic. In doing so, students will develop logical thinking skills as well as pay a closer attention to the connections between sentences and the presentation of certain scientific concepts. Students are given a list of sentences and asked to combine or sequence these sentences into a coherent story. Below is an example of such an exercise on omnivores.

a. Our brains have brought us out on top.
b. Our place in the food chain is right up there with the top predators
c. What we do have is intelligence.
d. Most of us are omnivores.
e. We don't have the teeth of a wolf, or the speed of a leopard, or the claws of a bear.
f. even though we don't have the right qualifications for the job.
g. Nor do we have the strength of a lion or the sight of a hawk.
h. We eat primary producers (plants) and primary and secondary consumers (animals).

Most of us are omnivores. We eat primary producers (plants) and primary and secondary consumers (animals). Our place in the food chain is right up there with the top predators, even though we don't have the right qualifications for the job. We don't have the teeth of a wolf, or the speed of a leopard, or the claws of a bear. Nor do we have the strength of a lion or the sight of a hawk. What we do have is intelligence. Our brains have brought us out on top. (From Anderson, M. *Food chains: The unending cycle*, p. 50. 1991.)

Reading and Diagramming

Diagramming either before reading, while reading, or after reading invites active reading for meaning and understanding and focuses on key issues or concepts under study (Schwab & Coble, 1985). For non-native English speaking students, this kind of graphic organizers can use fewer words but can tell a big story. Especially the pictorial presentation of the relationships between concepts and information not only further students' understanding of the reading material but also train their thinking skills.

a. Venn Diagram

A Venn Diagram includes two adjacent circles intertwined each other with an intersection in the middle, presents similarities in the middle intersection and differences on the sides. It illustrates the comparisons and contrasts of the two concepts and reading information very effectively. With the focus on comparisons and contrasts, students can jot down the similarities and differences on the two circles during their reading. This pictorial representation of the comparative relationships between concepts help students organize their thoughts, further their comprehension of the reading, and allow them to focus on manageable and meaningful chunks of information and their relationships between each other. This kind of purposeful reading can improve students' note-taking skills as well. Constant training can help students make notes for organizing their thoughts and for crystallizing ideas. In Figure 31, there is a Venn diagram of tundra and taiga based on students' textbook reading.

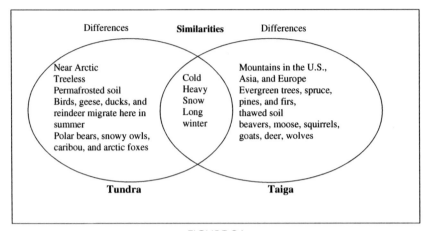

FIGURE 31

The tundra is a region that lies south of the ice caps of the Arctic and extends across North America, Europe, and Sibera. In the Southern Hemisphere, the areas that would be tundra are oceans. The tundra is characterized by a low average temperature and a short growing season of about 60 days. During the long, cold winters, the ground is completely frozen. During the short summer, only the topmost layer of soil thaws. The layers beneath this layer remain frozen. These layers are called permafrost. The average precipitation in the tundra is only about 10 to 12 centimeters a year. However, because of the low rate of evaporation, the region is wet with bogs and ponds during the warm season. Vegetation in the tundra is limited to lichens, mosses, grasses, sedges, and shrubs. There are almost no trees because of the short growing season and the permafrost.

Moving south across the tundra, the vegetation slowly changes. Groups of stunted trees begin to appear in sheltered places. Farther south, the trees become larger and closer together, at last giving way to evergreen forests. This belt of evergreen forest, which extends across North America, Europe, and Asia, is the taiga. The taiga has cold winters during which the ground is covered by deep snow. However, the growing season is longer than that of the tundra—about 120 days. The summer days are warmer than in the tundra, and the ground thaws completely. Precipitation is greater than in the taiga, averaging between 50 and 100 centimeters a year. As in the tundra, there are many ponds and bogs. Pines, firs, and spruce are the dominant vegetation, although some deciduous trees, which shed their leaves, are also present. (from Schraer & Stoltze *Biology: The Study of Life* p. 846-847, Prentice Hall, 1995).

b. *Relational Diagram*

In biology, many concepts and knowledge organizations fall into hierarchical or taxonomic relationships. A relational diagram illustrates the rela-

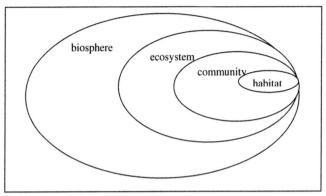

FIGURE 31

tionships between concepts that can illuminate the teacher's lecture and the students' textbook reading and promote a deeper understanding of the key concepts (Soyibo, 1995). When reading is for drawing or organizing information, students look for the main ideas and inter-relationship between ideas rather than simply memorize the text. Also, students can come up with different relational diagrams to compare and contrast in class and talk about the rationales behind their thinking. Figure 32 is a diagram illustrating the relationship between four concepts: biosphere, ecosystem, community, and habitat.

Guessing the Unknown from the Context

In training English language learners to be independent and active readers, a science teacher should convey the message that they don't have to understand every single word of the reading in order to comprehend the material. These students should learn to discover that they can guess for meaning from the context, and in doing so their reading will not be interrupted so frequently. Researchers in both first language and literacy development and second language and literacy development have shown that skilled readers use contextual clues more during reading than unskilled readers (Kern, 1989; Perfetti, 1995). For English language learners, this can be done in pairs or in groups, where students work together to understand a reading passage. In class reading the textbook, the students can be invited to predict what likely to happen at different stages of reading, such as the beginning, middle, and end. Responsibility can be later placed upon students associated with their development of note taking and questioning skills. Students will ask questions to each other, predict, or try to answer these questions. In addition, predicting and guessing meaning should be modeled by the teachers first to let students know the steps that s/he takes. Having modeled these strategies, then the students can proceed to these tasks. The following is an example of reading from the context.

Ecological Succession

Although ecosystems appear **stable** (calm), they do **undergo** (experience) change. Change **occurs** (takes place) because the living organisms *present* in the ecosystem **alter** (change) the environment. Some of the changes tend to make the environment more suitable for new types of organisms and less suitable for the existing organisms. Thus, the original organisms in an ecosystem are *slowly replaced* by other types. A new community *replaces* the original community in the ecosystem. Over time, this community *gradually replaced* by still another community. The process by which an existing community is *slowly replaced* by another community is called ecological succession. In land environments, ecological succession usually depends on the types of plants that are *present* at any given time. Plants **determine** (decide) the type of community that develops because plants are producers . The types of animals that can **survive** (continue to live) in the community depend, directly or indirectly, on the types of plants.—from Schraer & Stoltze *Biology: The Study of Life* p. 835, Prentice Hall, 1995.

In this typical textbook reading, with the help of the teacher, the students can learn to ask questions like "Why does a change occur in an ecosystem?" "Is the change always good or bad?" "Why do plants determine the types of community that develops?" "What does 'slowly/gradually replace' mean?" "How can we replace 'present' for another word?" By posing these questions, students are led into predicting and critically reading and actively guessing the unknown words. Sample strategies used to guess the word from contextual clues are as follows:
Structural clues:

- Look for affixes and suffixes in the word.
- Look at punctuation marks.
- Look at parts of speech to identify whether it is a verb or a noun, etc.
- Look at surrounding words for connection clues and relationships in sentences above and below, such as "and" "so" "because" "when", etc.

Semantic clues:

- Try to replace the unknown word with a word you know.
- Look at surrounding sentences to see any synonyms or antonyms used to describe the unknown word.
- Look at the title of the reading or the topic sentence of the paragraph for general ideas before guessing

- Keep reading to see whether the following sentences explain the unknown word.

Highlighting Organizational Links

In order to help non-native English speaking students with reading the textbook and academic language, one strategy is to direct students' attention to the organizational links that the textbook writer uses to present information. For example, the transitional words used in English to illustrate the relationships between the concepts and highlight the key facts and information. These links also reflect American academic ways of writing and thinking which might be foreign to these students. In making these links explicit, the teacher guides the students to think logically and use these links not only for understanding but also for writing. For example, the teacher can ask students to fill in the appropriate transitional words in a reading passage or ask students to use these words in sentences.

A population remains the same size **if** the birth rate and death rate are equal and no changes result from migration. In this century, the death rate in the industrialized countries has declined sharply **because of** improvements in medical care, food production, and sanitation. In many of these countries, **however**, there has also been a decline in the birth rate. This has led to a stable, **but** older population. In a few countries, the birth rate has dropped below the death rate, **resulting** a shrinking population. In the underdeveloped countries, the birth rate remains high. **At the same time**, the death rate in many of these countries has dropped **because of** improved living conditions. **Thus**, the continued high birth rate is causing a rapid growth in the populations.—from Schraer & Stoltze *Biology: The Study of Life* p. 865, Prentice Hall, 1995.

Some of the links that can be identified through reading this paragraph are: *if, because of, however, but, resulting, at the same time, because of,* and *thus.* Once the links are identified, the teacher can conduct a mini lesson on the functions and meanings of these links. These organizational links can be used as a note-taking device to reinforce the main concept and serve as a study guide. The following are a list of sample links frequently used in the science text.

Function	*Links*
Sequence	first, second, third, at the same time,
Cause/effect	because, consequently, therefore, thus, as a result, hence, resulting
Compare/contrast	than, by contrast, in comparison, however
Emphasis	in particular, specifically, in addition, moreover, furthermore,
Conditional	if, although, suppose

Matching the Headline with the Article

In order to train students to read for main ideas, a science teacher can bring to class a collection of news articles or short stories on the focused science topics under study. S/he will cut out the headline from each article and give the students the article to read first. Then they will be asked to pick and choose a title for their article from a collection of headlines. They will be asked to give reasons for their choice, or they will be also asked to come up with their own title for the article that they just read. During the exercise, the teacher can ask the class to pay attention to the ways that students use to come up with the main ideas for the article by reading topic sentences and reading the opening paragraph. An extension of this activity can be a combined writing activity that students will be given out headlines first and asked to compose an article based on the headline. Then they can compare and contrast their writing with the actual article.

Second Language Reading Instruction in Mathematics Classes

Folk knowledge often considers that mathematics contains only numbers and symbols, having almost nothing to do with the language. Therefore, as long as information is presented in numbers and symbols, people without language proficiency should be able to do the calculation. So, reading in mathematics classrooms should be kept as little as possible. However, actually mathematics involves as much language use as, for example, history, and complex reading comprehension and thinking processes using the language. Especially for students learning advanced mathematics in secondary schools, many calculations often come in after students understand the concept, comprehend the problem, and resolve the language issues. Also, because mathematics textbooks are often written at the reading level paralleling with the grade level with an assumption that the reader has grown up in this culture, non-native English students even though may have an edge over the content knowledge and calculation skills, they still are at a disadvantage when facing the advanced mathematics reading materials and learning mathematical concepts in another language (Borasi & Agor, 1990).

One of my graduate students encountered this when tutoring her tutee. One of the probability problems stated, "if you rolled a 'fair die' what is the probability of getting a number less than three?" The English language learner, who was strong in probability, had no idea what a "fair die" was. The textbook did not have any illustration to show students what a fair die was. It was not until the student's tutor drew the picture and explained a fair die before the student could do the problem. Some mathematics teachers are quick to assign students to do the practice questions by the end of the chapter, rather than go over the reading with the students. By avoiding teaching students how to read and comprehend the mathematical language, a mathematics teacher shortchanges these students and does not prepare them for advanced academic work. Esty (1992) and Esty and Teppo (1994) all emphasized the importance of language concepts in mathematics learning and demonstrated ways of teaching how to read and think in mathematical language. Every mathematics teacher needs to learn some basic reading strategies used to work with second language learners. The following are a few reading strategies:

Providing A Roadmap for Textbook Reading

Language use in mathematics textbooks often follows a distinctive syntactical structure of principle-explanation-application (Campbell, 1979). The challenge for the teacher is to provide a roadmap and to guide the students through the labyrinth. This is especially important for English language learners because their previous mathematics reading may follow a different structure in their native language. Unaware of this discourse pattern can throw many students off and make the reading tedious and unyielding. A typical mathematics textbook reading is like this:

The Probability of an Event

In the study of probability, any happening whose result is uncertain is an experiment. The various possible results of the experiment are outcomes, and the collection of all possible outcomes of an experiment is the sample space (S). Finally, any sub-collection of a sample space is an event (E).

To calculate the probability of an event, you count the number of outcomes in the event and in the sample space. The number of outcomes in event E is denoted by $n(E)$, and the number of outcomes in the sample space S is denoted by $n(S)$.

If an event E has $n(E)$ equally likely outcomes and its sample space S has $n(S)$ equally likely outcomes, then the probability of event E is

$$P(E) = n(E)/n(S)$$

Example: Two coins are tossed. What is the probability that both land heads up?

Let E = {HH} and S = {HH, HT, HT, TT}. The probability of getting two heads is

$$P(E) = n(E)/n(S) = 1/4$$

(from *Precalculus* by Larson/Hostetler, 1993, D. C. Heath and Company, pp. 716)

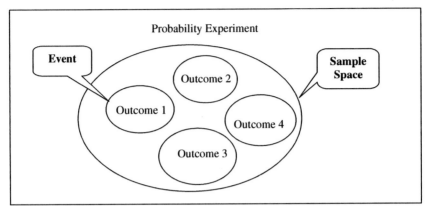

FIGURE 33

This principle → explanation → application language structure is used to develop and demonstrate certain abstract mathematical ideas and concepts. However, its complex sentence structure, loaded with mathematical terminology, introduces several concepts at once making this short passage unintelligible to regular readers, let alone to non-native English readers. As a result, students though assigned to do the reading, skip the passage going straight to the operational drills and practices without really understanding the concepts and terminology that set up the operation. To understand the above passage, we can use visuals to illustrate the meaning and relationship among these terms, such as outcome, event, probability experiment, and sample space like Figure 33.

Textbook Simplification

Research in second language literacy learning has shown a general gain in comprehension through the use of a simplified text when the original text is linguistically complex (Cervantes & Gainer, 1992; Jameson, 1998; Nation & Deweerdt, 2001). According to the input hypothesis (Krashen, 1982), when an oral or written input, such as a classroom discussion or a reading assignment is well above a language learner's proficiency level, the learner will be overwhelmed, thus anxiety sets in and the comprehension level goes down. Over the years, researchers in second language acquisition have been investigating an optimal level of comprehension using simplification strategies in reading. Despite varied findings, the consensus is that a simplification of the original text is necessary when a language learner does not achieve comprehension after reading. Also, a simplification that focuses on enriching the reader's reading experience using elaboration and re-organization of the reading proves more successful than simply cutting down information and watering down the content. An elaboration involves adding simple words to describe difficult words, signaling a clear transition or a train of thought, using graphics and visuals to illustrate the information, and shortening the sentence but preserving the original content (Oh, 2001). Table 35 is an adapted simplification strategy based on Jameson (1998).

Fictional Reading in Mathematics

Mathematics reading has long been oriented toward textbook or workbook reading, especially at the secondary level. However, research (Borasi & Sigel, 2001; Chappell & Thompson, 1999) has shown that by including other reading materials, such as folktales and non-expository text, such as stories and poems, the teacher can use reading as a tool to teach abstract mathematics concepts and promote interest and motivation in learning mathematics. Borasi and Brown (1985) compared and contrasted the two styles of writing and reading between the textbook and novel

	Novel	*Textbook*
Reader's motivation	high, intrinsic interest	low, being forced
Sequence of the knowledge	inductive	deductive
Conception of truth	negotiated	fixed
Amount of information	given in chunks	overloaded
Path to solve a problem	can be several	one way only
Reader's attitude toward the writer	read to make believe	believe before reading
Writer's attention to the reader	very much, showing appeals	less

According to these researchers, textbook writers need to improve their writing by learning from how fiction and non-fiction writers pay attention to their reader's prior experiences, feelings, ways of thinking, and beliefs. Also, the mathematics classroom should include the readings besides the textbook by including authentic and engaging materials. These works as shown in Appendix A use an exploratory and inductive text structure to discuss complex mathematics concepts, which ease the reading difficulty that English language learners tend to have with deductive hypothetical principle → explanation → application text structure. In dealing with culturally and linguistically diverse students, folktales work better to include non-Western culture in mathematics instruction and create cultural connections and capture students' attention.

TABLE 35
Five Guidelines for Simplifying Language in Mathematics Textbooks

Guideline	Original Text	Simplified Version
1. Make a long sentence into several short sentences.	The various possible results of the experiment are outcomes, and the collection of all possible outcomes of an experiment is the sample space (S).	A probability experiment has many results. These results are called outcomes. The sample space is a collection of all the outcomes.
2. Change passive voice into active voice.	The number of outcomes in event E is denoted by n (E), and the number of outcomes in the sample space S is denoted by n (S).	We name the number of outcomes in event E n (E). We name the number of outcomes in the sample space S n (S)
3. Underline key points or words and define these points or words if necessary.	To calculate the probability of an event, you count the number of outcomes in the event and in the sample space.	To calculate the probability of an event, you count the number of outcomes (results) in the event (a specific result) and in the sample space (a collection of all the results).
4. Turn narratives into lists.	To calculate the probability of an event, you count the number of outcomes in the event and in the sample space. The number of outcomes in event E is denoted by n (E), and the number of outcomes in the sample space S is denoted by n (S).	To calculate the probability of an event: 1. Count the number of all the outcomes in the sample space. 2. Count the number of the specific events that you are interested in. 3. Divide the number of the specific events from the number of all the outcomes in the sample space.
5. Use charts and diagrams to illustrate relationships among key concepts and words.	The various possible results of the experiment are outcomes, and the collection of all possible outcomes of an experiment is the sample space (S). Finally, any subcollection of a sample space is an event (E).	See figure above.

Note: The original text is taken from Precalculus by Larson/Hostetler, 1993, D. C. Heath and Company, pp. 716

Logical Connectors

Logical connectors, such as "if . . . then," "if and only if," or, "and," "either . . . or," used in mathematics vary in meaning compared to these connectors use in everyday English (Esty, 1992). They are used to link abstract thoughts and indicate the relationship between these thoughts in mathematics, which often extend beyond or are different from the common English language use. For English language learners, who just begin to learn the use of "and" and "or" in English, understanding the logical concepts of these words can be very challenging. However, proper understanding of the use of these connectors in mathematics reading is a critical aspect of high school mathematics learning. One way to deal with this is to use these learners' English grammatical knowledge to compare and contrast the use of these connectors in common English and mathematical language as in Table 36.

Word Problem Trouble Shooter

Word problems prove to be the most challenging mathematics reading for non-native English speaking students. Word problems often use conditional sentence structure and logical connectives with modifiers or clauses, thus creating a syntactical labyrinth for non-native English readers. Gerofsky (1996) discussed the three discourse components of a word problem:

1. a set-up component,
2. an information component, and
3. a question component.

TABLE 36

Example	Function of connectors	Equivalent Forms	Mathematical Meaning
If it stops raining, then I will go for a walk.	predicting a future action	If p, then q $(p \rightarrow q)$	p is true except when hypothesis p leads to a false conclusion q
You can pass the test only if you study.	stating a fact	p if and only if q $(p \leftrightarrow p)$	p and q are true only when p and q are both true or both false.
Sue likes golf and Lee likes swimming.	paralleling two statements giving cohesion	p and q $(p\ ?\ q)$	p and q are true only when both are true.
The school bus is late or my watch is fast.	giving choices and alternatives	p or q $(p?q)$	p or q is true when any one of the statement is true.

Although sometimes these three components may collapse into one or two lengthy sentences, they are still observable. In component one, there is often a story line offering a simple plot and characters, aiming at activating the reader's appropriate background knowledge about the problem. The background knowledge brought into the problem has to be relevant, specific, and sufficient, but not too much. However, for English language learners component one of the word problem can be problematic because these learners may not share the background knowledge that the word problem writer or the teacher of the word problem has in mind. Furthermore, complex sentences with frequent use of prepositions and connectors tend to make the reading difficult. Therefore, some cultural and language teaching is necessary to establish the background knowledge that the problem required and to simplify the problem. Look at the two examples below:

Distance and speed problem:

> A plane takes 5 hours to fly from Atlanta to Los Angeles and 4 hours to return from Los Angeles to Atlanta. If the wind velocity is 50 mph from the west on both trips, what is the airspeed of the plane in still air?

In this problem, considerations have to be taken in terms of the English language learner's familiarity with the geography of the United States so that they can know that Los Angeles is in the west of Atlanta and it takes more time to fly to Atlanta (because it flies against the wind) than it takes to come back from Los Angeles (because it flies with the wind). Second, two terms used to express the meaning of speed, one is velocity and the other airspeed, may not be in second language students' vocabulary. Even though airspeed is introduced, still, the term "still air" might need to be clarified to make sure that students understand the differences in speed between flying in still air and flying in the air that has wind velocity. Finally, acronyms such as "mph" have to be checked for students' understanding. A mathematics teacher can either engage students into rewriting the problem or use visuals to illustrate the problem to ensure comprehension. The following are illustrations of the above two procedures:

Rewriting the Problem:
A plane takes 5 hours to fly from Atlanta to Los Angeles. Los Angeles is west of Atlanta. It takes 4 hours to fly back to Atlanta from Los Angeles. The wind blows at 50 miles per hour from west to east, meaning from Los Angeles to Atlanta. Question: what is the plane's average speed without thinking about the wind speed? (Figure 34)
Once a language barrier is cleared, students can then proceed to solve the problem.

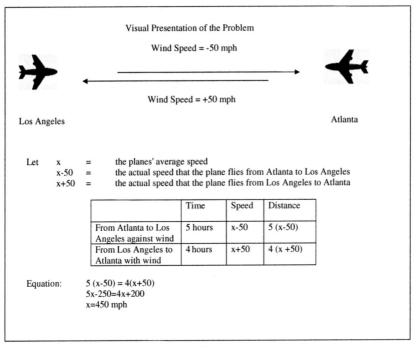

FIGURE 34

Mixture problem;

Forty liters of a 80 percent sugar lemonade are reduced to a 50 percent sugar lemonade. How much must be drained off and replaced with distilled water so that the resulting solution will contain only 50 percent sugar?

In this problem, several language issues have to be addressed to ensure comprehension. First several idiomatic phrases used here need to be rephrased to enhance understanding, such as reduced to (make it smaller), drained off (remove or take out), distilled water (water without any salt) and replaced with (changed into). Next, a repeated use of passive voice can confuse second language learners. Therefore, a change in sentence structure from passive voice to active voice is necessary. Finally, the condensed and long sentence structure has to be broken down into chunks of information for accurate comprehension. A teacher can rewrite the problem like this:

We want to reduce 20 liters of 80 percent sugar lemonade to 50 percent sugar lemonade. We want to add to some water to make the 80 percent sugar lemonade into the 50 percent sugar lemonade. How much 80 percent sugar lem-

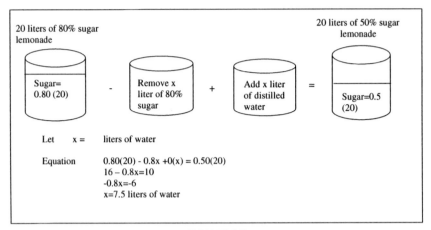

FIGURE 35

onade must we remove and how much water must we add to make the 20 liters of a 50 percent sugar lemonade? (see Figure 35)

Guided Reading

The style of textbook writing as shown in the above is based on the assumption that mathematics is taught and learned through explanations and practiced and students' reading skills have already developed from exploratory to expository and from inductive to deductive at the secondary level. However, the textbook writer is not aware of the change in the student body and given little consideration to their readers' previous language, educational, reading experiences, such as English language learners who may have just learned how to read and write in English. Even though some English language learners may appear very proficient with algorithm skills, they may not understand or are able to express the concepts or the reasoning behind their calculation. Since often the mathematics text is interwoven between written language with symbolic language, students tend to bypass the written language to do the exercises. If not taught how to read, these students may not be able to progress into the higher-level mathematics courses. Therefore, there is a need for mathematics teachers to teach appropriate ways of reading mathematics textbooks, to model the process, and to guide students rather than to simply assign the reading but never check for the students' understanding or show the students how to read a mathematics text.

One strategy called guided reading can be useful in this context (Manzo, 1975). Guided reading is a reading demonstration that the teacher first shows how she goes about making meaning using reading strategies and non-verbal cues, to paraphrase what she reads, and to summarize what she has read to the students, then guides the students along using the same strategies that the teacher just has modeled, and finally lets the students read independently. For example, look at the following (Figure 36):

> When two polygons can be moved in such a way that the sides and angles of one polygon fit exactly upon the sides and angles of the second polygon, we call these figures congruent polygons. In simpler terms, we say that congruent polygons have the same shape and the same size. As shown in the diagram, polygon ABCD is congruent to polygon EFGH. Notice that the congruent polygons were named in such a way that the order of their vertices indicates a one-to-one correspondence of points.

In reading this excerpt, a teacher can model to the students the following three reading strategies:

1. making sense of the passage using contextual clues or a dictionary.
2. asking questions about the key points in the passage.
3. retelling in your own words what this reading is about.

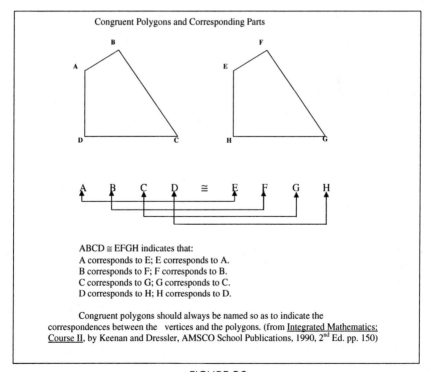

Congruent Polygons and Corresponding Parts

ABCD ≅ EFGH indicates that:
A corresponds to E; E corresponds to A.
B corresponds to F; F corresponds to B.
C corresponds to G; G corresponds to C.
D corresponds to H; H corresponds to D.

Congruent polygons should always be named so as to indicate the correspondences between the vertices and the polygons. (from Integrated Mathematics: Course II, by Keenan and Dressler, AMSCO School Publications, 1990, 2nd Ed. pp. 150)

FIGURE 36

In illustrating the use of the first reading strategy, the teacher can show to the students how to identify and highlight the unknown words and phrases, such as polygon, fit, figures, congruent, vertices, one-to-one, correspondence, etc. Making use of the diagrams and symbolic language on the side of the passage, the teacher can model how to actively guess the meaning of these words. During the reading, the teacher asks questions about their understanding, such as "Why do we call these two shapes 'polygon?'" "What is the meaning of 'congruence?'" "Does 'congruence' mean the 'same?'" "Why do we have to focus on a one-to-one correspondence of all the points?" "What does the 'vertex' have anything to do with the congruence of the two polygons?" By posing these questions, the teacher demonstrates her thinking process that allows her to derive meaning from the text. Finally, a retelling in her own words, the teacher directs the students' attention to reflect on what is read and to organize the new information in a meaningful and coherent way. Here is a sample retelling of the passage above:

> In order to know whether two polygons are congruent, we must make sure that these two polygons have the same shape and the same size. That means that each side of polygon A has to be the same as the matching side of polygon B.

SECOND LANGUAGE READING INSTRUCTION IN ENGLISH LANGUAGE ARTS CLASSES

Parallel Reading

Studying various versions of literary texts has been recommended by Anderson and Rubano (1991) as an aesthetic reading activity to engage the reader in critical and creative responses to literature. Although their examples were drawn from native English speakers, the same principle can be applied to second language learning situations. In order to make sure that English language learners have exposure to the original literature but at the same time their reading difficulties are taken care of, a parallel reading of different versions of the literature can work very well (Samuel, 1993). For example, each of the various versions of Shakespeare's *Romeo and Juliet* can offer something different—the dramatic language use of the original, a prose summary of a simplified version, and the visual impact of the comic book.

Shakespeare for Kids: His life and times by Colleen Aagesen and Marcie Blumberg, Chicago, IL: Chicago Review Press. 1999.
Shakespeare Can Be Fun! Romeo and Juliet for Kids by Lois Burdett, Firefly Books Ltd. 1998;

Shake Hands with Shakespeare: Eight Plays for Elementary Schools by Cullum, New York: Scholastic, Inc. 1985;

Tales from Shakespeare by Charles and Mary Lamb, Puffin Books, 1987;

Shakespeare Made Easy: An Illustrated Approach by Muriel J. Portland, ME: Weston Walch Publisher, 1990; and

Beautiful Stories from Shakespeare for Children by Nesbit, Totowa, NJ: Barnes and Noble Books, 2002

Together, they provide students with the opportunity to compare and contrast, to help with their reading, and to offer an insight which often one text might not be able to achieve. By exposing students to various versions according to students' language proficiency levels and progressing from simple to difficult reading levels and finally studying the original version of the text, students will not be intimidated by the text and reading and they will even have fun (Castantino, 1995). Reading discussion can then be moved beyond the comprehension level to a critical and creative level.

Slow-Paced Audio Book Reading

Research in second language classroom learning has supported instruction that involves the learner in learning using multi-modalities, such as listening, speaking, reading, and writing skills all at once. When an English language learner sits in an English class, s/he is expected to do a lot of listening, listening to the teacher's talk, classroom discussions, the read-aloud of the text, and sometimes the video or audio taped version of the literature under study. However, many times the classroom talks go by quickly and the read-aloud goes by in a rapid pace. The language learner does not have time to identify many language challenges such as idiomatic usage, figurative language, and humor in the listening. Raphan (1996) suggested micro-listening skill training for college English language learners by isolating language challenges and training students on these language components and presenting the listening material in both visual and audio formats to enhance comprehension. With the diverse literature works as an authentic listening resource, using slow-paced audio recorded reading can provide English language learners with rich language exposure and practice (Beers, 1998).

Audio-recorded books can expose the second language learner to the language modeled by native speakers, enhance the students' ability to make the sound and meaning connection in the new language, and immerse the student in a pure enjoyment of literature through audio impact which silent reading cannot achieve. Slow paced audio books adjusted to these students' language proficiency levels can be used as an effective learning tool for students. These books can also be used for whole class reading or listening activities. In the following is a list of selected titles of audio books compiled by Recorded Books (2700 Skipjack Rd., Prince Frederick, MD 20678, 1-800-638-1304, www.recordedbks.com).

The adventure of Huckleberry Finn by Mark Twain (8 cassettes/11.75 hours)
The adventure of Tom Sawyer by Mark Twain (5 cassettes/7 hours)
Animal farm by George Orwell (3 cassettes/3.25 hours)
Anne Frank: The diary of a young girl (6 cassettes/9 hours)
The call of the wild by Jack London (3 cassettes/4.5 hours)
The chocolate war by Robert Comier (5 cassettes/6.5 hours)
The contender by Robert Lipsyte (4 cassettes/5.25 hours)
Fahrenheit 451 by Ray Bradbury (4 cassettes/5.5 hours)
The light in the forest by Conrad Richter (3 cassettes/4 hours)
My Antonia by Willa Cather (6 cassettes/8.5 hours)
Number the stars by Lois Lowry (3 cassettes/3.5 hours)
The outsiders by S. E. Hinton (4 cassettes/5.5 hours)
The pearl by John Steinbeck (2 cassettes/2.75 hours)
The red badge of courage by Stephen Crane (3 cassettes/4.5 hours)
Shabanu: Daughter of the wind by Suzanne Fisher Staples (5 cassettes/6.75 hours)
Summer of my German soldier by Bette Greene (6 cassettes/7.75 hours)
Things fall apart by Chinua Achebe (5 cassettes/6.5 hours)
To kill a mockingbird by Harper Lee (9 cassettes/13.5 hours)
Where the red fern grow by Wilson Rawls (6 cassettes/7.75 hours)

Dual-Language Reading

Dual-language reading (reading in both the student's first language and English), especially in the beginning stage of second language learning, is an effective way for English language learners to make the transition from their native language to English. Research done by Edward and Walker (1996) and Miriam (1994) has found that dual-language reading materials (picture books that contain both English and the students' native language) are effective not only in easing second language learners' difficulty in reading English but also building a valuable bridge between home language and school language. Many picture books, trade books, and juvenile literature works are written in the students' native language. Reading a book in both the students' native language and in English can be used creatively to help students learn English. The following is a sample of such reading materials:

Spanish/English
Bofill, F. (1998). *Jack and the beanstalk—Juan y los frijoles magicos*. San Francisco: Chronicle Books

Johnston, T. (1996). *My Mexico—Mexico mio.* New York, G. P. Putnam's Sons.

Lachtman, O. (1998). *Big enough—Bastante grande.* Houston, TX: Pinata Books.

Reisner, L. (1993). *Margaret and Margarita—Margarita y Margaret.* New York: Greenwillow Books.

Reisner, L. (1998). *Tortillas and lullabies—Tortillas y cancioncitas.* New York: Greenwillow Books.

Humong/English

Campbell, R. (1992). *I won't bite.* Union City, CA: Pan Asian Publications.

Thao, C. (1993). *Only a toad.* Green Bay, WI: Project Chong.

Humong/Spanish/English

Coburn, J. R., & Lee, T. C. (1996). *Jouanah, a Hmong Cinderella.* Arcadia, CA: Shen's Books.

Vietnamese/English

Trugen, T. (1987). *The little weaver of Thai-yen village—Co be tho-det lang thai-yen.* San Francisco, CA: Children's Book Press.

Chinese/English

Ching, E., et al. (1991). *Two bushels of grain: forget the turnips!* Cerritos, CA : Wonder Kids Publications.

Ching, E., et al. (1991). *The Blind man & the cripple* Cerritos, CA : Wonder Kids Publications.

Ching, E., et al. (1991). *Sun valley: A stone carvers' dream = Thai yang kuo ti chin tzu: Shih chiang ti meng.* Cerritos, CA : Wonder Kids Publications.

Shepard, A. (2001). *Lady white snake: A tale from Chinese opera.* Union City, CA: Pan Asian Publications (U S A), Incorporated.

Zhao, Q. (1998). *Liang Shanbo and Zhu Ying Tai,* Beijing, China: New World Press.

Graphic Organizers in Reading Instruction

a. Literature Maps

Visual presentation of the story, whether a map or a chart or a graphic, can often help students untangle the complex plot of a long work and crystallize the key events or issues under study. Based on the work that they have read, students can create a map of the protagonist's journey, the relationships among characters, or a timeline of events. For example, students can map out Esmeralda's journey of coming to America, including the places and the obstacles that she encountered in her journey in their reading of *When I Was A Puerto Rican* by Esmeralda Santiago. They can draw a map identifying where major scenes took place, create a timeline of when the events happened, or write a narrative about the key events or places. Figure 37 shows Esmeralda's journey of coming to America.

b. Character Comparison Chart

A use of a character comparison chart, a student generated visual display of the characters' traits and their relationships among each other in the book, can help to deepen students' understanding of the major characters under study. A character chart can begin in the pre-reading stage and continue with students' reading and be completed after the reading is finished. By assigning groups of students to do a character chart, the teacher can really get students focused on descriptive language use, such as key vocabulary, when the author introduces each character and how each character develops in relation to other characters. Students can also write a caption of their characters or quote from their characters to make a textual connection with their characters. Students who are artistically talented can even create a character portrait along with the chart. The chart can be put on the wall for display and comparison. Table 37 is a character chart of *Stella: On the Edge of Popularity* by Lee.

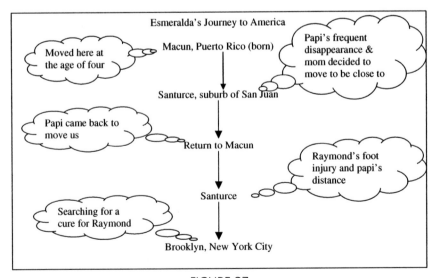

FIGURE 37

TABLE 37

Character	Appearance	Behavior	Personality
Stella Sung Ok	12 yr old Soft, rounded nose Soft dark hair in a braid Brown-black eyes Heart-shaped face Straight, small white teeth	excellent in school work Helps out house chores trying to be friends with Elieen	courageous strong innocent
Mother	smooth black hair well combed Swollen feet and wrinkled dress Dark circles under her eyes	Speaks little English worked as a nurse in Korea	Gentle strong
Father Apha	stern, serious Treats boys favorably	Only speaks Korean Works as an engineer in Korea	strong quiet, Hard working
Grandmother	old Gray hair pulled the tight at her temples Wears pink glasses Little nose	Does the house chores Controls the family Smokes Treats boys favorably Only speaks Korean	demanding hard working caring for Stella
Eileen	White Wear pink and purple Long hair loose Thin with blond hair	making racist remarks Popular among peers asks Stella to do her math	arrogant, ignorant superior, spoiled
Rachel	Jewish Wears gold-flecked Indian scarf Auburn hair	sympathetic for Stella excellent student disapproves Elieen's behavior	caring, friendly rivalry with Eileen, strong

Quotation Collage

An in-depth study of quotations in literary works has several advantages to English language learners. Many English teachers have included quotation study in their teaching to students for the Regents exam. Besides this, a quotation study can offer students an opportunity to closely examine language use in context. It can also deepen and broaden students' understanding of a concept or a theme (Morache, 1987). Finally, many English language learners claim that they have learned English through an intensive reading process back home in their native countries; therefore, any in-depth examination of the language will trigger these students' motivation and create a familiar environment for second language acquisition. One way of studying quotations is using collages or drawings to visually interpret and display the quote. Visual approaches can reshape and reinforce the written text. By purposefully combining visual and verbal approaches in instruction, the teacher provides concrete and meaningful connections for the students to make meaning of the verbal language. If the students are artistically inclined, they can create their own pictures to depict the concept or the theme of the quotation. Students can even use ready-made materials, such as newspaper and magazine pictures, photos, etc. to interpret and represent the meaning of the quotation.

Text Transformation

This is an exercise where students replace selected words or phrases in the original text to make a new text. It is often used to help students to actively construct meaning through context and to be active participants in reading a literary text (Anderson & Rubano, 1991). Students who have learned a second language in a word for word translation and memorization approach often have little tolerance for the unknown words in the reading passage. Over-reliance on the dictionary and a lack of skill in guessing meaning from contextual clues slow their reading and prevent them from become active readers. Thus, a use of a text transformation exercise when appropriate can force the students to extract meaning from the context and the overall meaning of the reading. Students will realize that they do not have to know every single word in order to understand a passage. Also, inserting their own words or phrases gives students the pleasure of recreating a text and practice in using language creatively. An after reading discussion of the words that students put in and a comparison of students' creations with the author's original text should be fruitful in exploring students' understanding and fostering literature appreciation. This helps students to focus their attention to holistic meaning and at the same time to the semantic and syntactic cues of the language. For example, an examination of word choice can lead to a study of language structure. Therefore, this has an additional benefit of training students' language skills. The following is an example of a cloze reading and writing exercise using an excerpt of Sandra Cisneros' *The House on Mango Street*.

The House on Mango Street by Sandra Cisneros (p. 28).
Those Who Don't

Those who don't know any better come into our neighborhood *scared*. They think we're *dangerous*. They think *we will attack them with shiny knives*. They are the people who are *lost and got here by mistake*.

But we aren't *afraid*. We know *the guy with the crooked eye* is *Davey the Baby's brother*, and *the tall one* next to him in *the straw brim*, that's Rosa's Eddie V., and the *big one that* looks like *a dumb grown man*, he's Fat Boy, though *he's not fat anymore nor a boy*.

All *brown* all around, we are *safe*. But watch us drive into *a neighborhood of another color* and *our knees go shakity-shake and our car windows get rolled up tight and our eyes look straight*. Yeah. That is how it goes and goes.

Cloze Writing Activity: Those Who Don't

Those who don't know any better come into our neighborhood
_____. They think we're _____ they think _____.
They are_____people who are_____.
   But we aren't _____. We know _____ is _____ and the
_____ next to him/her in _____ , that's _____ and the
_____that looks like _____
   All _____ all around, we are _____. But watch us drive into
_____ and _____Yeah. That is how it
goes and goes.

The following are some sample student writing based on the cloze exercise.

Those Who Don't

Those who don't know any better come to our neighborhood are puncha.
They think we're crazy. They think we'll beat them up. They are dumb peo-
ple who are lost in their own world. But we aren't worried.
   We know there is unity here and serk next to him in the buoincos suit,
that's laughable, and the Slack Sam that looks like a wolf in sheep clothing he
is really a snake. All of us are protected all around. We are wise to them.
   But watch us drive into a white neighborhood and with the music up loud.
Yeah. That is how is goes and goes.

Those Who Don't

Those who don't know any better come into our neighborhood open-
handed. They think we're rich. They think we will give them money.
   They are crazy people who are asking for money. They should hurry and
leave. But we aren't giving them a dime. We know what they want. And there
is only one thing, WHAT the tall one, and the skinny one next to him in the
white, that's the same one, and the little girl that looks like me is evil, she's
kind of cute.
   All of them are holding out there hands all around, we were getting
scared. But watch us drive into their neighborhood and tell their parents.
Yeah. That is how it goes and goes.

Those Who Don't

Those who don't know any better come into our neighborhood scared. They
think we're ignorant. They think we're stupid people. They mistake people
who are scared.
   But we aren't who they think we are. We know David is the boy with a snoty
attitude and the lady next to him in the car, that's his mother, and the man
next to him that looks like a dog, he's David's father.
   All light all around, we are not scared. But watch us drive into a neighbor-

hood were people look different and we'll get scared. Yeah. That is how it goes and goes.

Those Who Don't

Those who don't know any better come into our neighborhood wide-eyed. They think we're weird. They think we have very strange ways of living. They are outside people who are learning something new about people.

But we aren't odd. We know the guy with the flashy car is Tim, and the beautiful lady next to him in tight blue jeans, that's Hazel, and the little girl that looks like a kid, she's cool, too.

All people all around, we are happy. But watch us drive into your neighborhood and we will still be happy. Yeah. That is how it goes and goes.

Jigsaw Reading

A jigsaw reading activity is an exercise that the teacher first breaks a long piece of reading into manageable parts and then assigns students to be responsible for one part of the reading. After the reading, the students who read different parts come together in a group to share their reading and piece together the whole reading passage as a group. In doing so, the teacher can not only accomplish a whole reading passage in class, but also create opportunities for students to talk, listen, and work together to create meaning. For beginning second language learners, jigsaw reading works well in training them reading skills as well as listening, speaking, and writing skills. Because of the set up of the activity, each student is an "expert" in his or her part of the story; therefore s/he has something important to share with the group. The excitement of piecing together a story can motivate students to speak and to be actively involved in group work. After talking and sharing, students can write up their version of the story and present it to the class. The teacher can then compare and contrast the student's version with the original and give discussion questions for deeper understanding. The following is an example using Rudolfo Anaya's "Celebration of Grandparents":

Part 1

"Buenos dias le de Dios, abuelo." God give you a good day, grandfather. This is how I was taught as a child to greet my grandfather, or any grown person. It was a greeting of respect, a cultural value to be passed on from generation to generation, this respect for the old ones.

The old people I remember from my childhood were strong in their beliefs, and as we lived daily with them, we learned a wise path of life to follow. They had something important to share with the young, and when they spoke, the young listened. These old *abuelos* and *abuelitas* had worked the earth all their lives, and so they knew the value of nurturing, they knew the sensitivity of the earth. . . . They knew the rhythms and cycles of time, from the preparation of the earth in the spring to the digging of the *acequias* that brought the water to the dance of harvest in the fall. They shared good times and hard times. They helped each other through the epidemics and the personal tragedies, and they shared what little they had when the hot winds burned the land and no rain came. They learned that to survive one had to share in the process of life. . . .

Part 2

My grandfather was a plain man, a farmer from the valley called Puerto de Luna on the Pecos River. He was probably a descendant of those people who spilled over the mountain from Taos, following the Pecos River in search of farmland. There in that river valley he settled and raised a large family.Bearded and walrus-mustached, he stood five feet tall, but to me as if a child he was a giant. I remember him most for his silence. In the summers my parents sent me to live with him on his farm, for I was to learn the ways of a farmer. My uncles also lived in that valley, there where only the flow of the river and the whispering of the wind marked time. For me it was a magical place.

I remember once, while out hoeing the fields, I came upon an anthill, and before I knew it I was badly bitten. After he had covered my welts with the cool mud from the irrigation ditch, my grandfather calmly said: "Know where you stand. " That is the way he spoke, in short phrases, to the point.

Part 3

One very dry summer, the river dried to a trickle; there was no water for the fields. The young plants withered and died. In my sadness and with the impulse of youth I said, "I wish it would rain!" My grandfather touched me, looked up into the sky and whispered, "Pray for rain." In his language there was a difference. He felt connected to the cycles that brought the rain or kept it from us. His prayer was a meaningful action, because he was a participant with the forces that filled our world; he was not a bystander.

A young man died at the village one summer. A very tragic death. He was dragged by his horse. When he was found, I cried, for the boy is my friend. I did not understand why death had come to one so close. My grandfather took me aside and said: "Think of the boy as the death of the trees and fields in the fall. The leaves fall, and everything rest, as if dead. But they bloom again in the spring. Death is only a small transformation in life."

Questions to be answered as a whole group:

1. Why did Anaya say of his grandfather, "I remember him most for his silence"?

2. What are the lessons Anaya learned from his grandfather's words? What do these words mean?
3. Why did Anaya have tremendous respect for his grandfather?
4. What did grandfather say about the brought?
5. Why did Anaya say that his grandfather was a plain man?

SECOND LANGUAGE READING INSTRUCTION IN SOCIAL STUDIES CLASSES

Parallel Reading

Because a major component of social studies learning involves expository reading, such as textbooks, documents, articles, etc., there is a need for the social studies teacher to bridge the language and conceptual gaps to ensure an understanding of the concepts and ideas. One way of easing the difficulty of demanding social studies textbook reading is to use parallel reading materials drawn from juvenile's literature and ESL resources. A social studies teacher can even rewrite the sections of the textbook or engage the advanced learners in rewriting key sections of the textbook or summaries of the documents to use these as parallel reading materials for English language learners to first get the students past the barrier of comprehension. These parallel readings, especially juvenile literature, are written not only with simplified ways of communicating the social studies concepts but also using an inquiry-based and exploratory approach, well suited for new language learners' language learning needs. The following is an example of such parallel readings on the Greek Wars.

> Greece also had trouble with other countries. King Philip was the ruler of Macedonia. Macedonia was a country north of Greece. In 337 BC, King Philip began to conquer the Greek city-states. Sparta was the only Greek city-state that he did not conquer. When King Philip was killed, his son, Alexander, became the leader of Macedonia. Alexander went to school in Athens. There Aristotle taught Alexander philosophy. But Alexander was not known as a scholar. He was a mighty warrior. King Alexander lead an army made up of Macedonian and Greek soldiers. They conquered Persia, the rest of Asia Minor and the Middle East. That was most of the ancient western world. For this he became known as Alexander the Great.

After the death of Alexander the Great, his empire was split into three parts. Each part was ruled by one of his generals. The three parts were Macedonia, Syria and Egypt. Later most were conquered by the Romans. (from Field, R. J. *World history: Understanding our past* pp. 43-44, New York: Educational Services, Inc., 2000)

Alexander the Great

As a young boy, Alexander was taught by the great Greek philosopher Aristotle. He loved Greek poetry and art, and was interested in science. Just like his father, Philip of Macedon, he wanted to conquer other lands. He is best remembered as a brave solider. He conquered so much land in Europe, Asia, and Africa that he became known as Alexander the Great.

Alexander led his armies into Asia Minor, Syria, Palestine, and Egypt. He attacked Greece's old enemy, Persia. He defeated the King of Persia, Darius III. All the lands of Persia came under the Greek rule of Alexander. He treated the Persians carefully, they had once been rules of his empire. They could revolt at any time and defeat his empire. Alexander said that his men should marry Persian women. He set an example by marrying Roxane from Sogdiana. She was Persian.

Alexander was only 32 when he died from a fever in 323 BC He made no plans for his empire after his death. Eventually three of his generals took parts of his empire. They ruled over them as kings. Alexander's conquests paved the way for the blending of Greek civilization with the cultures of the ancient Middle East. (from Rees, R. *The Ancient Greeks* pp. 56. Heinemann, 1997)

The Rise of Macedonia

Greeks who worried about foreign invasion thought the danger was still the Persian Empire. A new kingdom, however, was arising in Macedonia, in the northern part of the Greek peninsula.

Philip

In 359 BC a young rule named Philip became a king of Macedonia. Philip built a strong army and won the support of some city-states that opposed Athens. A great Athenian statesman and public speaker, Demosthenes, warned of this new threat, but the quarrelsome city-states could not unite soon enough to stop the invaders. In 338 BC, at Chaeronea, Philip's forces crushed the Greek alliance. The Greek lost what they loved most—their independence.

Alexander the Great

Philip was assassinated in 336 BC, and his 20-year-old son Alexander became ruler. He is known to history as Alexander the Great. From his father Alexander had learned military skill, leadership ability, and a deep desire to conquer the Persian Empire. Alexander had also studied under Aristotle, developing scientific curiosity and a love for Greek culture. He knew Homer's epics well, and he dreamed of matching the deeds of the heroes of the Iliad and Odyssey.

Daring and intelligent, Alexander became one of the greatest military leaders in history. In 334 BC, he crossed the Hellespont and took over the Greek colonies held by the Persians in Asia Minor. Phoenicia was next to fall, and then Egypt. In 331 BC Mesopotamia came under Alexander's rule. After defeating the king of Perisa in battle, Alexander sped on to northwestern India. Between 334 and 326 BC Alexander's armies conquered the lands from Egypt to India without losing a battle.

In Babylon in 323 BC Alexander died of a fever. He was not quite 33 years old. His death ended the brief period of unity that had brought together Greece and the ancient Middle East. None of the Alexander's generals was able to control the vast empire, and it broke into three separate kingdoms. (Perry, *et al. History of the world*, p. 90-91. McDougal Littell Inc. 1995)

The above three readings are taken from an ESL adapted world history book as shown in passage one, juvenile literature as shown in passage two, and a regular social studies textbook as shown in passage three. Although the topic is the same, passages taken from ESL and juvenile literature sources have shorter sentences (about 9 or 10 words per sentence), while the regular textbook passages have about 15 or 16 words per sentence with varied clause structures and modified elements in the sentence. In addition, vocabulary in the ESL and juvenile literature pieces is easy to understand and as a result, the English language learner is not bogged down by many new words, and reading becomes less labor intensive. Ideally students who begin with passage one should continue to read passage two or even three to make sure that the content knowledge is reinforced, and in turn, students can read the original text with little difficulty.

Focused Reading

Focused reading or narrow reading (Cho & Krashen, 1994; Krashen, 1981; Schmitt & Carter, 2000) refers to reading on one specific topic through a variety of sources or genres or at different reading levels. Second Language acquisition research has shown that a sustained reading on one focused topic either for pleasure or class read-aloud can have a significant growth in second language vocabulary and reading. As a result, students' conceptual knowledge about the content area will be greatly enhanced also. Through focused reading or narrow reading, the reader has read in various contexts and been exposed to recurrent vocabulary used on that topic. Also, through reading on a focused issue in different genres or contexts or levels, the reader has become more familiarized with the topic, and therefore, understanding is increased. A social studies teacher can facilitate this by assigning English language students a range of readings at various reading levels on key topics or concepts. Table 38 is an example of some reading materials that can be used for focused reading.

TABLE 38

Topic: Confucius		
ESL material	**Juvenile Literature**	**Internet**
Field (2000) World History pp. 86-90	Hooblers (1997) Confucianism	http://www.friesian.com/confuci.htm (with Chinese characters)
Ahmad et al. (1993) World Cultures pp. 330	Wilker (1999) Confucius: Philosopher and teacher	http://www.enteract.com/~geenius/kongfuzi/ (with a biography)
	Rowland-Entwhistle (1987) Confucius and Ancient China	www.friesian.com/confuci.htm (The Analects of Confucius in both Chinese and English)
	Odijk (1991) The Chinese	

Textbook Simplification

Social studies textbooks are written in a parallel with students' grade-level reading proficiency. At the secondary level, the textbook discourse tends to be laden with passive verbs, long and complex sentence structures. For English language learners, the textbook reading poses a huge challenge. These students must reach a high or advanced level of language proficiency before they can fully understand the reading materials. Second language researchers have found that using a modification of the textbook reading can offer more opportunities for English language learners increase comprehension. Jameson (1998) provided five guidelines for such a modification of the content material according to English language learners' language levels to ease reading difficulties and enhance comprehension. These procedures are fairly simple and straightforward for a social studies teacher to use to make complex reading comprehensible for students at low English proficiency levels. The social studies teacher can either do it himself/herself to simplify key excerpts in the reading or they can engage the native English speaking students in simplifying these excerpts for their non-native English speaking peers. The focus should be on simplifying the language but not the content of the reading by paraphrasing the key social studies concepts and ideas. Three of the five guidelines (Jameson, 1998) and their applications are shown in Table 39.

Highlighting Organizational Links

Typical social studies reading materials have five major organizational links to represent ideas in a logical manner (Short, 1994a, 1994b). These five organizational links are: illustration, sequence, comparison and con-

TABLE 39

Guideline	Sample original text	Simplified text
1. Use short sentences and eliminate extraneous material.	Sea captains who ventured into uncharted oceans, explorers who penetrated unknown lands, soldiers who conquered vast overseas territories--all were driven by curiosity, the desire for adventure, and the hope of fame (p. 347).	Sea captains, explorers, and soldiers all wanted adventure and fame.
2. Change pronouns to nouns.	Other Europeans--especially the Portuguese --hoped to find a water route to the East that would allow them to trade directly with Asia (p. 347).	Other Europeans-- especially the Portuguese --hoped to find a water route to the East that would allow Europeans to trade directly with Asia.
3. Underline key vocabulary and give meanings.	Marx claimed that the exploitation of the "have nots" by the haves" has always caused a class struggle (p. 500).	Marx <u>claimed</u> (said) that the <u>exploitation</u> (treating unfairly) of the "<u>have nots</u>" (poor) by the "<u>haves</u>" (rich) has always caused a <u>class struggle</u> (a struggle between the rich and the poor).

(from Perry, *et al.* <u>History of the world</u>, McDougla Littell Inc. 1995)

trast, cause and effect, and problem and solution. In order to follow the writer's train of thought and make meaning of the reading, a reader has to be aware of these links or signals. Being aware of these links can help students read for relationships between the ideas, thus increase their deeper understanding of the reading material. A social studies teacher can survey the text for major organizational links and plan out how to approach them. If the organizational links are in conceptual understanding of the text, then the teacher needs to find a way to incorporate these links into the lesson by highlighting these links and their functions as shown below.

Many of the Buddha's teachings were consisted with Hindu beliefs. *However,* some sharp differences existed. *For example,* Buddhism placed *more* importance on how one lived *than* one's caste. *In addition,* Buddhists saw little value in the Brahmin's complex rituals *Also, while* the Buddha believed in reincarnation, he did not believe that it was necessary for becoming pure. He taught that a person could gain enlightenment in one lifetime *and so* escape Hinduism's cycle of rebirth (Perry, School, Davis, Harris, & Von Laue, *History of the world*, p. 133. McDougla Littell Inc. 1995).

Functions	*Transitional Links*
illustration	for example, also,
sequence	and, so
comparison and contrast,	however, more . . . than, while
cause and effect,	so, because,

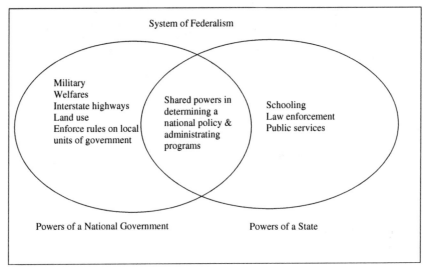

FIGURE 38

Graphic Organizers

Graphic organizers are diagrams used to clarify and illustrate a concept or a historical event and often provide a better visual representation than the textbook definitions and explanations. They are powerful learning tools for improving conceptual learning and enhancing critical thinking (DuPlass, 1996). Many concepts in social studies class may be foreign to many immigrant students whose prior knowledge is either non-existed or mismatched with the prior knowledge required for the study. In this situation, graphic organizers can facilitate comprehension and visualize the relationships among the concepts or the events. For example, many English language learners may easily be confused by the complex political system governed the country. They may have misconceptions about certain issues, such as paying taxes. Therefore, a close reading of the excerpts on these key topics is necessary. Figure 38 is an example of the reading passage describing the federalism and a Venn Diagram to show similarities and differences after reading:

"The basic political fact of federalism," writes David B. Truman, "is that it creates separate, self-sustaining centers of power, prestige, and profit." Political power is locally acquired by people whose careers depend for the most part on satisfying local interests. As a result, though the national government has come to have vast powers, it exercises many of those powers through state governments. What many of us forget when we think about "the government in Washington" is that it spends much of its money and enforces most of its rules not on citizens directly but on other, local units of government. A large part of the welfare system, all of the interstate highway system, virtually every aspect of programs to improve cities, the largest part of the effort to supply jobs to the unemployed, the entire program to clean up our water, and even much of our military power (in the form of the National Guard) are enterprises in which the national government does not govern so much as it seeks, by regulation, grant, plan, argument, and cajolery, to get the states to govern in accordance with nationally defined (though often vaguely defined) goals . . . States participate actively both in determining national policy and in administering national programs. Moreover they reserve to themselves or the localities within them important powers over public services, such as schooling and law enforcement, and important public decisions, such as land-use control, that in unitary systems are dominated by the national government. (From Wilson & Dilulio *American government: Institutions and Policies*, p. 50, 76. 1999.)

Jigsaw Reading

Based on the interactive approach to teaching of reading, jigsaw reading (Aronson, 1978) has shown a gain for second language readers' reading comprehension and communicative skills. In reading a social studies text, for example, a teacher can pair students or create groups of three or five. The reading passage is divided into two, three, or even more sections to make the reading manageable and efficient. The teacher first provides an introduction to the topic of the reading. Then s/he gives a reading handout to the pair or the group, having each read a different section of the passage. Students are encouraged to jot down the main ideas and key words. Afterwards, the students begin sharing their part of the reading and notes within their pairs or groups. Next, the students meet with other pairs or groups of the students who read different sections of the passage. This time, students share with each other what the reading is all about. Jigsaw reading is effective in that it divides the reading task into two or three manageable chunks and saves class time. Also, it fills the information gap because the reader has something to communicate to his or her peer of which the peer has no prior knowledge. That motivates the student to speak up. Finally, working in pairs or groups, students will feel comfortable in talking about their thoughts and using the language to communicate. In the following is an example of a jigsaw reading passage taken from Blassingame, McKivigan, and Hinks edited *Narrative of the Life of Frederick Douglass*:

Part 1

I was born in Tuckahoe, near Hillsborough, and about twelve miles from Easton, in Talbot county, Maryland. I have no accurate knowledge of my age, never having seen any authentic record containing it. By far the larger part of the slaves know as little of their ages as horses know of theirs, and it is the wish of most masters within my knowledge to keep their slaves thus ignorant. I do not remember to have ever met a slave who could tell of his birthday. They seldom come nearer to it than planting-time, harvest-time, cherry-time, spring-time, or fall-time. A want of information concerning my own was a source of unhappiness to me even during childhood. The white children would tell their ages. I could not tell why I ought to be deprived of the same privilege. I was not allowed to make any inquiries of my master concerning it. He deemed all such inquiries on the part of a slave improper and imperti-nent, and evidence of a restless spirit. The nearest estimate I can give makes me now between twenty-seven and twenty-eight years of age. I come to this, from hearing my master say, some time during 1835, I was about seventeen years old.

Part 2

My mother was named Harriet Bailey. She was the daughter of Isaac and Bet-sey Bailey, both colored and quite dark. My mother was of a darker complex-ion than either my grandmother or grandfather. My father was a white man. He was admitted to be such by all I ever heard speak of my parentage. The opinion was also whispered that my master was my father; but of that correct-ness of this opinion, I know nothing; the means of knowing was withheld from me. My mother and I were separated when I was but an infant—before I knew her as my mother. It is a common custom, in the part of Maryland from which I ran away, to part children from their mothers at a very early age. Frequently, before the child has reached its twelfth month, its mother is taken from it, and hired out on some farm a considerable distance off, and the child is placed under the care of an old woman, too old for field labor. For what this separation is done, I do not know, unless it be to hinder the development of a child's affection toward its mother, and to blunt and destroy the natural affection of the mother for the child. This is the inevita-ble result.

Part 3

I never saw my mother, to know her as such, more than four or five times in my life; and each of these times was very short in duration, and at night. She was hired by a Mr. Stewart, who lived about twelve miles from my home. She made her journeys to see me in the night, traveling the whole distance on foot, after the performance of her day's work. She was a field hand, and a whipping is the penalty of not being in the field at sunrise, unless a slave has special permission from his or her master to the contrary—a permission which they seldom get, and one that gives to him that gives it the proud name of being a kind master. I do not recollect of every seeing my mother by the light of day. She was with me in the night. She would lie down with me, and get me to sleep, but long before I waked she was gone. Very little communication ever took place between us. Death soon ended what little we could have while she lived, and with it her hardships and suffering. She died when I was about seven years old, on one of my master's farms, near Lee's Mill. I was not allowed to be present during her illness, at her death, or burial. She was gone long before I knew anything about it. Never having enjoyed, to any considerable extent, her soothing presence, her tender and watchful care, I received the tidings of her death with much the same emotions I should have probably felt at the death of a stranger.

SQ2R Reading

SQ3R (Survey, Question, Read, Recite, and Review) is a reading strategy developed by Robinson in 1961. It has been widely used in expository reading instruction, especially when the reading demand is high and the text is long and difficulty. While reciting is not necessary, the reader definitely can benefit from survey, question, read, and review (SQ2R). In social studies, with an increasing use of primary sources, such as historical documents in the reading, one topic is read from different points of views and from texts produced in different historical times. Often students are buried in mountains of documents and lose the main ideas of the reading. Therefore, learning an effective reading strategy such as SQ3R can make the reading experience more effective and productive and less frustrating (Call, 1991; Scott, 1994). Here is an example:

Nazism's Appeal

Hitler's political strategy was simple but effective. Over and over he repeated what he wanted people to believe. He gave them an enemy to hate and a cause to fight for. He played on their emotions with spellbinding speeches and used violence to impress them with the Nazi Party's power. Calling himself Der Fuhrer (the leader) he said that he would bring Germany out of chaos.

As in Italy, many people in Germany were unhappy with the democratic government and eager for strong leadership. Nazism had a powerful appeal for the less wealthy people of the middle class—shopkeepers, small farmers, office workers, teachers, and artisans. These people believed that Hitler would protect them from the large industrialists and from the Communists.

Many unemployed young men joined the "storm troopers" (Brown Shirts), Hitler's private army. They were given food, shelter, uniforms, and a chance to devote themselves to a cause—the strengthening of Germany. "For us National Socialism is an idea, a faith, a religion," one of them wrote. Bands of storm troopers broke up rival political meetings, attacked Jews, and fought street battles with the Communists.

By the end of 1932 the Nazis had become the strongest political party in Germany. They were still far, however, from a majority in the Reichstag (German parliament). At this point Hitler received much-needed help from a small group of powerful industrialists, landowners, and bankers, as well as some generals. Most of these men did not share Hitler's extreme views, but they were impressed by his anti-communism and his promises to rebuild Germany. They felt they could use Hitler to advance their own interests. In January 1933 they persuaded Paul von Hindenburg, the 86-year-old war hero who had become president of the Weimar Republic, to make Hitler chancellor. (from Perry, *et al. History of the world*, p. 666-667. McDougla Littell Inc. 1995.)

How did Hilter Come to Power?

A German sees Hitlerism as Germany's "salvation (protection) from Communism."

Hitler was a simple soldier, like millions of others, only he had a *feeling* for masses of people, and he could speak with passion. The people didn't pay any attention to the Party program as such. They went to the meetings just to hear something new, anything new. They were desperate about the economic situation, 'a new Germany' sounded good to them; but from a deep or broad point of view they saw nothing at all. Hitler talked always against the government, against the lost war, against, the peace treaty, against unemployment. All that, people liked. By the time the intellectuals asked, 'What is this?' it had a solid basis in the common people. It was the *Arbeiter, Sozialist* Party, the Party of workers controlling the social order; it was not for intellectuals.

The situation in Germany got worse and worse. What lay underneath people's daily lives, the real root, was gone. Look at the suicides; look at the immorality. People wanted something *radical*, a real change. This want took the form of more and more Communism, especially in middle Germany, in the industrial area, and in the cities of the north. *That* was no invention of Hitler; *that* was real. . . .

Hitlerism had to answer Communism with something just as radical. Communism always used force; Hitlerism answered it with force. The really absolute enemy of Communism, always clear, always strong in the popular mind, was National Socialism, the *only* enemy that answered Communism in kind. If you wanted to save Germany from Communism—to be *sure* of doing it—you went to National Socialism. The Nazi slogan in 1932 was, 'If you want your country to go Bolshevik, vote Communist; if you want to remain free Germans, vote Nazi'. . . .

The middle parties, between the two millstones, played no role at all between the two radicalisms. Their adherents were basically the bourgeois, the 'nice' people who decide things by parliamentary procedure; and the politically indifferent; and the people who wanted to keep or, at worst, only modify the status quo.

. . . A dictatorship, or destruction by Bolshevism? Bolshevism looked like slavery and the death of the soul. It didn't matter if you were in agreement with Nazism. Nazism looked like the only defense. There was your choice."

Of my ten friends, only two, Tailor Schwenke and Bill-collector Simon, the two *alte Kampfer*, wanted to be Nazis and nothing else. They were both positive—still are—that National Socialism was Germany's and therefore their own, salvation from Communism, which, like the much more sensitive bank clerk, they both called "Bolshevism," "the death of the soul." "Bolshevism" came from outside, from the barbarous world that was Russia; Nazism, its enemy, was German, it was their own; they would rather Nazism. Did they know what Communism, "Bolshevism," was? They did not; not my friends . . . they knew Bolshevism as a specter which, as it took on body in their imaginings, embraced not only the Communists but the Social Democrats, the trade-unions, and, of course, the Jews, the gypsies, the neighbor next door whose dog had bit them and his dog; the bundled root cause of all-their past, present, and possible tribulations . . . . —From Milton Mayer, *They Thought They were Free: The Germans*, 1933-1945, pp. 95-97. University of Chicago Press, 1955.

QUESTION: How common is the tendency to be "for" or "against" something that one does not completely understand?

Using SQ2R method to read the above two passages on Hitlerism, one a primary source and the other the textbook, a social studies teacher can help English language learners to establish active reading habits and skills. A systematic training in this enables students to become independent readers. Let us go through this method using the above reading passages step by step.

First, survey the material. The reader will preview the title, headings, questions, topic sentences, etc. to get an idea of what the reading is about. For example, a preview of the titles of the above readings tells us that the two reading passages are about how German people believed in Hilter and followed him at the time. Skimming over the topic sentences of the readings reveals that the two readings are about the political, economic, and social aspects that Hitlerism appealed to German people at the time. Dealing with non-native English speaking students with varied English proficiency levels, a social studies teacher should prepare a glossary or provide some background information on the reading handout.

Once the reader has a general idea about the reading, s/he then can pose questions about these issues. If the reading already has a question or two at the end or on the side, or there are assigned review questions attached to the reading, then all that can become the reader's questions too. Some of the reader generated questions can be: Why did German people see Hitler as a hero? What are some of the strategies that Hitler used to attract German people? What was the economical situation at the time? Why were German people afraid of Communism? What is Communism? How common is the tendency to be "for" or "against" something that one does not completely understand? These questions should be written down as a guideline for the reading.

With the above questions in mind, a reader then can read with a focus and purpose. In doing so, reading becomes an active searching for answers. They can either highlight the key points related to answering their questions or jot down answers to the questions in their own words while doing the reading in a form of reading notes. For second language readers, they can consult a dictionary if they find a new word or two that prohibits their understanding. If not, they should be encouraged to continue with the reading or guessing the meaning of the word from the context.

After the reader finishes with the reading, s/he then can check the questions and answers to see any inconsistencies or inaccuracies. For example, the question "What is Communism?" is not answered in the reading. Why wasn't it answered? The reader then can go back to the last portion of the reading to re-read that portion for understanding. Also, going through the questions, the reader can assess whether s/he has had any difficulty in answering them. If so, the reader can re-read the section.

The final step involves reviewing the entire reading. The reader re-reads the key portions of the reading to see whether the questions posed are answered and whether s/he has had a solid understanding of the reading. Also, this is the time for the reader to evaluate the reading critically by examining the points of views, how is it different or similar from what the reader had in mind before the reading, and whether the reader believes in what the author has written and why.

In all, SQ2R method can be effective if the student is systematically trained to read this way. Also, reading by actively asking and answering questions can be a useful experience that helps students not only become independent readers but also critical learners.

CHAPTER 7

SECOND LANGUAGE WRITING INSTRUCTION IN MAINSTREAM CLASSES

SECOND LANGUAGE WRITING INSTRUCTION IN SCIENCE CLASSES

Picture Captions

One theory of second language acquisition (Krashen, 1982) argues that adolescent's competence in a second language is a function of the amount of "comprehensible input" acquirers receive and understand. In order to promote second language acquisition, science teachers have to think beyond the textbook to create ample comprehensible input for English language learners to learn and to use the language. With many non-fiction picture books available on science, a biology teacher can collect these books and magazines on certain biological themes for training non-native English speaking students' writing and thinking skills in biology. For exam-

Teaching Language and Content to Linguistically and Culturally Diverse Students:
Principles, Ideas, and Materials; pages 167–205.
A Volume in: Language Studies in Education
Copyright © 2004 by Information Age Publishing, Inc.
All rights of reproduction in any form reserved.
ISBN: 1-59311-088-X (paper), 1-59311-089-8 (cloth)

ple, lower-level non-native English speaking students can come as a group creating captions for a series of pictures and compare their captions with the original captions in the book. As the students progressed in language and content learning, they can be asked to make a picture book on certain topics and share their books among each other. For example, *Who eats what? Food chains and food webs* written by Patricia Lauber and illustrated by Hooly Keller has a series of telling pictures. Students can be given these pictures first and then be asked to create captions for the pictures. Afterwards, they will compare their captions with the original caption in the book.

Poems

Poetry stimulates language acquisition and expression. Visualization and poem can go hand in hand. After getting to know the vocabulary items used to describe certain scientific concepts, students can be encouraged to use these words either to write a random word association poem or come up with a shape filled with words related to it. High school students enjoy lyrics, rap, Jazz chant, or poetry that they can relate. Second Language learners especially are likely attuned to easy rhymes and alliteration aspects of poetry, which offers rich opportunities for oral language development (Graham, 1996). Writing and reading aloud poetry provides an excellent way for these students to learn the language and reinforce the scientific content. Three sample poem writing ideas and student writing are as follows:

a. Picture Poems
One example is poetry writing and sharing in science classes is picture poems. They consist of shapes or pictures with words, which suits beginning students very well. They also provoke strong visuals for the reader as well as for the writer. (see Figure 39)

b. Diamante
Diamantes are simple poems in seven lines. The first four lines are about one topic and the next three lines about the other. Students first think of a plant or an animal or a scientific concept as their topic to focus, such as the animal cell in this poem below. The opposite topic is the plant cell. Then they come up with two adjectives and three verbs used to describe the animal cell. For example, what are the shape, characteristics, and functions of the cell. Next, they generate four nouns used to label these functions that they have learned. For the next three lines, they focus on the plant cell and brainstorm the shape, characteristics, and functions

The eagle died & decayed

In a wild world the tree says to the sun,
"Thank you for giving me food and energy, and
for making green grass and a world so pretty."
The mouse underneath the tree thanks the tree
for giving him nuts and a nice play ground.
The owl thanks the mouse for becoming her food
so that she can be powerful and see far and good.
The snake says "Wait a minute, I have to thank the owl
for my feast. Otherwise I will be starve to death."
The eagle flies in and he cannot wait to eat the snake at once.
"Then, what happens to you?" everyone asks the eagle.
The tree flaps his big leaves and says proudly,
"when he dies he will be all mine."

FIGURE 39

of the plant cell and focusing on the differences between the two as shown
in Figure 40.

c. Sensory Poems

Five senses are basic but powerful tools for human communication and
expression. They can also be used to foster students' understanding of scientific concepts, which are difficult to explain or describe verbally. Creatively using five senses also tap into students' creative and imaginative
abilities to enable them to see how scientific concepts are used beyond the
disciplinary boundaries. In a sensory poem, students are asked to first
select a scientific concept of vocabulary item to focus their poem on. Then
they will brainstorm a list of words or phrases that come to their minds
associated with that concept, using five senses (below are sample questions
to guide students' writing). Students are encouraged to use similes or metaphors to express their concept. They can use a dictionary or thesaurus for
this task. After that they will use these words to write their poems. In doing
so, students find a new way to discover meaning of the concept they
learned. Also, using poetry to talk about the topic under study can add a
new dimension to the expository writing of the textbook and can stimulate

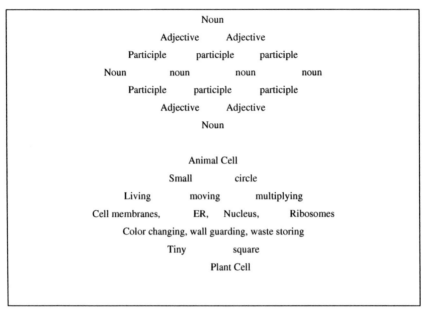

FIGURE 40

students' interest in the subject as well as in the language. The following is an example of such a poem writing process.

Choose a color for your topic: Osmosis: white

1.   What osmosis would look like? It looks like a broadened river.
2.   What osmosis would smell like? It smells like smoke.
3.   What osmosis would taste like? It tastes like a raisin.
4.   What osmosis would sound like? It sounds like a quiet classroom.
5.   What osmosis would feel like? It feels like less crowded in the subway.

Osmosis is white.

It looks like a waterfall rushing down the mountain to broaden the river bank.

It smells like lingering smoke weeks after 9/11.

It tastes like a swollen raisin sitting in water for days.

It sounds like a quiet classroom after a hot debate.

It feels like a getting into a bigger subway car with the same amount of people.

Writing for A Different Audience

Writing can help all students in general and English language learners in particular to develop better understanding of biological concepts and the ability to communicate their understanding to others. A common difficulty that faces English language learners is that often they write only science papers or lab reports, which are distant from their own lives and interests. Research has shown that school writing which focuses only on the teacher and the formulaic school assignments tends to result in students' negative responses to writing and limited language use (Applebee, 1984). In writing for a different audience, students are asked to rewrite a textbook excerpt or write something on a given topic, for example a student to a newspaper editor, a 9th grader to a 3rd grader, a daughter and a son to a parent or grandparent back in their home country, or a student to a scientist, etc. In these real situations where students are genuinely involved for real learning purposes, second language acquisition will occur naturally. A modeling activity is necessary where the teacher demonstrates some basic elements such as a typical language structure and an appropriate choice of words. Writing for a real audience rather than writing for the teacher creates purposes for authentic communication and thus speeds up the second language acquisition process (Lindfors, 1989). Sample writing prompts are:

Write a letter to your grandparents or the elders or your school friends back in your home country comparing pollution here in the US and that in your home country

Make a picture book for a 3rd grade class about the importance of ocean biome

Write a letter to New York Times Editor to argue the side effect of the pesticide spray to kill West Nile virus

Write a journal describing a day in your backyard or a local park or a local wetland observing and researching like an ecologist

Keep a record of your family's grocery shopping for a week and write an analysis tracing the food chain and food web.

Compare what you have in the ecosystem where you lived back home in your native country with the one you are living now. Design your own ideal ecosystem and tell it to your major.

Investigate human population growth in your neighborhood for the past 10 years and report it to an ecologist in your community.

Interview scientists or ecologists in local environmental centers or gardens about pressing environmental issues and report these issues to the local newspaper or radio station.

The following is an example of one ELL student's writing to New York Times editor on cloning.

Dear Editor,

After learning genetics in my biology class, I have some thoughts about the current human cloning debate. I think it's not an easy thing to have a clear idea about something like cloning. However, by this entire picture that I was given, I think that any supporting and approving the idea of "cloning" destroys the saintly concept of the family. We should value a healthy family that nature gives us, and we should not try to control the nature no matter how advanced science is.

From a Headline to an Article

This writing activity involves the whole writing process, including pre-writing, writing, revising, and publishing. The teacher will first cuts out the headlines and articles from a magazine of a newspaper and bring them to class. Students are given a headline but not the article about a science issue, such as a biological issue to read. Then they are asked to compose an article as group about the topic given in the headline. Students are expected to expand the headline as much as they can by adding detailed information about what is in the news using what, where, when, why, who, and how. Once their writing has completed, they will pass the writing onto the next group for revision. Each group will have a chance to be the writer first and then the editor. The editorial group can ask the writing group questions and give suggestions for revision. Finally, they can read about the original article for further insights and compare and contrast their writing with the original and revise their article. The revised piece will be published either by reading aloud or putting on the bulletin board with the headline, the original writing, the revision, and the final piece. New York Times science section serve this purpose very well.

Sample headings:

- Surviving on the Siberian Tundra
- Five Beneficial Ways Insects Affect the Food Chain
- Save the Tropical Rain Forest
- Trees for Life: Exploring Organisms Live in A Tree
- Observing Our Living Earth: Our Day at A Botanical Garden

Journal Writing

Journal writing has been frequently used by science teachers to make the lesson relevant to students' lives and to build up students' habit for scientific observations and writing. Journal writing can also be used as a language learning tool to train students' language skills in a specific area and to develop students' critical and creative scientific thinking skills. Research in second language acquisition and teaching has shown tremendous promise for using journal writing to increase students' writing fluency and motivation (Peyton, *et al.,* 1990; Taylor & Sobota, 1998). For example, a journal that requires students to use a conditional structure of "What if . . . " or "If I were . . . " can expose students to experiencing a particular language situation and lead to a creative and critical use of scientific knowledge learned to express themselves. Also, prompts like "There" and "Then" can set students into practicing specific language structures, such as the past tense while thinking about a biological issue in a different time frame.

Some of the journal writing topics are:

- If dinosaurs were still alive, which feeding level and niche would it be in and why?
- What happens if the decomposers all died?
- What happens if there were no producers in the world?
- Imagine your home in different biomes, such as tundra, tropical rain forest, ocean, desert, and the lake, what would they look like?
- How different are the abiotic factors comparing your native home with the home here in the US?

Below there is an excerpt of a 9th grader's month-long journal on her observations of a tree in her yard.

March 15, 1998
Today I realized how much it takes to really understand a tree. I have been observing this tree for a while. Before, I often thought it was silly for me to eyeball a tree everyday. It seems to me it won't take a couple of minutes before I get everything down about the tree in my yard. As it turns out, it is not that simple once the teacher has given us guidelines for observations. For example, I have to use my math knowledge and skills to measure the height and the circumference of the tree. A closer examination of the tree trunk, I see damages made by insects or animals. Who are they? Where do they live? The tree leaves are interesting too. Some leaves are in fine green color and a good round shape, but others are obviously eaten by insects or birds, still others turned yellow already. What happened? Why? I have seen squirrels on the tree. As it becomes warmer and warmer, I believe there will be more animals visiting this tree. I need to keep a record of these visitors. Also, factors such as the soil, humidity, rainfall, etc. have to make some impact on the tree also. My tree in the yard is no longer an ordinary tree anymore. Now I look forward to all the discoveries I will make to learn about it.—A Korean Student

Sentence Combining

Sentence combining exercises were first used with native English speaking students to develop their writing maturity (Christensen, 1968) by teaching students to expand their simple sentences to complex sentences using more sophisticated language structures, such as clauses, modifiers, and transitional words, etc. Even though adolescent second language writers have good ideas to express, still limited language and writing skills prevent them from expressing themselves effectively and maturely. Beginning second language writers have many characteristics parallel to lower grade native language learners. For example, their sentences are short, simple, and choppy. This activity can be a follow-up to the previous reading for organizational links. Once students have learned about the organizational links in the reading, the next step is to guide them to use these links in their writing. Since scientific writing uses many connectors to draw clear and logical relationships between concepts and facts, it is important for English language learners to learn to use them appropriately in their writing. One effective way of doing so is to ask students to combine two or more sentences into one using appropriate connectors. This can be done by the teacher selecting sentences from the textbook, newspaper, or magazines, breaking them down into short and simple sentences, and then asking students to combine these sentences using appropriate connectors. The following are two examples of such a writing exercise.

Combine the following sentence into one using appropriate transitional words:
a. An existing community is slowly replaced by another community.
b. This process is called ecological succession.
The process by which an existing community is slowly replaced by another community is called ecological succession (p. 835).
Combine the following sentence into one using appropriate transitional words:
a. Pines, firs, and spruce are the dominant vegetation in taiga.
b. Some deciduous trees are also present.
c. The deciduous trees shed their leaves.
Pines, firs, and spruce are the dominant vegetation, although some deciduous trees, which shed their leaves, are also present in taiga (p. 847).
(From Schraer & Stoltze, *Biology: The study of life*. (1995). Needham, MA: Prentice Hall).

Reader Response

A reader response approach has been taken by many English teachers to teaching literature reading comprehension, interpretation, and appreciation. It is based on Rosenblatt's (1978) theory that when a reader interacts with the reading using his or her experience, the comprehension and motivation for reading increase. Beginning readers such as English language learners tend to resort to recitation and memorization of the reading due to limited reading strategies and complex and dry reading materials used in science classrooms. Many of the English language learners' past science learning experience in their home countries was memorization oriented and teacher centered; as a result, they had no interaction with the reading or in the science classroom. Therefore, there is a special need for them to experience the wonder for discoveries and imagination by using non-traditional science reading materials. These materials can also be used to develop a student's scientific reading skills, too. Figure 41 is a poem written by Joe Miller (1998) engaging students visually as well as aesthetically in conversing about issues we all care about. Scientific issues addressed in a form of poem asking students for their personal views make it easier for ELL students to understand and lead to more active responses on the part of the student.

If the earth were only
A few feet in diameter, floating a
few feet above a field somewhere, people
would come from everywhere to marvel at it.
People would walk around it, marveling at its big
pools of water, its little pools and the water flowing
between the pools. People would marvel at the bumps
on it, and the holes in it, and they would marvel at the
very thin layer of gas surrounding it and the water suspended in the gas. The people would marvel at all the creatures
walking around the surface of the ball, and at the creature in
the water. The people would declare it precious because it
was the only one, and they would protect it so that it would
not be hurt. The ball would be the greatest wonder known
and people would come to behold it, to be healed, to
gain knowledge, to know beauty and to wonder how it
it could be. People would love it, and defend it with
their lives, because they would somehow know
that their lives, their own roundness, could
be nothing without it. If the earth
were only a few feet in
diameter

Do you agree with the author? Why? Or Why not?
How can we save our planet?

FIGURE 41

I agree with the author. When the earth is small, everybody will take care of it. When it is huge, nobody can take care of it. Since the earth is so big, people cannot see that we are destroying the earth by killing lots of living things in order for people to survive. I think the earth is a beautiful thing full of wonders. It's nature, animals, plants, and people are all special, and most of all it is the only one planet that has water and oxygen. For future generations, I just want to say "People should take care of this earth. We should not care about ourselves only. We should take care of the animals, fish, trees, etc. We cannot lose them because if we lose them, we lose the earth and we lose our own lives."—A Bangladeshi student

SECOND LANGUAGE WRITING INSTRUCTION IN MATHEMATICS CLASSES

With an increasing interest in using writing to learn and writing to think mathematics, more and more mathematics teachers have explored ways to engage their students in writing, thinking, communicating their thoughts and beliefs about mathematics learning, and assessing students' understanding (Masingila & Prus-Wisniowska, 1996; Miller, 1991). Research in second language acquisition and in second language writing has supported the argument for writing to learn, writing for social interaction, and writing for language development (Enright & McClosky, 1988; Faltis & Wolfe, 1999; Freeman & Freeman, 1994). For English language learners, unlike speaking, writing has time advantage, providing an opportunity to process information, translate English into their native language and vice versa, and reflect on their learning. Writing can also ease the anxiety of speaking. Planned speech by asking students to first write down their answers or responses before speaking up can increase participation and interaction. Therefore, English language learners need to be exposed to writing in the mathematics classroom whenever is necessary. Initial writing or writing for the low English proficiency students can be basic and short, such as words and phrases. Many second language learners may have acquired fluency at using numbers and symbols in their native language, so learning to translate the mathematical language into English is critical in developing students' thinking and writing skills in English. Below is a sample of few ideas for writing instruction in the mathematics classroom.

Symbolic Language to Written Language Translation

Very often non-native English speaking students have difficulty in translating universally used mathematics symbols into the written language. Teachers tend to think that with more exposure to the second language,

TABLE 40

Symbolic language	Written language
$\angle ABC + \angle DBC = 90°$	Angle ABC plus angle DBC equals ninety degrees.
$l \mathbin{/\mkern-3mu/} m$	Line l is parallel to line m.
$A\,(-2, 2)$	The coordinate of point A is negative 2 and positive 2.
$_4P_4=4!$	The permutation of four objects taken 4 at a time.
$0°\,?\ \ x\,?\ 180°$	x is greater than or equal to zero degree and less than or equal to 180 degrees.
$p\,?\,q$	p and q (p and q are true only when *both are true*.)

they will catch up with the language aspect of mathematics. However, without writing instruction and emphasis on language from the teacher, this may not happen. One way to get even beginning English language learners to write, is to do a translation between symbolic language and the written language as shown in Table 40.

Double-Entry Journal

A double-entry journal is a journal written on a loose-leaf paper in two columns, one column is a layout of the student's mathematics calculation and the other is a prose of the thinking process that the student went through while doing the problem. Research findings have demonstrated repeatedly that double-entry journals provide a medium for English language learners to record, communicate, and reflect on mathematics using the written language (Countryman, 1992; McIntosh & Draper, 2001; Norwood & Carter, 1994; Powell & Ramnauth, 1992; Tovani, 2000). Even if the learner has already caught up with the procedural aspect of mathematics learning, writing can still develop declarative knowledge and language skills and the habit of using writing to develop their thinking. The journals can include steps in the thinking process and questions that the learner has afterwards. All this offers the teacher an opportunity to gain insights into students' understanding, identify the strengths and weaknesses and the thought process. The prose on the right hand column can reveal or at least give the teacher a point of departure for inquiry. For English language learners, journal writing provides them with a chance to articulate their understandings or difficulties in a non-threatening environment. If the students have trouble beginning their journals, suggest some lead sentences such as "This is how to . . . " or "The problem/question I am having with this is . . . " Some kind of writing prompt to ask students to respond to an answer or to explain a problem to somebody is another way to get students quickly involved in the writing. The journal can go beyond summarization of the operational procedures to reveal alternative ways of solving the problem or to question what has learned, which merit serious developments on the part of the students otherwise may not discover in the whole class discussion. Table 41 is an example of a non-native English speaking student's journal entry.

Word Problem Questions

One difficult area of second language and mathematics learning is to learn how to ask a question. Questions that begin with what, where, when, why, which, and how are more challenging linguistically for second language learners than yes or no questions. Asking questions also involves learning to think actively and deeply, constructing meaning, analyzing, and synthesizing what students have learned. Normally in the mathematics classroom, often the teacher is the one who asks the questions and the students are the one to respond to the teacher's questions. The teacher gets the chance to practice his or her questioning techniques and expand them to include questions paralleling Bloom's taxonomy. Students, however, do not have the opportunity to ask questions (Tovani, 2000). Therefore, there is a need for students to be included in the questioning process by actually designing questions in writing first and then orally. For English language learners, they learn the statements like "I am a student." first before learning various question formations (what, why, where, when, who, and how) in their second language acquisition process. Since these question involve an inversion of the subject and the verb in the sentence like in "Who are you?" they are more difficult for English language learners to master (Krashen, 1982). So by encouraging students to ask questions about real problems in the mathematics class the mathematics teacher enhances these students both mathematics learning and language learning. One way to do so is to give the students a word problem but leave a word problem's question out in order for them to design appropriate questions (Menon, 1996). This way, not only the students get the chance to practice their questioning skills, but also to think critically about the information given using their mathematics knowledge. Table 42 has are few examples of the students' questions based on the word problems.

Personalizing the Mathematics Text

Textbooks in the mathematics classroom often play a privileged and authority role, though they tend to fall behind the rapid changes in the educational landscape and fail to acknowledge alternative ways of doing

TABLE 41

Mathematics Operation	Written Reflection
5x2·2x3 =(5·2) (x2·x3) =10 (x2·x3) =10 (x2+3) =10 x5	Thinking process: Since x to the second power and x to the third power are like terms, I first grouped them together (x2·x3). Then I multiplied the numbers (5x2) and got 10. Afterwards, using the power law of exponents, I added the exponents of the x (2+3) and got 5. My final answer to the question is ten x to the fifth power. Question: What happens when the exponent is negative?

In the quadrilateral below, if PQ=SQ=RQ and PS=SR, then x=?	**Student one:**
	Since PQ=SQ=QR, and PS=SR,
	$\triangle$PQS is congruent to $\triangle$SRQ (side-side-side)
	Therefore, $\angle$PSQ = $\angle$QSR (Congruent triangle's corresponding angles are equal.)
	Since $\angle$QSR = 70° , $\angle$PSQ=70°
	Also, since PS = SR and $\angle$PSQ = $\angle$QSR, then
	   $\angle$POS = $\angle$SOR = 90°
	($\triangle$POS and $\triangle$SOR congruent triangles: side-angle-side.)
	Then $\angle$OPS = 180° - 90° - 70° = 20°
	Finally, $\angle$x = 70° - 20° = 50°
	
	Student two:
	Since PQ = SQ = QR, and PS = SR,
	$\triangle$PQS is congruent to $\triangle$SRQ (side-side-side)
	Therefore, $\angle$QPS = $\angle$QRS = 70° and $\angle$PSQ = $\angle$QSR = 70°
	   (Congruent triangle's corresponding angles are equal.)
	Since $\angle$QSR = 70°, $\angle$PSQ = 70° So $\angle$PQS = $\angle$SQR = 40°
	In $\triangle$PQO and $\triangle$OQR
	Since PQ = QR and QO = QO,
	then $\triangle$PQO is congruent to $\triangle$RQO (side-angle-side)
	Finally, $\angle$x = 50° (180 - $\angle$PQO - $\angle$QOP = 50°)
	
	Student three:
	Since PQ=SQ=QR, and PS=SR,
	$\triangle$PQS is congruent to $\triangle$SRQ (side-side-side)
	Therefore, $\angle$QPS = $\angle$QRS =70° and $\angle$PSQ = $\angle$QSR =70°
	   (Congruent triangle's corresponding angles are equal.)
	Since $\angle$QSR = 70°, $\angle$PSQ = 70° So $\angle$PQS = $\angle$SQR = 40°
	In $\triangle$PQR, since PQ = QR, so $\angle$PRQ = $\angle$RPQ = $\angle$x
	   ($\triangle$PQR an isosceles triangle)
	$\angle$PQR = $\angle$PQS + $\angle$SQR = 80° ($\angle$PQS = $\angle$SQR = 40°)
	$\angle$QPR + $\angle$QRP + $\angle$PQR = 180°
	Since $\angle$PRQ = $\angle$RPQ = $\angle$x and $\angle$PQR = 80°
	Then $\angle$x = 180° - 80 - 2x = 100°/2
	Finally, $\angle$x = 50°

TABLE 42

Given information:	Student generated questions
If 10 identical coins weigh 21 grams,	How many coins weigh 63 grams?
	What about the weight of 15 coins?
	How many coins do I deduct in order to get 12.6 grams?
If Sally can write an essay in 5 hours and John can write an essay in 6 hours,	How long would it take for both Sally and John to write an essay together?
	How long would it take Sally to finish if John helps her out for the first two hours?
	How long would it take John to finish if Sally helps him out for the first hour?
Lisa's father is three times as old as Lisa. Five years ago, he was five times as old.	How old is Lisa's father now? How old is Lisa now? How old would Lisa be five years from now? How old would Lisa's father be ten years from now?
In right triangle ABC, altitude CD is drawn to the hypotenuse. If AD=3 and DB=4	How long is CD? How long is AC? What is the relationship between ? ABC and ? ACD? What are the corresponding angles comparing ? ABC and ? ACD? How long is BC?

mathematics. In addition, the typical textbook writing, formal, dense, and expository, makes the reading difficult. For example, in discussing the angle theorems, a typical textbook gives the definition of each theorem like below.

Theorem 23: If two parallel lines are cut by a transversal, then the alternate interior angles formed are congruent.

Theorem 24: If two parallel lines are cut by a transversal, then the corresponding angles formed are congruent.

Theorem 25: If two parallel lines are cut by a transversal, then two interior angles on the same side of the transversal are supplementary. (from Keenan and Dressler *Integrated Mathematics: Course II,* 1990, AMSCO School Publications, Inc. p. 218)

Even with illustration, these theorems are still very abstract and far removed from what students' lives. One way to make mathematics learning an active process and assist English language learners' understanding is to personalize the key concepts under study. For example, in teaching the above angle theorems, instead of solely reading the textbook and explaining, the teacher can ask students to bring in their city map, subway map, or bus map to study. The teacher breaks students into groups and asks them to identify as many angles that they learned, such as alternate interior angles, corresponding angles, and vertical angles as they can and discuss the angle relationships. After the discussion, students write down their thought process and use what they have written to personalize the textbook reading. In doing so, students have opportunities to explore mathematics concepts, to justify mathematics principles, and to apply mathematics knowledge. This type of personalized writing can also be a natural way for English language learners to bring multiple language skills together, such as reading, listening, speaking, and writing, and practice these skills in a holistic way. Figure 42 is an example of such an exercise.

Our group, Jose, Lee, Sue, Kim, and Edward studied Queens bus map. We chose it because we ride the bus everyday to school, and we are familiar with the map. Jose brought in the most recent map for our study. Looking at the map, we found out several parallel lines such as Union Turnpike is paralleling with Hillside Avenue and Northern Blvd is paralleling with Long Island

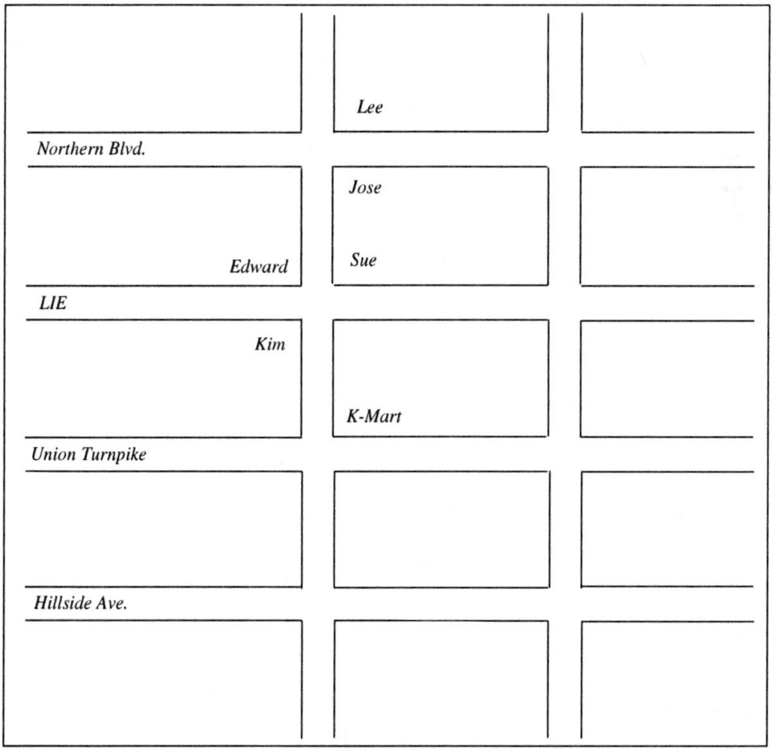

FIGURE 42

Expressway (LIE). We are surprised to find that we live really close to each other and some of our homes have interesting angle relationships between each other as shown on the map. For example, Jose's home and Sue's home form a supplementary relationship, while Lee's home and Sue's home is in a vertical angle relationship. K-Mart and Kim are in a corresponding angle relationship. Now we know where we live, we might want to visit each other when we have time.

Interviews about Real-world Mathematics Application

Concrete and authentic experiences involving mathematics problems in real-world often provide students with a firm ground of understanding mathematics concepts. Real world connections enable students to see the value of learning, thus motivate them to learn. Also, by including everyday problems into mathematics classes, the teacher gives the students, especially English language learners, an opportunity to use context embedded language, everyday vocabulary, thus pushes the students to use the second language. Personal narratives of real-world mathematics encounters or reports on the interviews about mathematics use on jobs or everyday life are activities for such writing. Students can go to their family, neighborhood, or community to ask, read, and write about how mathematics plays a role in a situation or helps resolve a dilemma and make a decision. They are seeking, interpreting, evaluating information. They also bring their everyday experiences and perspectives to bear on the findings. Students' writing thus becomes rich and meaningful. Sample interview ideas are as follows:

Mathematics Topics	Interview sources
Geometry	Taxi drives
	Construction workers
	UPS delivery workers
	Firemen
	Postal workers
	Environmental centers
Number	Supermarket cashiers
	Pharmacists
	Restaurant waiters and waitresses
	Bank tellers
	Clinic receptionists
	Gas station assistants
Statistics	Athletes
	TV and radio station workers
	Policemen and policewomen

Mathematics Topics	Interview sources
	Librarians
	Teachers
Algebra	Bank tellers
	Pharmacists
	Auto dealership
	Accounting offices
Logic	Court houses
	Weather people
	Food factories

Mathematics Learning Autobiography

Telling stories about one's own mathematics learning history and personal encounters with real-life mathematics is an effective way to learn about students' backgrounds and needs and their beliefs and perceptions about mathematics. Since mathematics is a subject in all schools cross-culturally from grade one, everyone, including English language learners, has a story about mathematics learning to tell. The autobiography writing also gives students, especially English language learners, permission to explore their feelings about mathematics learning and to capitalize on what they have already known, their strengths, and things that they are familiar with when they are comparing mathematics learning back home in their native country with mathematics learning in America. This writing exercise can be used along with mathematics survey (see in Chapter Four) to assist the mathematics teacher in the beginning of the semester or when a new English language learner comes to the class. Sample autobiography writing probing questions are:

- Do you remember your first mathematics lesson? If you do, describe it.
- What are your feelings about your mathematics class? Do you like mathematics? How so?
- What differs in learning mathematics as compared to your elementary school days and high school days or as compared to your mathematics learning back home in your native country and mathematics learning here in America?
- What are your strengths or weaknesses in mathematics?
- What is the most useful mathematics concept or principle that you have learned so far? How so?
- Describe your real-life encounters with mathematics.

Reader Responses to Mathematics Readings

Writing to respond to the readings about mathematics requires students to read deeply for not only comprehension of mathematics knowledge but also for personal involvement and critical understanding. Non-textbook readings (see Appendix A) often engage students personally, provoke their thinking, and crystallize mathematics concepts that they have learned. These readings can also explain and describe certain mathematics concepts in a different way. In addition, the readings, such as folktales and biographies of famous mathematicians, bring out social, cultural, and human aspect of mathematics learning. Writing about the reading like this can be a fun and engaging activity. Students can keep note cards during the reading and then write about their readings afterwards. The following is an example of such writing after reading *A Grain of Rice* by Pittman (1996):

> I first learned about this story in Chinese, back in China before coming over here. I was so glad to read the English version of the story here in the US I admire Pong Lo, the young farmer, for his knowledge and determination. He outwitted the emperor and won over his daughter using his brain. Before I like to think that the high level of mathematics such as exponential function had no use in real life. The story makes me think again. The only thing that I don't like were the pictures. People in the pictures don't look like Chinese people. After reading, I still have two remaining questions: How did Pong Lo know about the emperor's daughter in the beginning? What made him so determined to marry her?—A Chinese student

Riddle Writing

Riddles are fun, and with the simple sentence structure, a riddle provides a framework for writing. Playing with language is a way of learning about the language. By including riddle writing into mathematics classes, teachers can help English language learners understand various functions of language and be a part of it. It also gives students freedom to imagine and to experiment creatively ways of illustrating a mathematics concept without giving it away (Evered, 2001). Students can work as a group first to come up with ideas or concepts to be the focus of the riddle, then to create a semantic web around that concept, generate all relevant words or images that come to their minds, and finally write their riddle. For English language learners, some modeling by using a simple sentence structure, such as "I am . . . " and "What am I?" is necessary. The following is an illustration of few riddles created by the students.

I am long
I am irrational.
I am dancing in the circle.
What am I? (π)

I am a powerful tool.
People use me to cut through big numbers.
Big numbers are broken apart.
Wherever they share a part.
What am I? (factoring)

I am in the shape of a house roof.
Under me the number can be greater than or equal to zero
But never negative.
What am I? ($\sqrt{}$)

Mathematical Concept Comparisons

Many concepts in mathematics can be explored through comparative writing, the writing comparing and contrasting the similarities and differences between the concepts and their use. The paired concepts can be both similar concepts and different concepts that students have trouble grasping. Some pairs of concepts can be chosen with a close relationship between each other or without an apparent relationship at all. Students can first work in pairs creating Venn Diagrams comparing and contrasting a pair of words. Then based on what they have found out, they can write prose describing and explaining these points. The writing can clarify students' thinking and help students gain a deeper understanding of these concepts. In selecting similarities and differences and elaborating these points in writing, the comparison and contrast demand higher order thinking skills such as analyzing, evaluating, and synthesizing (Spivey, 1997). For English language learners, comparative writing also offers them a chance to practice specific language structures used in writing comparisons and to use appropriate mathematical vocabulary. The comparative writing often helps students discover new meaning of the old words, thus lead the students to another level of learning. Sample paired mathematics concepts are as follows:

How are these two terms different?	*How are these two terms similar?*
Factor vs. multiple	line and plane
Permutation vs. combination	circle and ellipse
Vertices vs. points	linear equation and quadratic equation
Line vs. segment	radian and arc

SECOND LANGUAGE WRITING INSTRUCTION IN ENGLISH LANGUAGE ARTS CLASSES

Literature Double-Entry Journals

Literature journal writing has been a common practice in the English classroom to engage readers and link reading to writing and thinking. Tovani (2000) discussed the benefit of using a literature double-entry journal to establish active reading habits by asking questions, identifying confusions, and making associations between the text and their own lives. For English language learners, literature journals can also be used to check for students' understanding of the reading and invite students to express their confusion or reading difficulties. Very often, English language learners are shy about asking a question or admitting that they do not understand in class. The journal provides a safe net for them to talk about their confusions or lack of comprehension. In a double-entry journal the student copies down a phrase, a sentence, or a section in the book, which confuses him or her on the one side of the page and asks questions about it or makes some inferences or association or predictions about the possible meaning on the other side. The teacher can use the journal to gauge students' comprehension of the unfolding plot or the evolving characters and tailor his or her instruction to the students' needs. The following is a sample of such a journal entry on reading the *Great Gatsby* by Fitzgerald.:

Copied excerpt	*Student's journal*
In my younger and more vulnerable years My father gave me some advice that I've Been turning over in my mind ever since. "Whenever you feel like criticizing any-one," he told me, "just remember that all the people in this world haven't had the advantages that you've had." Pp. 6	I have several new words in the opening part of the *Great Gatsby*. For example, "turning over in my mind" and "vulnerable" I tried to guess on my own. I think that "turning over in my mind" means thinking over and over again, and vulnerable years maybe younger years. The advice that the author's father gives him was confusing to me. I don't understand it. But I tried to think about any advice my parents give to me like "Don't eat food without thinking about who toil and harvest it." I sense his father is talking about something like this too, but I am not sure.

Clustering

For beginning English language learners who have limited vocabulary and grammatical knowledge about the language, writing, even sentence production, can be a challenging task. Bereiter and Scardamalia (1987) discussed the interplay of the two domains of knowledge in composing: content knowledge and discourse knowledge. Even when a second language writer has something to say, it often requires tremendous effort and determination to find equivalent words in English, retrieve these words, and sequence the words into sentences. Often the time involvement and mental process demands are so high that students are left with almost no higher order concerns for the content or organization. Therefore, prewriting activities such as a clustering technique are especially beneficial to these students in learning to compose. To cluster, students either work in groups or as a whole class to associate the topic of the writing with all the relevant ideas they can come up with. In a class with second language learners, this technique can go beyond brainstorming ideas by asking students to elaborate on their ideas in phrases or sentences or by the teacher modeling a few sentences using these ideas so that students can see how the words are put into sentences. Once the ideas are generated in phrases or sentences, students then can work on organizing them into an outline and generating the topic sentence of each paragraph. Below is a sample of such a technique in action when an English teacher works with an English language learner to compose a poem on "My Sacred Place" after reading Dunn's poem.

My Sacred Place by Stephen Dunn

After the teacher asked if anyone had
  a sacred place
and the students fidgeted and shrank
in their chairs, the most serious of them all
  said it was his car,
being in it alone, his tape deck playing
things he'd chosen, and others knew the truth
  had been spoken
and began speaking about their rooms,
their hiding places, but the car kept coming up,
  the car in motion,
music filling it, and sometimes one other person
who understood the bright altar of the dashboard
  and how far away
a car could take him from the need
to speak, or to answer, the key
  in having a key
and putting it in, and going.

Sample Clustering
Step One: Clustering

My sacred place: my bed.

SEE:	TOUCH:
White walls	knob on the radio
blue blanket	
TV-MTV	
Dirty clothes under the bed	HEAR:
	Soccer ball
	Spanish music, Ekimosis
TASTE:	ACTION WORDS
Coke	relaxing in the bed
Chocolate chip cookies	listening to the music

My Sacred Place by A Colombian Student:

My bedroom is where I go to be alone.
The walls are white.
My blanket is blue.
Sitting on my desk is my TV
Under my bed are some dirty clothes.
Next to my bed rests a lonely soccer ball.
I am standing by my radio turning the knob.
   When I hear Spanish music.
My favorite band is called Ekimosis.

In-role Writing

Writing by using different characters' voices and personalities can offer all students a chance of stepping into the character's shoes and promoting aesthetic appreciation. For English language learners, this activity is important linguistically in that students can learn to use varied language structures and expressions in a meaningful way. Students can work as groups of three to recreate a dialogue or a scene from the perspectives of the characters in the book or bring in new characters to write about their points of views. In reading Lee's *To Kill A Mockingbird*, for example, students can retell the trial scene from the perspective of Jem, Aunt Alexandria, Atticus, Tom Robinson, Judge Taylor, a New York Times Reporter, etc. The recreation will enhance students' understanding of the characters' motives, provide them with the opportunity to use varied language structures to communicate for real purposes, and encourage students to express their feelings and reactions from an insider's point of view. The following is an example of such writing on *How the Garcia Girls Lost Their Accents* by Julia Alvarez:

Yolanda

I am really scared with these men and their guns in my house. Why are they here? Last time I did something wrong and almost got my father killed. My mom looks so calm. How can she act like that when we all know why they are here? Rudy bothers me. I feel like I want to live up to my "old world" and parents' expectations. But I have to be me. I am not just Dominican, I feel I am American also. Who do I let Rudy treat me this way? Would my mother let my father treat her like this?

Sandi

Tonight I am both excited and nervous. We are all going to dinner and Mami insists we don't mess up in front of her and Papi's friends. She always gets so nervous that we will disappoint her. Oh, well! I can't wait to put on my beautiful dress and eat in the fancy restaurant. My first "mistake" at dinner was that I stood up to greet the Fannings when they arrived at the table. I didn't know what to do, so I just followed Papi's lead. Anyway, Mami gave me the eyes, so I knew I was wrong. Then we ordered cokes. We weren't supposed to, but we couldn't resist. Hmmm! They were so good. One problem I had at dinner was with the ways Mrs. Fanning was acting. She drank so much wine, then she kissed Papi on the lips. I'm still shocked. Papi seemed uncomfortable, but he didn't stop her. If Mami knew, she wouldn't be pleased. I won't say anything to her.

Picture Poetry

An English teacher can bring in posters, postcards, photos, or pictures to class and ask students to work as a group to first view the picture and then write down images that come to mind. Then based on a list of the imagery generated by the group, the teacher can have students generate as many words as they can which rhyme with the images they just came up with by saying the words out loud and writing them down. Afterwards, students will work together to compose a poem using the imagery and the words they generated together. Dannie Abse's *Voices in the Gallery* is a wonderful collection of poems on paintings with one poem and a painting placed side by side. Rhyming words are words that share the same vowel sounds, such as cake, lake. By asking students to purposefully practice these sounds, students will get an audio feel of the language and develop their speaking abilities. Using language to recreate what they have seen gives English language learners a common base and a rich context for communication. The activity can go even further by the group sharing their poem with the class and letting the whole class that has not seen the picture, postcard, photo, or the painting guess what the poem is about.

Then share the picture to see how well the group has communicated it to the class. Second Language learners are often fascinated with rhyming words. This exercise is also a good speaking and listening activity to develop students' skills to the sounds and meanings of the language. Here is an example of such a response to a postcard that featured a sculpture by Isamu Noguchi, a Japanese sculptor and architect:

Images that you see:	*Rhyming sound associated with that image:*
snake	awake, make, fake, shake, lake
black	back, attack, cat, act,
red	head, bread, dead, bed
crawling	saw, small, broad, straw, withdraw
tree	free, we, freeze, breeze

Poem

A snake is coming to awake,
Scared, it's beginning to shake.
Red and black,
It's ready to attack.
Crawling under the tree,
Waiting for its opportunity.

Multilingual Text Exploration

Gail Reisin (1993) shared the idea of having her students pick a few striking lines, such as an excerpt of a soliloquy, or a dialogue, and transform it into a multicultural text using students' native language or home dialect, and present it to the class. By encouraging English language learners to use their native language in this activity, the teacher offers them a chance to share something that other students are lacking. Doing the translation and sharing it with the class gives second language learners an edge over others, which they normally do not have. This can boost their self-esteem. The exercise can also get students engaged in the literary experience and use their language background to deepen their understanding of a difficult text, such as *Romeo and Juliet, Hamlet, Macbeth,* etc. Through the translation students can easily compare and contrast different versions of the lines and ways of speaking, such as intonation, rhyme, and facial expressions that presenters use to convey meaning. Through a purposeful translation, students can be led to a discussion of how some universal themes and concepts are depicted in different languages and how language influences our thinking about these themes and concepts. The following are a sample of multilingual texts of *Romeo and Juliet.*

Original English version

Romeo: O, she doth teach the torches to burn bright.
It seems she hangs upon the cheek of night
As a rich jewel in an Ethiop's ear-
Beauty too rich for use, for earth too dear.
So shows a snowy dove trooping with cows
As yonder lady o'er her fellows shows.
The measure done, I'll watch her place of stand,
And touching hers, make blessed my rude hand.
Did my heart love till now? Forswear it, sight.
For I ne'er saw true beauty till this night.
(*Romeo and Juliet*, Scene one, Act five. Folger Shakespeare Library Series, 1976, Simon & Schuster Adult Publishing Group.)

Chinese Version

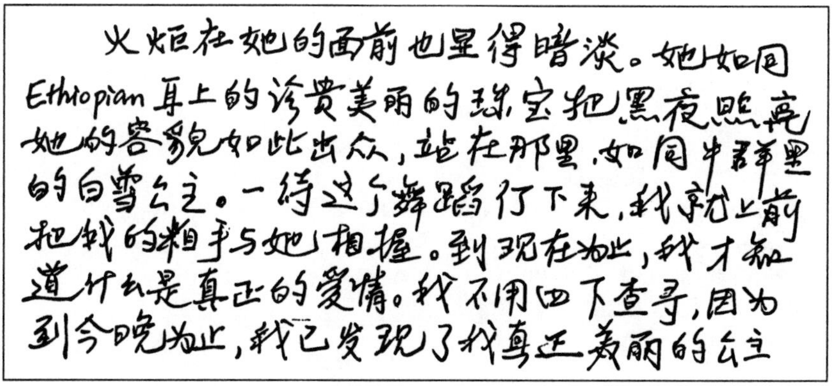
火炬在她的面前也显得暗淡。她如同
Ethiopian耳上的珍贵美丽的珠宝把黑夜照亮
她的容貌如此出众，站在那里，如同牛群里
的白雪公主。一待这个舞蹈停下来，我就上前
把我的粗手与她相握。到现在为止，我才知
道什么是真正的爱情。我不用四下查寻，因为
到今晚为止，我已发现了我真正美丽的公主

FIGURE 43

Spanish Version :

Romeo: ¡El Oh, antorchas parece dévil al lado de ella! Ella noche de los embellishes como una joya rica en un ear?too de Ethiopian?s hermoso para el uso diario, demasiado valioso para este mundo. Ella está parada hacia fuera como una paloma nieve-blanca entre los cuervos. La danza una vez encima, I?ll ve donde ella está parada y hace mi mano áspera bendecida tocando el suyo. ¿Mi corazón sabía amor verdadero hasta ahora? Mis ojos necesitan la mirada no más futura: El hadn?t I considera belleza verdadera hasta esta noche.

French Version:

Romeo: Ah, torches semblent faible près d'elle! Elle nuit d'embellishes comme un bijou riche dans un ear?too d'Ethiopian?s beau pour l'usage journalier, trop valable pour ce
monde. Elle se tient dehors comme une colombe neige-
blanche parmi les corneilles. Une fois la danse plus de, I?ll
voient où elle se tient et font mon main approximative
bénie en touchant le sien. Mon coeur a-t-il su le vrai
amour jusqu'à maintenant? Mes yeux ont besoin de
regard pas autre: Le hadn?t I voient la beauté vraie
jusqu'à ce soir.

Writing for A Different Audience

Audience awareness plays an important role in effective communication. However, in dealing with non-native English speaking students, often
it is not sufficient to just assign the audience and the topic of writing. Task
II in the New York State English Regents exam requires students to use
their knowledge about the audience to recreate a piece of writing that they
have read. Students write to a particular audience, such as the mayor, the
newspaper editor, or a school principal. A good strategy to use is to create a
profile of the audience by asking students specific questions about the
audience and then modeling a few examples of language use appropriate
to that audience in the prewriting stage. The following eight audience pro-
filing questions are adapted from Kirby and Liner's (1987):

1. What age is the audience?
2. Where do they live?
3. What are their cultural backgrounds?
4. What are their educational backgrounds?
5. What kind of job do they have?
6. What kinds of leisure activities do they participate in?
7. Is there anything atypical about them?
8. What is the language typically used to address to this audience?

The following is an example of a student writing a speech from the perspective of a business manager:

A Business Speech

Hello my name is John Gonzales, owner and boss of the Davila Manor. To our
newcomers this speech is a word of warm welcome and introduction. In this
speech we will get to learn about each other, working in my nursing home.

This is a special place. This makes you a very special person. The welfare of those who come to us for care and treatment is our first concern. With this in mind we will provide the highest quality of patient care available. The first 60 days of your employment is considered an introductory period. One of the most important things is to be kind to the elderly and do not use foul language around them. If there is a problem, write a note in my mailbox and tell me. Your week begins on Monday and ends on Saturday. Payday is every Thursday. Your normal workload is 40 hours per week, and a 45-minute lunch break. If you leave you must punch you time card. It is mandatory you come to work every single day. If a person is late it could interfere with resident care. You must be here at 9:00 am. Late 5 times look for a new job, buddy. You must take a urine test. In your introductory days you are paid $8.65 an hour, after that you get $1.75 raise. Any questions?

Literature Mimic Writing

Unlike in elementary schools or middle schools, in secondary schools language is only taught or alluded to during writing instruction. However, it makes more sense to have students learn about language use from literature which students are most often exposed to in their English classrooms. Literary discourse has many language characteristics, which provide language learners with a rich context for learning. One way of using literature for language learning is to select passages that are specifically rich in certain language characteristics and literary techniques, such as the use of pronouns, verbs, prepositions, adjectives, or the use of imagery, symbolism, etc. and ask students to mark the elements under study and alert students to the effective language use by the writer. In the following poem, students are asked to identify all the human qualities of Chicago (personification) by highlighting the words and phrases, such as adjectives, verbs, or nouns that give the city these human characteristics. Also, the striking parallel structure use in this poem is worth exploring. Noden (1999) suggested the idea for such a focused writing exercise to develop students' writing skills in the needed areas. Once the students have a good grasp of the language and literary elements the poet used here, they can then write a poem on their own city or town using similar words or phrases.

Chicago by Carl Sandburg

Hog Butcher for the World,
Tool Maker, Stacker of Wheat,
Player with Railroads and the Nation's Freight
   Handler;
Stormy, husky, brawling,
City of the Big Shoulders:

They tell me you are wicked and I believe them, for I
   have seen your painted women under the gas
   lamps luring the farm boys.
And they tell me you are crooked and I answer: Yes,
   it is true I have seen the gunman kill and go free
   to kill again.
And they tell me you are brutal and my reply is: On
   the faces of women and children I have seen the
   marks of wanton hunger.
And having answered so I turn once more to those
   who sneer at this my city, and I give them back
   the sneer and say to them:
Come and show me another city with lifted head
   singing so proud to be alive and coarse and
   strong and cunning.
Flinging magnetic curses amid the toil of piling job on
   job, here is a tall bold slugger set vivid against
   the little soft cities;
Fierce as a dog with tongue lapping for action,
   cunning as a savage pitted against the wilderness,
      Bareheaded,
      Shoveling,
      Wrecking,
      Planning,
      Building, breaking, rebuilding,
Under the smoke, dust allover his mouth, laughing
   with white teeth,
Under the terrible burden of destiny laughing as a
   young man laughs,
Laughing even as an ignorant fighter laughs who has
   never lost a battle,
Bragging and laughing that under his wrist is the
   pulse, and under his ribs the heart of the people,
      Laughing!
Laughing the stormy, husky, brawling laughter of
   Youth, half-naked, sweating, proud to be Hog
   Butcher, Tool Maker, Stacker of Wheat, Player
   with Railroads and Freight Handler to the Nation.

Student's Mimic Poem

New York City
They tell me you are the city of the world and I believe them, for I
   have seen so many people from all over the world
      since I came over to the US
And they tell me you are the city of action and I answer: Yes,
   Day and night subway pounds, Broadway shines
      and people never sleep.

And they tell me you are a ghost city with ashes only and my reply is:
There has never been this big and the city has not been this alive.
And having answered so I turn once more to those
who trash my city, and I give them back what they deserve:
Come and show me another city with lifted head
singing so proud to be the center of the world and the heart of the people
tough, cunning, and never be broken.

Word Association Poem

A Word Association poem is an activity inviting students to experience the creative power of words. Students are asked to generate a word list by their parts of speech, and they can either use their own words or they can choose words in their literature work. They then are asked to use the words from the list to create a poem. This is a good way to study words by using them. English language learners can use this exercise to deepen their understanding of certain words on the list and enjoy the power of words. Below is an excerpt from Octavio Paz's "The Blue Bouquet." Students first make note of the verbs used by the author here that are powerful by underlining all the verbs and putting them in one column.

> I **shrugged** my shoulders, **muttered** "back soon," and **plunged into** the darkness. At first I couldn't see anything. I **fumbled along** the cobblestone street. I lit a cigarette. Suddenly the moon **appeared** from behind a black cloud, lighting a white wall that was crumbled in places. I stopped, **blinded by** such whiteness. Wind **whistled** slightly. I **breathed** the air of the tamarinds. The night **hummed,** full of leaves and insects. Crickets **bivouacked** in the tall grass. (from Paz's *The Blue Bouquet,* pp. 164)

Then the teacher asks the class to generate another column of color words, another column of words with feelings, and another column of words of people or objects. Once the four columns of words are on the board, the teacher then ask students to work in pairs or groups to create sentences using these words creatively across columns.

Emotional nouns	Verbs	Colors	Nouns
Fortune	shrug	black	sky
Excitement	mutter	yellow	chimney
Confusion	fumble	purple	language
Fear	breathe	orange	melon
Frustration	whistle	blue	tune

Word Association Poem

My good fortune shrugs off the black sky.
Confusion mutters about yellow language.
Excitement breathes the air of orange melon.
Fear makes me fumble into the purple chimney.
Frustration whistles a blue tune.

"I am . . . " poem

An "I am . . . " poem is a nice icebreaker for students to introduce each other in the beginning of the semester or a writing exercise to further study characterization by writing from the character's perspective. Augusto Monterroso's "The eclipse" is a short story about a Spaniard who was lost in the Guatemalan jungle. He tried to use his Euro-centric thinking to persuade the natives not to sacrifice him, yet he was killed by it. The story is told in the third person. Student could write an "I am . . . " poem retelling the story from the first person as a tribe elder, the Spaniard who got killed, the tribe children, a *New York Times* reporter, etc. For English language learners, this exercise enables them to reveal their understanding of the story. Also, by using different perspectives but using "I am . . . " structure, the students practice the varied techniques of story telling. Though similar to in-role writing, this writing exercise provides more structure, and therefore, helps English language learners get started. The following is an example of the writing structure and a sample of such poem writing.

Sample Writing Prompt

I am _____(two characteristics of the character)
I wonder _____(something the character is curious about)
I hear _____(what the character hears)
I see _____(what the character sees)
I want _____(what the character desires)
I am _____(repeat the first line)

Sample Student's Writing

I am a wise and respected tribe elder.
I wonder why the white man invades our sacred ground.
I hear his nonsense talk to persuade us to spare his life.
I see my ancestor angered, rose to scold us for being so weak and naïve.
I want the white man's heart spilled over the altar.
I am a wise and respected tribe elder.

I am a superior and civilized European man.
I wonder why these savages cannot understand my mission from God.
I hear they chanting and yelling,
I see the altar, the mask, and blood,
I want them to understand the scientific principle behind the eclipse.
I am a superior and civilized European man.

I am an objective and fair *New York Times* reporter.
I wonder why the European man is so arrogant and foolish.
I hear the natives chanting the dates of the lunar eclipse.
I see the fear and helpless in the white man's eyes.
I want to stop all this, but I can't.
I am an objective and fair *New York Times* reporter.

SECOND LANGUAGE WRITING INSTRUCTION
IN SOCIAL STUDIES CLASSES

Timeline Caption

A timeline, as shown in cultural history studies, is frequently used in social studies classrooms as a visual aid to help students develop a clear

TABLE 43

Persians conquered the Greek colonies in Asia Minor. Later they conquered Athens too. with Spartans help, Greeks battle with Persians.	When King Philip was killed his son, Alexander became the leader of Macedonia. He led an army conquered Persia, the rest of Asian Minor and the Middle East.	Julius Caesar became the dictator of Roman Empire in 44 BC. He made many reforms and gained popularity. A group of Roman nobles and Senate were not happy and they plotted and killed him on March 15, 44 BC
Greeks defeat Persians /	Alexander the Great /	Julius Caesar assassinated /
400 BC 509 BC	336 BC	44 BC 31 BC

/ Roman Republic	/ Start of Roman Empire
Romans established a Republic without a king Or queen. Citizens had the right to elect their Leaders who were aristocrats called patricians. They formed laws known as the Twelve Tables.	Octavian, Caesar's adopted son, won the battle with Antony and Lepidus after Caesar's death and became a king called Augustus, meaning honored and majestic.

chronological sense of the historical events. Besides its visual effect, a time-line can also be used as a writing activity to engage English language learn-ers in a series of caption writing about the timeline. Writing captions along with the timeline gives these students a chance to describe or explain a his-torical event occurred on the timeline. The teacher can engage the class first talk about the key points on the timeline, make a semantic web, and elaborate each point using key words and phrases. For example, Table 43 is a timeline of Ancient Greeks and Romans.

Sentence Combining

Sentence combining is a technique used in teaching first and second language learners how to use varied short sentences to form clear and coherent sentences. The technique, though old, is effective in stimulating the growth in students' writing and in promoting logical thinking skills (Christensen, 1968; Weaver, 1996). It can be introduced as a game in which grammatical structures are being learned or practiced without stu-dents knowing about it. A social studies teacher can either select a complex sentence in the textbook reading and break it down into short and simple sentences or can pick short and choppy sentences from students' writing for a sentence combining exercise as shown below.
Sentences to be Combined:

There was a conflict.
The conflict occurred with the appointment of bishops.
The conflict became a struggle over who should have supreme authority: the Holy Roman Emperor or the Pope.

Combined Sentence:

The conflict over the appointment of bishops had grown into a struggle over who had supreme authority—the Holy Roman Emperor or the Pope. (from Perry et al. *History of the world,* p. 243, by McDougal Littell, Inc. 1995)

Photo Essays

A photo essay can be either a series of photographs or pictures with writ-ten captions on a theme or concept or one photo with a narrative attached to it. When used with English language learners, a photo essay combines verbal and non-verbal thinking into the writing and engages students in a close study of the visual representation of a social studies concept. This helps develop non-native English speaking students with their visual and culture literacy. Some typical social studies themes and concepts are: independence, the ways of life, migration and acculturation, war and peace, age and family, ecology, religion, men and women, individual and society, etc. The photographs or pictures can be either students' own production or the existing work collected by the teacher or it can be a photo in the textbook. The visual imagery presented by the photographs and pictures gets second language learners to a starting point with their writing and ease some of the anxiety produced by the word "essay." Also, centering round a theme or a concept, a photo/picture essay can build a connection between past and present, history and students' personal lives. A photo essay can also strengthen conceptual understanding, expand their language abilities, stretch their imagination, and create enjoyment of learning (Moulton & Tevis. 1991). The following is an example of a group photo essay after students' viewing a photograph of the harsh life of child laborers in *New York Times* in the 1900s.

Questions to ask during the viewing:
- What is the first thing you saw in the photo?
- What is going on here?
- Give three adjectives to describe this photo.
- List three things that you might not see today.
- Give the photograph a title.

Group photo essay: Child in Pain

We first saw a boy in the photograph. He is younger than us. He is carrying a big rock on his head. There are more rocks behind him. We guess he is not happy, but looks tired and sad. He wears those old clothes, which tell us that the picture was taken in the old days. Also, the pavement looks old and worn-out. The three words came to our minds: heavy, tired, and dirty. Since there are no other people around, we do not know why the boy is carrying a rock. It seems so heavy that we would assume someone helped him to get the rock up on his head. His dress and his facial expression tell us that he is not doing it for fun. Is he working for someone? Why has someone pushed him to do the job that is so dangerous and heavy? Since we are learning about the Industrial Revolution, we think this is about child labor. We don't think that children in his age could do something like this today unless they are crazy. Also, we don't dress up like him and the pavement on the streets in New York City are no longer like this. Child labor is illegal nowadays in the US. We title it "Child in Pain."

In Other Words . . .

Detailed writing in social studies demands students acquire skills of paraphrasing and summarizing. Coming from different cultural backgrounds and educational traditions, many Asian students might have different views toward using the writer's original words. In some Asian cultures, for example, Mainland China, direct copying of the writer's words or phrases without acknowledging the author is acceptable in the apprentice stage of writing (Dong, 1999a, 1999b; Matalene, 1985). Many teachers encourage students to do that. A famous Chinese saying goes: If you have memorized three hundreds Tang poems, you can write beautiful poems yourself. It stresses the importance of having a bank of famous sayings or other's words before you can produce your own writing. In American schools, however, these students might find it difficult to change the writer's words not only due to language issues but also due to varied cultural values. They might find it insulting or disrespectful to change or reword the original words. As a result, they might plagiarize. Therefore, teaching how to paraphrase and summarize becomes an important task for all teachers.

Once the students understand the varied cultural norms observed in different countries, they will be open to ways of paraphrasing and learning how to do citations. It is preferable that the teacher models what a good paraphrase looks like by routinely sharing his or her own paraphrased sentence or comparing different paraphrases with the original sentence or paragraph. Research in second language learning has demonstrated that paraphrasing demands deeper reading comprehension and develops students writing skills (Odean, 1987). Vocabulary learning can be enhanced with students' learning how to do a paraphrase. Students with limited knowledge of synonyms will benefit from paraphrasing by learning how to use words with similar meaning. The following are some procedures of paraphrasing and a sample.

1. Read the original text and get the main idea of the text.
2. Focus on the key words or phrases in the text and try to find similar words to substitute these words or phrases.
3. Try to connect the key words by using your own words.

The growth of the slave trade

Original:

Inequality began to increase in African society. At the upper end of society, wealth and power became concentrated in the hands of a few families that belong to the ruling and merchant classes. At the other end of society there was an enormous increase in slavery. Since ancient times, Africa's exported to the outside world had included slaves. The wealthy classes in many lands wanted African slaves as servants and laborers ((from Perry, *et al. History of the world*, p. 306, by McDougal Littell, Inc. 1995).

Paraphrased Version:

In African society, rich and powerful people governed the society. The poor people became slaves. Starting from ancient times, these poor people were shipped to other countries as slaves to serve and labor for the rich people there.

Cross-Cultural Perspective Comparison

Even though there has been some change in social studies curriculum in recent years, such as including more non-Western cultures and people, textbooks have been slow in reflecting the changing world and including multiple perspectives towards an issue. Very often historical events are still more frequently depicted from a Western perspective. Last year when a class of English language students was discussing the Korean War, Korean students revealed that they never thought the Korean War was portrayed like the way that the US textbook depicted it. They felt that their side of story was not told in the textbook. The textbook was seven years old. Zarnowski (1991) suggests the idea that students engage in a critical inquiry by rewriting portions of the old textbooks. In dealing with multicultural and multilingual students, a social studies teacher must draw on students' knowledge of their home cultures and allow them to present multiple perspectives, update the information, and enhance understanding between the worlds. A critical comparison and contrast of a portion or even a chapter of the US textbook with that of the textbook used in other countries can be done as a whole class or a group project. A social studies teacher should be aware of possible different points of views from his or her students (Gross, 1996). Students should be invited to share their perspectives gained from their schooling in their home country. Students should also be encouraged to research their views gained back in their home country either by reading the textbook in their native language or by doing oral interviews with people from their cultures and communities. As they actively get involved in doing history and writing about what they have learned, students will find history fascinating and see the relevance of what they bring to the classroom, which in turn, helps them gain a deeper understanding of the issue. The following is an example of such a comparison on the treatment of Native Americans portrayed in a US textbook and a Chinese textbook.

Chinese Version

The process of the westward territorial expansion of the United States was also a process in which the Indians were driven out and killed, their land and property stolen. Bloody massacres sharply reduced the population of the Indians from one million to 240,000 in the late 19th century. The survivors were driven to the reservations where they led a miserable life. The peaceful, pastoral westward movement advocated by the ruling class of the United States was, in fact, the Indians' history written in blood and tears. (*Senior High World History*, Vol. 2, 1982, 23, by Chinese Department of Education.)

American Version

Then in 1637, the Puritans set out to destroy the Pequots. They surrounded a fortified Pequot village, and set fire to it. Nearly 400 Pequots—mostly women, children, and the old men—burned to death or were shot as they tried to escape. Others were hunted down and killed or sold into slavery. The Indians had once claimed all the North America continent as their own. By 1890, their conquerors had stripped them of most of their land, and confined them to reservations. (From Todd and Curti *Triumph of the American nation*, p. 38, 494. Chicago: Harcourt Brace Jovanovich, 1986)

Written Debates

In recent years social studies curriculum, instruction, and assessment have emphasized developing students' critical thinking skills on issues by examining the strengths and weaknesses of opposing views. A frequent use of primary and secondary sources to complement one-sided views depicted in the textbook is based on the assumption that students at the secondary level are able to entertain different positions. They can also learn to construct their own historical interpretation through a guided inquiry approach in which students play the role of "detectives" or "jurors" to find out what was going on. A debate is an excellent forum for students to develop their own position, demonstrate their critical thinking process, and articulate their views using sources. For second language students, a written debate can be more appropriate in providing sufficient time for students to think and write their arguments. Once students are comfortable with their views in writing, they can then form teams and debate orally. A written debate topic can be any controversial issues that students are learning using sufficient numbers of primary and secondary sources on opposing sides. Topics might include the use of the atomic bomb against Japan: fair or unfair? Imperialism in Africa: good or bad? Industrial Revolution: positive or negative? etc. Students can choose first which side they will be on, read the materials, and then write arguments and evidence to support their arguments. For English language learners, they could be asked to do an oral history investigation by interviewing their parents or grandparents and by constructing their arguments drawn from their rich home culture resources. In doing so, they can evaluate the sources that they read by reflecting on the following questions:

1. Who is the author, and when and where was this writing published?
2. What does the author's perspective tell you about his or her possible intention?
3. Why did you choose this side?
4. How were you convinced or persuaded by what you have read?
5. Who did you talk to and what did you find out about your topic?
6. What did you learn about this topic back in your home country? How is it different?
7. What evidence did you gather from interviewing your family or from your schooling back home?

Media Analysis

Technology is progressing at a breathtaking speed. Film excerpts, videotapes, Internet sources, and TV new reports have become more and more an integral part of classroom instruction to stimulate students' interest, to create an immediate effect of mood and feelings that often reading a textbook can hardly achieve. They can also reinforce concepts and themes under study. For second language learners, the use of these media sources can actively engage students in the use of language (Penfield, 1987).

Discussing the effects of media and how teenagers learn, Zevin (2000) stresses the importance of critical viewing by engaging students in a series of reflections. Media can be a useful resource for students' content knowledge learning and authentic language learning if the students are taught to critically examine the source. A media analysis is a writing report on what the student has seen or not seen after viewing a film excerpt, a movie, or a TV news report. The students compare and contrast the media source with other sources they are reading about the issue and they pose a question for further investigation of the issue or to challenge one perspective, or provoke deeper thinking about the issue.

For English language learners, the teacher can ask them to jot down the part they don't understand. Then students can be put into groups going over the main ideas about what they just watched. Through peer interaction, English language learners have a chance to use their social language to make sense of academic language. Also, by using multiple senses, such as viewing, listening, speaking, writing, English language learners' language skills are developed along with their acquisition of social studies knowledge (Collier, 1992). A sample outline for a media analysis report is like this:

Topic under Viewing: Racial Discrimination after Sept. 11

Summary of historical period covered by the film, video, or TV news:

Time:
Place:
People:
Event:
Analysis:

- What was the most meaningful part of the film, video, or TV news?
- List one part of the film, video, or TV report which you don't understand.
- What was the mood, attitude, or feelings you experienced from viewing it?
- How well did the sound and moving imagery portray the historical period?
- Explain possible motivation behind this film, video, or TV news.
- How was the position taken by the film, video, or TV news report different from or similar to the other sources that we are reading?

Biographical Interview Report

This activity asks students to play the role of an interviewer to get an in-depth understanding of a historical figure under study by writing up an interview report (Whitman, 2000). Students will read more about that historical figure, and biographies on the historical figure can be used to enrich their reading experience. By reading these biographies, students can step into the character's shoes and transform a narrative version of the biographical account into a dialogue. The transformation pushes students in general and English language learners in particular to use specific language appropriate, such as switching pronouns, using the present tense, etc. to write up their interview. Reading biographies can stimulate students' interest and excitement of bringing history to life and promote reading for enjoyment and reading for interaction (Zarnowski, 1990). In order to do the project, students also need to generate relevant questions, and through the process, they have to think like an interviewer and a historian. Students can be grouped and assigned one historical figure to write about. The following is a sample of student's report on her interview with Mao.

Biographical Interview With Mao

It was about 2 o'clock in the afternoon, I arrived at Zhong Nan Hai and met Mr. Mao. He looked great and seemed happy to meet me. After we greeted each other, we sat down and began the interview.

Jessie: Sir! I am really glad to meet you.

Mao: Hi, nice to meet you, too, Jessie.

Jessie: You had a successful leadership during your ruling of the Communist Party. Is there something in your early life that affected you?

Mao: I was born in 1893 in a peasant's family, which didn't place much value on education. When I was 13 years old, I left these relatively comfortable surroundings to continue my studies on my own. By 1911, I was studying at a secondary school in the capital of my native Hunan province, Chang-Sha. At this time a revolution broke out to overthrow the Manchu dynasty in the hope of creating a new China based on the Western model. I served six months in the Revolutionary army, where I began to develop some of the skills that would make me a military leader in the years to come.

Jessie: Could you explain the famous "Long March" to me briefly?

Mao: Sure. When our Jiangxi province was surrounded by the Nationalist army led by Chiang Kai-shek, some 90,000 men and women broke through and went on the Long March. It was in Oct., 1934 and we marched westward to Guizhou province. During the Long March, we overcame many obstacles, you know, constant harassment by Nationalist troops and the armies of provincial warlords, countless mountains and rivers. More than half of the original marchers were lost their lives in this incredible journey.

Jessie: When I was a kid, I read many stories about the Long March. I'm really glad to have a wonderful conversation with you, sir. I wish that I can have another interview with you next time.

Mao: You are always welcome, Jessie. Our China needs you young people to make our country better. Take care, Jessie!

CHAPTER 8

SECOND LANGUAGE LISTENING/SPEAKING INSTRUCTION IN MAINSTREAM CLASSES

SECOND LANGUAGE LISTENING/SPEAKING INSTRUCTION IN SCIENCE CLASSES

Tongue Twister

Many times non-native English speaking students are reluctant to speak up because they are embarrassed by their strong accent and mispronunciation. Taking a few minutes a day for both the teacher and the students to write and choral read tongue twisters can help them improve their pronunciation and speaking skills on difficult sounds, the sounds that are absent in their home language, thus reinforce concepts learned. Many words in biology are new to all learners not only in writing but also in speaking, therefore experimenting with them using tongue twisters sounding words out in a game like situation creates fun and excitement in learning, forcing

Teaching Language and Content to Linguistically and Culturally Diverse Students:
Principles, Ideas, and Materials; pages 207–227.
A Volume in: Language Studies in Education
Copyright © 2004 by Information Age Publishing, Inc.
All rights of reproduction in any form reserved.
ISBN: 1-59311-088-X (paper), 1-59311-089-8 (cloth)

students to pay attention to the words they learn. A science teacher can ask students to say the tongue twister together as a class or as a group to avoid spotlighting individual students. Below are some sample tongue twisters created by the teacher and the students using biological ideas.

- Land biome, ocean biome, they are all biomes in the biosphere.
- Deciduous trees, confinerous trees, deciduous trees, and confinerous trees.
- Three trees with green leaves breathing the morning breath.
- Herbivores, carnivores, omnivores, and what are you?
- Drip, drop, dribble, a rain drop drizzle.

How to . . .

In this activity, students are asked to give advice on how to cope with a science situation they find in reading science, such as biology. This can be done with a connection to reading and writing activities. After students read about a biological issue, for example, a decline in the number of local humming birds, they will write about steps they would take to solve the problem. In doing so, English language learners practice certain language structures used to describe a problem and the solution, such as transitional words and appropriate word choice. After writing, they will report back to their group or the whole class. Topics for writing and speaking "How to . . . " can be found in newspapers and popular science magazines or can be something students care about or curious about. The following are a few "How to . . . " prompts.

- How to collect organisms living in a pond?
- How to tell the differences in trees in a park?
- How to observe the ecosystem in your backyard?
- How to examine abiotic factors around your school?
- How to solve the termite problem in your neighborhood?

Guess Who I Am.

This oral activity encourages English language learners to speak up in class using scientific knowledge they have learned. Before the activity, the teacher instructs the students to put down on a card of the name of the animal or plant they like to be. If several students have chosen to be the same plant or animal, they can group together and plan their presentation. Once the students have made a decision on which plant or animal they want to be, they are supposed to come up to the front of the classroom and ask the class to guess who they are. The students can write down their questions they are going to ask. The person or the team being questioned can only answer yes or no or give short answers without revealing the name of the plant or the animal. The teacher can model the guessing game for the class first, asking questions like: Is it an animal or a plant? Is the animal living in tundra or a tropical rain forest? Does the animal eat plants? Which level of the food chain is this animal in? The following are a few sample "Guess Who I am" questions:

Guess One Herbivore: (giraffe)

Does it eat grass?
Is it big?
Does it produce milk?
Which biome does it live in? Forest
Does it live in trees?
Which kind of species does it interact with?
Does it sleep in the night time.
What is its favorite food?

Guess One Decomposer: (fungi)

Is it small?
Does it live on land?
Is it a type of the plant?
Is it green?

Guess One Law: (Boyle's Law)

Does it have anything to do with liquid/gas?
Is the temperature kept constant?
Does it related to pressure?
Does it related to volume?
Does the law describe a direct or inverse relationship?

Guess one environmental phenomenon: (Ozone)

Does it have anything to do with our air or water?
Is it harmful or beneficial to humans?
Does it block or pollute?
How big an impact does this have on our environment?

Conversational Cooperative Learning

Engaging English language learners in cooperative groups working on some scientific problem is an important part of science learning. Normally the teacher would like to see students are all on task during cooperative learning with a minimum noise or conversation. However, the truth is an extended talk in English among each other is often lacking for English language learners in particular when they have limited resources or opportunities both in school and back home. With a well-designed, challenging, and interesting task, students are eager to talk through ideas and make decisions on how to solve the problem In addition, group talks during the cooperative learning can also arouse curiosity, extend thinking, and develop a scientific point of view (Lemke, 1990). Even English language learners who are constantly silent in class may open up to group talks. Therefore, the teacher should encourage everyone to use oral language in cooperative learning groups. It is during these talks that students get to practice on their listening and speaking skills, such as posing a question, clarifying a word, commenting on each other's performance, joking, demanding, etc. These communication functions are often achieved only in real verbal communication like cooperative learning groups rather than learned by listening to the teacher's talk.

The following is an example of such a conversational episode where students learn how a sickle cell disease is inherited, a topic of genetics, by randomly choosing two beans from the mix of the red and white beans representing sickle and normal cell alleles repeatedly. The sickle cell alleles, represented by red beans decreased as the population reproduced itself from one generation to another.

Student 1: I got AA. (meaning two white beans)
Student 2: Yeah, I got SS. (meaning two red beans)
Student 3: Oh, cool, she got SS. What did you get?
Student 4: SS.
Student 3: Put them back.
Student 1: You screw up, you cannot put these beans back. These are with sickle diseases. They are dead already. What did you get? (the one did not close his eyes in picking)
Student 3: AA.
Student 4: All right, let's count them.
Student 3: (report to the teacher) We got 15 AAs, 2 SSs, and 4 ASs.
Teacher: Why are there always more white beans than red beans in this population?
Student 3: Because we have more white beans.
Teacher: Why do we have more white beans?
Student 2: Because white is dominant.

Teacher: Why is it dominant?

Student 1: Because they don't have disease and they are going to live longer.

Teacher: That's it, that's it. Does everybody hear that? If you have two SSs, the individuals are going to die and not to pass their genes on. So therefore, that number of SSsis going to decrease in the population.

SECOND LANGUAGE LISTENING/SPEAKING INSTRUCTION IN MATHEMATICS CLASSES

Mathematics and second language research literature has shown how verbal interaction can play a powerful role in mathematics learning and language acquisition between the teacher and the students and among students themselves (Usiskin, 1996). However, misconceptions about English language learners' readiness for mathematics participation often lead the teacher to exclude these students like the anecdote I gave in the introduction, where mathematics teacher considers that he has done his English language learners a big favor by leaving them alone. With more and more emphasis on classroom participation and an articulation students' thought process, there is a real need for mathematics teachers to support English language learners in developing listening and speaking skills (Moschkovich, 1999). The following are four strategies used to engage English language learners in the mathematics classroom listening and speaking activities:

Think-Pair-Share (TPS)

Think-pair-share is a three-step cooperative learning activity designed to build students' active learning habits by first thinking on their own about a question or a problem, then pairing up with their neighbors to share each other's thoughts about the problem, and finally coming up with a collective idea about the solution. In a large class, think-pair-share can work effectively to get students involved in the learning task and communicating with each other in a focused and efficient manner. The spontaneous thinking and sharing often lead to a whole class discussion on a deep level. In working with English language learners, the cooperative activity can be expanded to think-write-pair-share to ensure enough time for thinking and putting thoughts into writing before sharing. The topic for such an activity can also be concept oriented or theme-based. For example, the mathematics teacher can ask: What is the commutative property in addition? Give everyday examples to illustrate it. After pair worked through their problems they can share their findings with the class. The following is a sample of student responses to the above question.

Kim's response	Luke's response
A commutative property is an order we use to do additions. When the order changes, the result is not changing.For example, $a + b = b + a$ Everyday examples: Put on your coat and pick up your boots. Hang up the telephone and say goodbye.	When we do additions, we can switch back and forth the two or more numbers. It does not matter which number we put first or second, the sum will always be the same. For example, $4 + 6 + 8 = 6 + 8 + 4 = 18$ An everyday example: Put on your left shoe and put on your right shoe.

Homework Challenger

A homework assignment is normally evaluated by students putting their answers on the board for the teacher and class to check in the mathematics class. In working with English language learners, a mathematics teacher needs to change relatively silent homework writing into a verbal exchange. One way to do it is a use of the homework challenger. Students take turns to be a homework challenger of the day. The challenger is assigned to pose a question or two or reveal difficulties about the homework assignment of the previous day. The challenger will read aloud some of these questions and concerns for both the teacher and students to respond. To help English language learners learn questioning and clarification techniques, the teacher can put some commonly used mathematics classroom talk structures on the board or in a handout, for example, "I don't understand . . . " "I am confused about . . . " "Why do you do . . . ?" "What is the meaning of . . . ?" Being a challenger puts a student into the role of an active learner. For English language learners, they can be challengers, too, once they have learned to raise a question or talk about their understandings. By using a planned speech, a speech prepared in writing, the English language learner will feel less nervous about her or his speech and more confident about what s/he is going to say. Finally, the preparation for the question or concern creates a mystery and excitement.

Fishing for Questions

In this activity, instead of the teacher being the one reviewing the lesson given the day before and preparing the lesson for the day, the students are the ones who write down questions about what they have learned the previous day and what they will be learning and put them into a hat or a bag or an empty tissue box once they come into the mathematics class. The teacher can put her questions into the container, too. Then the teacher asks one student to pull out a question and read it aloud to the class, using it either as a review or a motivational tool for the class to be ready for the new topic. This again demands students to pay close attention to the lesson and to be reflective about what they have learned. Students are welcome to use examples beyond the textbook, such as real life math to ask questions. The assignment demands students' use of the appropriate language structure, such as a correct use of tenses to describe the lesson learned the previous day and the lesson to be learned. Those who are shy and do not like to openly share their own questions can have a chance to read aloud someone else's questions, thus reduce the anxiety of speaking publicly. Sample questions can be:

> Yesterday we learned the interest formula to solve problems. My question is what about zero interest for the first year and 1.9 percent starting from the second year as the car commercial shown on TV? How does that influence my dad's car payment in the long run, say five years? By the way the car cost $12,000 and our down payment was $5,000.

Say Something

This exercise is based on the assumption that verbal interaction among the students during the learning task can promote language growth and thinking skills (Harste, Short, & Burke, 1988). In a "Say Something" activity, the teacher gives out the reading material for students to read and talk about in pairs. The reading material can be selected from newspapers, magazines, local ads, or supermarket flyers. Make sure to include both numerical information and the description about the numerical data. In order to promote students' talking, the teacher needs to select the reading that has the need for discussion among students. Students are required to read and say something about the reading rather than do silently reading alone. After reading the pair is required to report to the class the main idea of their reading. They are welcome to draw a picture or use the visuals presented in the reading to facilitate their presentation. However, they must use oral language by describing and explaining the problem. For English language learners who have trouble with certain parts of the reading, they should be encouraged to say something about their trouble, too by either privately telling the teacher or sharing it with the whole class. The following is a list of possible readings for this activity.

- Car dealership ads for possible interest or rate problems
- Weather report and graphics in the local newspaper for probability problems
- Travel brochures or ads in the local newspaper for distance and geometry problems
- Graphic information of numerical data in the newspaper on a population change or a political campaign or Gallop polls for statistical information
- Scientific articles in the newspaper or magazine required some kind of mathematical knowledge
- Sports scores and averages in the newspaper

Speak in a Full Sentence

Very often students like to give out a single one-word or a single number answer rather than say it in the full sentence in the mathematics class. They feel that this is a mathematics class not an English class, and the mathematics teacher usually does not require students to speak in a full sentence. However, in order to assist students with language and literacy skills, a mathematics teacher should require her students to respond in a full sentence. The teacher can model this response by posing a question first and then respond to it. For example, the teacher can ask: What is a prime number? After settling down the students' urge to yell out 2, 3, 5, 7, the teacher should demonstrate the correct response: A prime number is a number that can be only divided by 1 and itself.

Requiring students to respond in a full sentence not only offers an opportunity to train students' spoken language, but also a chance for the teacher to get a sense of the student's understanding of the concept under study to evaluate whether the student's answer is a thoughtful one, or just simply a yell-out answer (Usiskin, 1996). By speaking in a full sentence, the students also internalize their mathematics concepts and develop their verbal skills in translating their mathematical concepts into English. Gradually, this positive habit will transfer into their writing by using the language to define, to describe, to explain, to compare, and to argue.

SECOND LANGUAGE LISTENING/SPEAKING INSTRUCTION IN ENGLISH LANGUAGE ARTS CLASSES

Dramatic Adaptations

Dramatic adaptations can be a simple skit with a planned storyline during the reading or after reading of the book. Students are encouraged to select a scene or a powerful line to produce a dramatized dialogue and present it to the class as a group. By stepping into the characters' shoes and living through the story, students can develop a deeper understanding of the characters' voices and development and how the plot unfolds. The conflicts in the story or the morals of the story become clear by the students' personal involvement in the literature. Dramatic adaptations are particularly helpful to second language learners who can get to practice various language use by speaking, listening, and acting in a playful setting. Texts used for dramatic adaptations can be an excerpt from a novel, a folktale, a line or two in a play. The following is an example of students' dramatic adaptation of Shakespeare's *Macbeth*. Students are asked to work as a group of three to come up with a short skit with the audience observing and identifying the possible quotation from the drama. The following is a sample handout that students will be given to come up with the skit.

Quotes from **Macbeth:**
"There are daggers in men's smiles."
Setting:
School cafeteria

Characters:	Mood
Girlfriend	depressed, hatred
Boyfriend 1	happy
Boyfriend 2	frustrated
Girl friend's girl friend	Romantic

Choral Reading

Poetry, rhymes, and tongue twisters can be used as an effective instructional tool to reinforce English language pronunciation patterns besides their possibilities for aesthetic explorations. Reading aloud a rhyme, a tongue twister, or a poem together as a whole class can offer students an enjoyable experience while experimenting with voice, rhyme, intonation, and stress and improving pronunciation (McCauley & McCauley, 1992). Also, students can be encouraged to pay special attention to certain rhymed words or the sounds that they may have trouble pronouncing during the read-aloud. Choral reading provides an opportunity for all learners to participate orally without one student being singled out to read aloud. In doing so, individual mispronunciations or accents are absorbed by the overriding voices of the group, even beginners will read along and experience the excitement of participation in the new language, not being afraid of making errors. Also, by reading aloud to an audience or even to oneself, students can enjoy the pleasure of literature and add a group expression to the work under study, which might not be achieved by using silent reading or the teacher's reading aloud. Almost all the poems and excerpts of the play or even a quote in novel can be read chorally. Varied choral reading strategies are broken down by line, couplet, stanza or dividing the class by gender or rows and assigning parts to the students to do the reading. Also, the teacher can ask the class to pause and re-examine a word or phrases to make sure that students understand the meaning and are able to pronounce it.

Tongue Twister

Tongue twisters provide students with brief encounters of language that are fun and challenging oral exercises for English language learners. They can be said either in unison or individually. Stumbling is acceptable and predictable. A teacher can select or even create specific tongue twisters designed to solve some pronunciation or accent problems tailored to her students' needs. Or students can write their own tongue twisters to practice on certain sounds that they have difficulty with.

- She sells seashells in the sea shore.
- Alice asks for axes.
- Crisp crust crackles.
- Elegant elephants.
- For fine fresh fish, phone Phil.
- Peter Piper picked a peck of pickled peppers.

Some Internet sources used to search for tongue twisters:

- http://members.tripod.com/~ESL4Kids/tongue.html
- http://www.geocities.com/Athens/8136/tonguetwisters.html
- http://www.uebersetzung.at/twister/ for multilingual tongue twisters

Speaking with a subtext

A subtext is an "underlying thinking of the character during speaking." It is used in plays and movies when the characters vary their intonation, stress, rhythm, and pause to convey an underlying meaning between each other and with the audience. Speaking with a subtext is a good way to immerse non-native English speaking students in subtle differences of speaking and using voice to convey meaning. It is also a good way to practice on typical troubling sounds, to sensitize students to appropriate use of intonation, stress, rhythm, and pause for communication purposes. In addition, it trains these students to read into speech, body language, and facial expressions and use these communication functions to their advantage and for literature appreciation. For example, the sentence "You're going to miss the bus" can have different meanings when speaking with a different subtext. It can mean the mother telling the child to hurry up to catch the bus in the morning, or it can mean a peer informing each other that the bus is leaving soon, or it can mean the school security guard warning the students of the bus leaving and stopping fooling around in the hallway. In reading plays in the English class, the teacher can assign students to act out a few lines with different subtexts to let the class experience varied ways of oral communication. Class can be divided into groups of three or four. Each group will be given a dialogue with a specific communication situation like the following:

Character 1: Hi,
Character 2: I got what you asked.
Character 1: Just leave it there.
Character 2: Can I come in?
Character 1: No, no way.

Use varied voices when speaking with the following subtexts:

- The relationship between character 1 and 2 is husband and wife after a fight.
- The relationship between character 1 and 2 is a pizza deliveryman and a customer.
- The relationship between character 1 and 2 is a young brother with an elder brother.
- The relationship between character 1 and 2 is friends.
- The relationship between character 1 and 2 is a boss and his employee.

Talk Show

Given that teenagers grow up in a media oriented environment, it is invaluable to constructively use media as a source for motivation and as a teaching tool to create a learning environment. For English language learners, media plays an important role in exposing these students to diverse language use, rich visual, audio stimuli, and cultural insights. Instead of passive participation, students can be active in creating certain media environments in class to promote authentic and meaningful discussion and make active use of their newly learned spoken language. Talk shows or trials in particular invite the audience to participate and allow thoughtful probing and insightful explorations of issues between the host and the guests or a jury and the judge as well as between the speakers and the audience. After reading a literary work, students can work as groups of three or five to rewrite part of the work in a talk show script, assign roles to each other, and play it out to the class. The following is an example of such a role play by a group of 11th graders after reading *A Lesson Before Dying* by Ernest Gaines.

Tara: Welcome to English World News Tonight. Now here is the man responsible for the murder of three men in a robbery of the store, Jefferson. How are you doing?

Jefferson: Can't get any worse, I suppose.

Tara: Why don't you appeal?

Jefferson: Why should I appeal? No hog needs appeal.

Tara: And do you consider yourself human?

Jefferson: No, hogs are not human. Like I said I am just a hog and people want to fatten me up before they kill me.

Tara: Why do you say this?

Jefferson: Why do you ask so many questions? No hog even deserves this. Y'all just look at me and say: that man killed three people.

Tara: Well, did you?

Jefferson: No, hogs cannot kill anything, but none that matters anyway. It ain't the problem of Grant. It ain't the problem of no man. It ain't even my problem. (Someone in the audience shouts out "It's the country.")

Tara: Tell us how it's like waiting to die?

Jefferson: Everyday last year and every hour last day until the day comes near, I had most hidden fear. But in all this there is no need in this world for a hog.

Tara: There you have it, people, an explosive dramatic scene of what appears to be an innocent man being sentenced to the electric chair very soon. How do you feel about this? We would like to hear your response. You may reach us by email at WWW.WENG News.com. Thank you and good night.

Music Story Telling

Second Language acquisition research has shown that music, especially slow beat and pleasant music, can not only stimulate and enrich learning in class, but also has the benefit of enhancing memory and language acquisition. In the 1970s, a psychologist from Bulgaria created Suggestopedia, a method using Baroque music and a relaxed environment to promote foreign language learning (Lozanov, 1979). Even though the method requires resources and aimed at memorization, music has an intriguing role to play in second language learning (Graham, 1996; Abbott, 2002). Music without a lyric works better as a listening activity. It can stimulate imagination and create a chance for an open exploration and interpretation. Students are asked to listen carefully and pay attention to any sound, beat, or note that intrigues them and brings memory or images to them. They will jot down anything that comes to mind and try to make a story out of the music. Once they are done with the listening, they will create a story either in pairs of individually based on what they have heard. Finally, they will share their stories with the class or within the group. Some interesting pieces of music by Georgia Gershwin are as follows:

- An American in Paris
- Strike Up the Band
- Someone to Watch Over Me
- Rhapsody in Blue
- I Got Rhythm
- S'Wonderful

SECOND LANGUAGE LISTENING/SPEAKING INSTRUCTION IN SOCIAL STUDIES CLASSES

Group Decision Making

Cooperative learning groups are regular part of class format of learning in the social studies classroom, an ideal environment to train students' listening and speaking skills through extended talks (Ghaith, 2002; Johnson, 1994). Traditionally, much learning in the social studies classroom is done through the teacher's lecture or the didactic teaching method, with the teacher concerning about time and large amounts of information to be covered. However, research has shown that students who learn better through learner-centered cooperative groups when they discussing and internalizing the information (Joyce, *et al.,* 1992). In the activity shown below, one social studies teacher uses a creative group design, using a series of reading, listening, speaking, and writing exercises to teach WWII to a class of English language learners. Each group is given a set of questions with a problem to solve. They are encouraged to converse with each other to come up with a group decision. After the group has made the decision, they have to write down their reasons for the decision that they have made and present it to the class. The class has to listen to the response first and then they have to write to the group who made the decision responding to their decision. The series of cooperative activities provoke students' imagination and critical thinking as well as listening and speaking skills.

Question for Group 1

If you were a Congressman or a Congresswoman, how would you vote in terms of the US action when Great Britain and France declared war on Germany in 1939?

Response

There are a couple of reasons why we should choose to declare war on Germany and send troops to help the British and French. One of the reasons is that we should be repaying the British's kindness to our country and we should help and support them as our friends. The British have always been loyal to the US and this is time to help them. Another reason why we should vote to declare war on Germany would be that we are aware that Adolf Hitler's greed to re-establish Germany which might lead him to do more harm to the rest of the world.

Question for Group 2

After the Japanese attack on Pearl Harbor, Congress approved President Franklin D. Roosevelt's request for a declaration of war against Japan. If you were a Congressman or a Congresswoman, what would you do to increase military forces in a short period of time?

Response

We chose to vote for a selective service act to draft men between the ages of 18 and 45. The situation is critical and if the citizens do not volunteer, then they should be drafted. In the time of war, there is not enough time to wait for volunteers. We need to act quickly to recruit as many people as possible and to get ready to attack Japan.

Question for Group 3

The Axis Powers (Germany and Italy) had expanded their territory and conquered many European countries in 1939. The US and other Allied Forces were concentrated in Great Britain. If you were General Dwight D. Eisenhower, the commander of the Allied Forces in Great Britain, which strategy would you use to attack Germany and Italy?

Response

During this time when the Axis Powers (Germany and Italy) were at the height of their conquests, it was difficult to attack them head on. When the enemy forces are together, they are stronger and they will attack the Allied Forces. We chose to transport most of the Allied forces across the North Sea to Denmark, and then move south into Germany. This way we could attack on the weak spot of the enemy forces and we would have a better chance of defeating them.

Question for Group 4

After Japan attacked Pearl Harbor, the US fought for years against Japanese forces. It was now 1945 and scientists had just completed work on the world's first atomic bomb. If you were President Truman, who just succeeded President Roosevelt, what action would you take to bring about the final defeat of Japan?

Response

We chose to hold a blockade against Japan to prevent the importation of needed supplies. It was sad news when President Roosevelt died at the beginning of the war with Japan. President Roosevelt took the country from the Great Depression and brought it back to normal. It was a hard decision to make in terms of how to defeat Japan. If we were President Truman, we wouldn't have dropped the atomic bomb on Japan, because then we would have to be ready to carefully guard the west side of the USA. But what we would have done was to block Japan and to prevent the importation of needed supplies. Japan needed the import supplies because it didn't have solid land. Of course after 60 years, the choice would be different. Still it was a difficult choice. And we still think that President Truman's decision was a very harmful one.

Guessing Who S/he Is

One way of releasing the boredom of memorizing and defining a list of historical figures and historical events and energizing social studies learning is using game activities. One activity is called Guessing who s/he is, like a bio-poem but without releasing the name of the person. The guessing game can be played during the unit review or even before learning a new topic to stimulate interests. The game can be played by the teacher modeling one poem or by assigning students to write about these poems. This activity can be combined with reading biographies so that students have access to these historical figures' lives. The poem can be written either individually or as a group. Students will then come up to the front of the classroom or stay within group to read aloud their poems and let the class or the group guess who they are describing. Finally, the poem and the picture of the person can be put on the wall for exhibition.

The poem is composed like this:

Step 1: Structure of the poem

Line 1:   Three words of description about the person
Line 2:   Believer in two things or ideas
Line 3:   Fighter for two things or ideas
Line 4:   Who loves two things or ideas
Line 5:   Who hates two things or ideas
Line 6:   One quote from this person's writing
Line 7:   Resident of (one or two places)

Step 2: Creating the poem

Heavily bearded, intelligent, and a newspaper editor
Believer in class struggle and revolution
Fighter for the workers and the poor
Who loves economy and equal opportunities
Who hates capitalists and oppression
"The history of all hitherto existing society
is the history of class struggles."
Resident of Germany and England.

How to . . .

Talk about or write about "how to . . . " can train English language learners' speaking skills by telling the audience how somebody did something or how something occurred step by step. It can engage students in thinking and using certain language functions and structures used to talk about "how to . . . " Certain language structures are best practiced in this type of speaking or writing, such as a chronological sequence or sentence connectors used in a cause-effect relationship. It can also help them understand and appreciate the complexities and contexts of a historical event. English language learners can write about their answers first and then talk about them in pairs or in groups or share with the whole class. Topics for "how to . . . " can be current events, issues that students care about, and controversial issues. Some of the examples of talking about "how to . . . " are:

- How to stop the Israeli and Palestine conflict?

- How to get people to vote?
- How to be not influenced by the media?

Role Play

Role playing has proven extremely beneficial not only in regular content classes but also in language classes. By assigning students roles, such as the narrator and characters, students can use multiple skills all at once, including listening, speaking, acting, and reading. Also, by involving students into such a read-aloud, the teacher enables them to gain a deeper understanding of the social studies issues. Students at all levels of language proficiency can participate in such activities. For example, beginning English language learners can use non-verbal communication skills to act out certain parts while the advanced learners can play a larger role by narrating. Even listening takes on a new meaning. Like the example shown below, students can play the role of audience to take notes on their listening and viewing and respond to the actors. The following is a role-playing on schools of thought in Ancient China:

Schools of Thought in China

Prince:	Nobody tells me what to do or how to think. I am the one who tells people what to do, whether they are Chinese peasants who work for me or barbarians whose land I've taken.
Confucian Scholar:	Nobody tells you what to do? Not even the Emperor of the Zhou Dynasty who gave you such power? What would your ancestors say about your behavior?
Prince:	Who cares what they would say?
Confucian Scholar:	I care. Confucian would care. He would say that you're not striving for a just and harmonious society. Those who rule must be smart. They must work hard.
Prince:	I am, and I do, so what are you complaining about?
Legalist Scholar:	Intelligence has nothing to do with being a good ruler, my foolish friends. A ruler must be strong. A ruler must be strict and harsh because people are naturally evil. We can't help it. The dark side of human nature leads us. Rulers must be all-powerful to keep people from doing evil.
Prince:	Just because I'm smart and work hard doesn't mean that I'm weak. I'm strong, very strong. And harsh. Anyone will tell you that. And strict. Ask anyone.

Taoist Scholar:	All this arguing, my dear friends, is unnecessary—just as strict government is. People are neither good or evil, and the world cannot be changed by people's actions. Nature determines what happens in the world. If people live in harmony with nature, then they will find true happiness. They will not need rulers.
Confucian Scholar:	But the population of China continues to grow and grow. The princes fight among themselves and invade other people's territories. We must have rules to tell everyone, from the emperor to the poorest of the poor, how to behave. We begin with the five different kinds of relationships: ruler and ruled, husband and wife, parents and children, older and younger brothers, and friends.
Prince:	Here we go again. The rules set out for your family will not work with my family. We are natural leaders. We don't think—we do. We prefer action.
Taoist Scholar:	But you don't consider the consequences of those actions.
Prince:	Why should I?
Legalist Scholar:	All this talking around and around is very boring. Strict laws are the key. Let me tell you a story that will explain everything. Once there was a farmer. A tree stump sat right in the middle of his field. He plowed around it. One day, a hare ran out of the woods, ran right into the stump, broke its neck, and died. The farmer decided to leave his plow in the field to watch the stump. He thought that would prevent other hares from dying. What happened? Weeds took over the field. The farmer had no crops to sell or eat. He became poor. Here is my message: Rulers who abandon the laws to protect their people, as a farmer would, are foolish and will suffer for it! (From Erin Fry's *25 Mini-Plays: World History*. Scholastic Professional Books, 2000, pp. 50-51.)

Simulation Game

Simulation games are the games that construct an environment or a historical event by engaging participants in a series of imaginative and genuine learning tasks to experience and to promote inquiry and discovery learning. Many educational theorists such as Piaget (1947, 1972), Bruner

(1990), and Vygotsky (1978) have argued for this strategy by students actually experiencing and interacting with each other on a real social issue. During the experience, students use language naturally and creatively to accomplish real communication goals. Often English language learners may tense up when called on to give an answer during the lecture in class. However, in a simulation game situation, the fear and the embarrassment can be mitigated because these students are "not so starkly on public display" (Brown, 1991) and there are many possible answers depending on students' experiences. As a result, these students are often found quite vocal and active in these learning environments. Johannessen's (2000) mine-and-booby-trap Vietnam War simulation and various war and peace simulations pushed students to think beyond the text, experience the trauma and crises, and gain a deeper understanding of the concepts. The following are a few ideas taken from the professional literature.

- Students plot routes to specific locations on maps in urban areas to train map and compass skills (Kirman, 1996).
- Class is divided into different countries and students are asked to select three countries they would like to migrate to and three they would not like to migrate. Then they go through the experience of forced migration (Clark, 2000).
- Students are given a job as a market trader with a collection of items to be traded to see who has the skills to get most items. The game demonstrates the market supply/demand structure (Brozik & Zapalska, 1999).
- Students experience the life in the Colonial Days by dressing up and cooking food (Hennessey, 1994).

Closed Captions and the Muted TV

Closed captioning has shown effectiveness as a second language and literacy learning tool (McDonell, 1998; Soyibo, 1995). With an increased captioning of all program types since 1993, more and more closed captions have been used to teach English language learners' listening and speaking skills. Closed captioning is a process by which audio portions of television programs are transcribed into words that appear on the television screen at the same time as the program. English language learners can benefit from watching both visual, verbal, and audio display of the material simultaneously or one at a time to increase their listening and reading comprehension. Use of closed captions makes classroom viewing less time consuming for teachers and a rich experience for students. In a large class with both English language learners and regular students, the teacher can provide English language learners with closed captioning to enhance their comprehension. Or students will all watch the regular TV or videotape first and then consult the captions for any confusions or disagreements.

A variation of this activity can be a use of the muted TV for students to guess and read silently for the characters' mood, non-verbal cues, and the theme. The muted TV or a silent watching requires students to be more observant than when they view the regular TV. As a result, they can capture things that they would not see if the sound of the TV is on. The teacher can ask the students to write down their observations using the excerpts of the muted TV first and then compare and contrast their observation with what they see later with the sound on.

CONCLUSION

Right after the first day of my graduate class: Reading and Writing for Diverse Learners, Lee a high school English teacher came to me sharing with me something special. Lee took my multicultural literature class the previous semester and she did her final project on engaging her class of reluctant and struggling readers in reading Langston Hughes' "Mother to Son" and then follow Hughes structure and write their own poems to their parents called "Son/daughter to Mother." Lee told me with excitement that one of her most troubled students, who never wrote anything and had difficulty in passing her class, who happened to be an ELL student, wrote such a beautiful poem about his mother that Lee mailed it home to his mother. Lee did not imagine that the mother sent her a big bouquet days later with a card, thanking her for what she did for her son, who had never written anything as this powerful like this. Deeply touched by the parent's gesture, Lee talked about how rewarding teaching diverse learners can be.

Working with linguistically and culturally diverse students can be a really rewarding and exhilarating experience for the teachers. I feel a certain kinship with those English language learners after listening to their stories and watching their struggles with English. I too was an ESL learner coming to The University of Georgia to work on my graduate degree from Mainland China years ago. Fortunately, I was with a group of supporting faculty members and sensitive fellow graduate students characterized by their "southern hospitality." To this day I still remember especially the faculty members who viewed my foreignness as a resource rather than a burden, who saw my bilingual and bi-cultural status as a strength rather than a weakness, and who did not benignly neglect me but included me in the class discussions, challenging and nurturing me to grow both cognitively, linguistically, and socially. Their willingness to listen to my voice of silence, to spend time learning about my native culture, and their persistence in helping with my second language learning serve as motivation and examples for my later career.

This book is no way providing "solve all" recipes for mainstream teachers. As a matter of fact, as I was finishing up with this book, several teachers reminded me of a sea of Internet resources and computer technologies that can be used to integrate language into their subject matter classes. Some of these commonly-used ESL resources are in Appendix C. Of course, there are many other ideas, strategies, and resources. It is my hope that the book has opened a way of teachers' thinking about those often silenced English language learners in their mainstream classes. I hope the strategies and ideas have served as points of departure for their journey to serve linguistically and culturally diverse students, and I wish them good luck on that journey.

APPENDIX A

TOPIC ORIENTED MATHEMATICAL NON-FICTION READING

Topic	Authentic reading
Symbols	Davis, P., & Hersh, R. (1998) *The mathematical experience,* pp. 122-123. Boston: Houghton Mifflin Company.
Proof	Davis, P., & Hersh, R. (1998) *The mathematical experience,* pp. 47-151. Boston: Houghton Mifflin Company.
Decimal	Temple, R. (1986). *The genius of China: 3,000 years of science, discovery, and invention*, pp. 139. New York: Simon and Schuster.
Zero	Temple, R. (1986). *The genius of China: 3,000 years of science, discovery, and invention*, pp. 140. New York: Simon and Schuster.
Negative Numbers	Temple, R. (1986). *The genius of China: 3,000 years of science, discovery, and invention*, pp. 141. New York: Simon and Schuster.

Teaching Language and Content to Linguistically and Culturally Diverse Students: Principles, Ideas, and Materials; pages 229–231.
A Volume in: Language Studies in Education
Copyright © 2004 by Information Age Publishing, Inc.
All rights of reproduction in any form reserved.
ISBN: 1-59311-088-X (paper), 1-59311-089-8 (cloth)

Topic	Authentic reading
Decimal fraction	Temple, R. (1986). *The genius of China: 3,000 years of science, discovery, and invention*, pp. 142. New York: Simon and Schuster.
π	Davis, P., & Hersh, R. (1998) *The mathematical experience*, pp. 369-374. Boston: Houghton Mifflin Company.
	Temple, R. (1986). *The genius of China: 3,000 years of science, discovery, and invention*, pp. 144. New York: Simon and Schuster.
Square root	Adler, I. (1990). *Mathematics*, pp. 30-31. New York: Doubleday.
Number theory	Adler, I. (1990). *Mathematics*, pp. 8-10. New York: Doubleday.
Even and odd numbers	Adler, I. (1990). *Mathematics,* pp. 12-13. New York: Doubleday.
Prime number	Adler, I. (1990). *Mathematics*, pp. 22. New York: Doubleday.
	Davis, P., & Hersh, R. (1998) *The mathematical experience*, pp. 209-216. Boston: Houghton Mifflin Company.
Polygons	Adler, I. (1990). *Mathematics*, pp. 27, 40-41. New York: Doubleday.
Angles	Adler, I. (1990). *Mathematics*, pp. 18-20. New York: Doubleday.
Triangles	Adler, I. (1990). *Mathematics*, pp. 26. New York: Doubleday.
Cubic equation	Davis, P., & Hersh, R. (1998) *The mathematical experience*, pp. 196-198. Boston: Houghton Mifflin Company.
Circles	Haven, K. (1998). *Marvels of math: Fascinating reads and awesome activities.* pp. 75-80. CO: Teacher Ideas Press.
Irrational number	Davis, P., & Hersh, R. (1998) *The mathematical experience*, pp. 180. Boston: Houghton Mifflin Company.
Mathematics and real world	Davis, P., & Hersh, R. (1998) *The mathematical experience*, pp. 89-93. the Boston: Houghton Mifflin Company.
Mathematics and war	Davis, P., & Hersh, R. (1998) *The mathematical experience*, pp. 93-96. Boston: Houghton Mifflin Company.
Probability	Haven, K. (1998). *Marvels of math: Fascinating reads and awesome activities.* pp. 85-91. CO: Teacher Ideas Press.
Permutation	Haven, K. (1998). *Marvels of math: Fascinating reads and awesome activities.* pp. 15-21. CO: Teacher Ideas Press.
Pythagorean theorem	Haven, K. (1998). *Marvels of math: Fascinating reads and awesome activities.* pp. 5-11. CO: Teacher Ideas Press.
Topology	Haven, K. (1998). *Marvels of math: Fascinating reads and awesome activities.* pp. 106-112. CO: Teacher Ideas Press.
Women	Haven, K. (1998). *Marvels of math: Fascinating reads and awesome mathematicians activities.* pp. 131-137. CO: Teacher Ideas Press.

Topic	Authentic reading
	Perl, T. (1978). *Math equals: Biographies of women mathematicians.* CA: Addison-Wesley.
	Perl, T. (1978). *Women, number and dreams: Biographies, mathematical discoveries and activities.* CA: Wide World Publishing.
Analytical geometry	Haven, K. (1998). *Marvels of math: Fascinating reads and awesome activities.* pp. 53-58. CO: Teacher Ideas Press.

APPENDIX B

MULTICULTURAL LITERATURE

LANGUAGE PROFICIENCY LEVEL: BEGINNING

Title	Year	Author	Ethnicity	Subject
A day's work	1994	Eve Bunting	Mexican	A Mexican boy's learning about his grandfather
Aekyung's dream	1988	Min Paek	Korean	A Korean girl's story of growing up in America
A sky full of kites	1996	Osmond Molarsky	Chinese	A Chinese boy's pursuit of his art
Almond cookies and dragon well tea	1993	Cynhthia Chin-Lee	Chinese	A Chinese American girl's discovery of her culture heritage
Annushka's voyage	1998	Edith Tarbescu	Russian	A story of two young Russian sisters coming to America with their grandmother's candlesticks
Aunt Lilly's laundromat	1994	Melanie Greenberg	Haitian	Aunt Lilly's memories of her native land

Teaching Language and Content to Linguistically and Culturally Diverse Students:
Principles, Ideas, and Materials; pages 233–238.
A Volume in: Language Studies in Education
Copyright © 2004 by Information Age Publishing, Inc.
All rights of reproduction in any form reserved.
ISBN: 1-59311-088-X (paper), 1-59311-089-8 (cloth)

Title	Year	Author	Ethnicity	Subject
Day of the dead	2000	Tony Johnson	Mexico	Mexican holiday commemorating the dead
Giving thanks: A Native American good morning message	1997	Jake Swamp	Native American	A story about Native American ritual of giving thanks.
Grandfather's journey	1993	Allen Say	Japanese	A Japanese grandfather's journey to America
How the sea began	1993	George Crespo	Caribbean	Caribbean myth
How Iwariwa the cayman learned to share	1995	George Crespo	Latin	A Venezuela myth
I hate English!	1989	Ellen Levine	Chinese	A Chinese girl's struggle with the new language
I speak English for my mom	1989	Muriel Stanek	Mexican	A Mexican teenager's story of helping her mother with English
Journey to Topaz: A story of the Japanese-American evacuation	1971		Japanese	A Japanese teen's and her family's life after the Pearl Harbor bombing
Juan Bobo: Four folktales from Puerto Rico	1995	Carmen Bernier-Grand	Puerto Rican	Puerto Rican folktales
So far from the sea	1998	Eve Bunting	Japanese	Surviving Japanese internment camps
Tam's slipper: A story from Vietnam	1997	Janet Pallazo-Craig	Vietnam	A Vietnamese legend
The firebird	1994	Demi	Russian	A Russian folktale
The gift of Wali dad: A Tale of India and Pakistan	1995	Aaron Shepard	India and Pakistan	A collection of Indian and Pakistani folktales
The old woman and red pumpkin	1999	Betsy Bang	Bang-ladeshi	A Bengali folktale
The tangerine tree	1995	Regina Hanson	Jamaican	A Jamaican teen's father is leaving for the U.S.
Two bad boys: A very old cherokee tale	1996	Gail E. Haley	Native American	Native American folktale
Watch the stars come out	1985	Riki Levinson	Latino	A young Mexican teen learns about her grandmother's journey to America

Title	Year	Author	Ethnicity	Subject
Who belongs here?	1996	Margy Burns Knight	Cambo-dian	A Cambodian boy's encounters in the new culture.
Why owl comes out at night: A story from Haiti	1999	Janet Pallazo-Craig	Haitian	A Haitian myth

LANGUAGE PROFICIENCY LEVEL: INTERMEDIATE

Title	Year	Author	Ethnicity	Subject
An Ellis Island Christmas	1994	Maxinne Rhea Lexington	Polish	A Polish teenager coming to the U.S. on Christmas Eve
Baseball in April	1990	Gary Soto	Latino	A collection of stories of Latino teens' dreams and struggles
Cool Salsa	1994	Lori M. Carlson	Latino	A collection of bilingual poems about growing up Latino in America
Dragon gate	1995	Lawrence Yep	Chinese	A story of a fifteen-year-old Chinese boy's coming to America
Dragonwings	1977	Lawrence Yep	Chinese	A young Chinese boy's helping his father realize his dream
Fitting in	1996	Anilu Bernardo	Cuban	Stories about Cuban teenagers growing up in the new culture
In the year of the boar and Jackie Robinson	1984	Bette Bao Lord	Chinese	A story of a Chinese American girl growing up in America
Jade and iron	1996	Hugh Hazelton	Latin America	A collection of Latin American myths and legends
Josefina learns a lesson: A school story	1997	Valerie Tripp	Latino	Latina teen sisters' coming of age in the new culture
Make a wish, Molly	1995	Barbara Cohen	Russian	A young Russian immigrant learns about the new culture

Title	Year	Author	Ethnicity	Subject
Mountain light	1985	Lawrence Yep	Chinese	A nineteen-year-old Chinese boy's journey to America
My Name Is Maria Isabel	1995	Alma Flor Ada	Puerto Rican	Puerto Rican girl's story of fitting in the new culture
Sea glass	1977	Lawrence Yep	Chinese	A Chinese boy's struggle with the new culture
Seasons of Splendour	1995	Madhur Jaffray	Indian	A collection of Indian folktales
Shadow of the dragon	1993	Sherry Garland	Vietnamese	A Vietnamese teenager's struggle with the two cultures
Talent night	1995	Jean Davies Okimoto	Japanese	A young Japanese American musician's learning to live in two cultures
The Great Kapok Tree	2000	Lynne Cherry	Brazilian	A Brazilian folktale
The house on Mango street	1984	Sandra Cisneros	Latino	A Latino family's struggle in the new culture
The magic shell	1995	Nicolasa Mohr	Dominican Republic	A young boy's use of a magic shell to help him learn living in two cultures
The moved-outers	1992	Florence Crannell Means	Japanese	Young Japanese Americans' life after Pearl Harbor's bombing
The war between the classes	1985	Gloria D. Miklowitz	Japanese	A story of seventeen-year-old Emiko's coming of age in America
Where is Taro?	1994	Elizabeth Claire	Japanese	A Japanese junior high student got lost in New York City
White bread competition	1997	JoAnn Yolanda Hernandez	Latino	A 9th grade Latina student's success and struggle in the new culture

LANGUAGE PROFICIENCY LEVEL: ADVANCED

Title	Year	Author	Ethnicity	Subject
All that glitters	1981	Michael Anthony	Caribbean	A Caribbean teenager coming of age in his culture

Title	Year	Author	Ethnicity	Subject
Annie John	1983	Jamaica Kincaid	Antigua	A story of a young girl coming of age in Antigua
A way out of no way	1996	Jacqueline Woodson	African-American	A collection of short stories about growing up African American
At the bottom of the river	1992	Jamaica Kincaid	Caribbean	A collection of stories of childhood in the Caribbean
Children of the river	1989	Linda Crew	Cambodian	A Cambodian teenager's coming to America
Donald Duk	1997	Frank Chin	Chinese	A Chinese teen's struggle with his bicultural identity
Down these mean streets	1967	Piri Thomas	Latino	A Latina boy's growing up in New York City's ghettos
Farewell to Manzanar	1973	Jeanne Wakatsuki Houston & James D. Houston	Japanese	A survival story of a Japanese girl and her family at internment camp
Having our say	1993	Sarah L. Delany and A. Elizabeth Delany	African-American	Two African American sisters' lives
How the Garcia girls lost their accents	1991	Julia Alvarez	Dominican Republican	Four sisters' struggles and successes in the new culture
I yo!	1997	Julia Alvarez	Dominican Republican	A young Dominican woman's story of growing up in America
Like water for chocolate	1989	Laura Esquirel	Mexican	A Mexican women's story
Miguel street	1959	V. S. Naipaul	Trinidadian	A teenager's story of growing up in Trinidad
Narrative of the life of Frederick Douglass	2001	Ed. Blassingame, McKivigan, and Hinks	African-American	A young African American's story of growing up as a slave
Shabanu	1989	Suzanne Fisher Staples	Pakistani	A coming of age story of a Pakistani teenager in her culture
Silent dancing	1991	Judith Ortiz Cofer	Puerto Rican	A Puerto Rican girl's childhood in two cultures
The color of water	1996	James McBride	African-Jewish American	An African-Jewish American boy's growing up in New York City

Title	Year	Author	Ethnicity	Subject
The joy luck club	1989	Amy Tan	Chinese	Four Chinese girls' and their mothers' lives in two cultures
The learning tree	1963	Gordon Parks	African-American	An African American family's struggle
The light in the forest	1953	Conrad Richter	Native American	A bicultural boy's pursuit of his identity
The magic orange tree	1978	Diane Wolkstein	Haitian	A collection of Haitian tales
The white-haired girl	1996	Jaia Sun-Childers & Douglas Childers	Chinese	A Chinese girl's growing up during the years of the Cultural Revolution in China
Tiger, burning bright	1992	Kathleen J. Crane Foundation	Korean	A collection of Korean myths about Korean tigers
When I was Puerto Rican	1993	Esmeralda Santi-ago	Puerto Rican	A Puerto Rican teen's coming of age in two cultures

APPENDIX C

ESL RELATED INTERNET RESOURCES

Dave's ESL Café

http://www.eslcafe.com/
A comprehensive list of links to ESL learning and teaching. It has a rich banks of teaching ideas using

http://www.nanana.com/esl.html
Includes tons of teaching ideas and learning activities focusing on using games, chat rooms, songs, to learn English as a second language.

http://www.smc.maricopa.edu/sub1/lac/esl007_%20links.html
This is a master link to many online ESL learning and teaching resources.

http://ilc2.doshisha.ac.jp/users/kkitao/online/www/student.htm
Includes students writing, setting up pen-pal relationships, students' published journals, etc.

Teaching Language and Content to Linguistically and Culturally Diverse Students:
Principles, Ideas, and Materials; pages 239–240.
A Volume in: Language Studies in Education
Copyright © 2004 by Information Age Publishing, Inc.
All rights of reproduction in any form reserved.
ISBN: 1-59311-088-X (paper), 1-59311-089-8 (cloth)

http://home.gwu.edu/~meloni/gwvcusas/

A practical site for both the teachers and students, including reading, writing, grammar, listening, discussion.

http://Home.InfoRamp.Net/~teslon/jims_links.shtml

Here you can find CNN News room for ESL, English Word Games, and ESL Multimedia Language Lab

REFERENCES

Aagesen, C., & Blumberg, M. (1999). *Shakespeare for kids: His life and times.* Chicago, IL: Chicago Review Press.

Abbott, M. (2002). Using music to promote L2 learning among adult learners. *TESOL-Journal, 11* (1), 10-17.

Abse, D. (1986). *Voices in the gallery: Poems and pictures.* London, UK: The Tate Gallery.

Achebe, C. (2002). *Things fall apart.* [Narrated by Peter Francis James] Cassette Recording No. RE-886-DJ. Prince Frederick, MD: Recorded Books, LLC.

Acton, W. R., & Felix, J. W. (1986). Acculturation and mind. In J. M. Valdes (Ed.) *Culture bound: Bridging the cultural gap in language teaching* (pp. 20-32). Cambridge, UK: Cambridge University Press.

Adamson, H. D. (1993). *Academic competence: Theory and classroom practice: Preparing ESL students for content classes.* New York: Longman.

Adelson-Goldstein, J. (1998). Developing active vocabulary: Making the communicative connection. *ESL Magazine, 1* (3), 10-14.

Ahmad, I., Brodsky, H., Crofits, M. S., & Ellis, E. G. (1993). *World cultures: A global mosaic.* Englewood Cliffs, NJ: Prentice Hall.

Allen, K., & Marquez, A. (1998). Word calendars. *TESOL Journal, 7* (6), 35-37.

Allen, V.G. (1989). Literature as a support to language acquisition. In P. Rigg & V.G. Allen (Eds.), *When they don't all speak English: Integrating the ESL students into the regular classroom* (pp. 55-64). Urbana, IL: National Council of Teachers of English.

Teaching Language and Content to Linguistically and Culturally Diverse Students:
Principles, Ideas, and Materials; pages 241–254.
A Volume in: Language Studies in Education
Copyright © 2004 by Information Age Publishing, Inc.
All rights of reproduction in any form reserved.
ISBN: 1-59311-088-X (paper), 1-59311-089-8 (cloth)

Allen-Sommerville, L. (1996). Capitalizing on diversity: Strategies for customizing your curriculum to meet the needs of all students. *The Science Teacher, 63* (2), 20-23.

Alvarez, J. (1991). *How the Garcia girls lost their accents.* New York, NY: A Plume Book.

Anaya, R. (1998). Celebration of grandparents. *In Homecoming* (pp. 458-460). Evanson, IL: McDougal Littell.

Anderson, M. (1991). *Food chains: The unending cycle.* Hillside, NJ: Enslow Publishers, Inc.

Anderson, P., & Rubano, G. (1991). *Enhancing aesthetic reading and response.* Urbana, IL: National Council of Teachers of English (NCTE).

Applebee, A. (1984). *Contexts for learning to write: Studies of secondary school instruction.* Norwood, NJ: ALBEX.

Aronson, E. (1978). *The jigsaw classroom.* Beverly Hills, CA: Sage.

Asher, J. (1977). *Learning another language through actions: The complete teacher's guidebook.* Los Gatos, CA: Sky Oaks Productions.

Ausubel, D. P. (1964). Adults versus children in second-language learning: Psychological considerations. *Modern Language Journal, 48* (6), 420-424.

Bahns, J. (1993). Lexical collocations: A contrastive view. *ELT Journal, 47* (1), 56-63.

Ballard, B., & Clanchy, J. (1991). Assessment by misconception: Cultural influences and intellectual traditions. In L. Hamp-Lyons (Ed.) *Assessing second language writing in academic contexts* (pp. 19-36). Norwood, NJ: ABLEX Publishing Corporation.

Banks, J. (1993). Multicultural education: Historical development, dimensions, and challenges. *Phi Delta Kappa, 75* (1), 22-35.

Banks, J. A., & Banks, C. A. M. (3rd Ed.). (1997). *Multicultural education: Issues and perspectives.* Boston, MA: Allyn & Bacon.

Barillas, M. R. (2000). Literacy at home: Honoring parent voices through writing. *The Reading Teacher, 54* (3), 302-308.

Beers, K. (1998). Listen while you read: Struggling readers and audio books. *School Library Journal, 44* (4), 30-35.

Bereiter, C., & Scadamalia, M. (1987). *The psychology of written composition.* Hillsdale, NJ: Lawrence Erlbaum Associates.

Bernhardt, E., et al. (1996). Language diversity & science: Science for limited English proficient students. *The Science Teacher, 63* (2), 24-27.

Blassingame, J. W., McKivigan, J. R., & Hinks, P. P. (2001). *Narrative of the life of Frederick Douglass.* New Haven, CT: Yale University Press.

Bofill, F. (1998). *Jack and the beanstalk—Juan y los frijoles magicos.* San Francisco, CA: Chronicle Books.

Borasi, R. & Agor, B. (1990). What can mathematics educator learn from second-language instruction? The beginning of a conversation between two fields. *Focusing on Language Problems in Mathematics, 12* (3 & 4), 1-27.

Borasi, R., & Brown, S. (1985). A "novel" approach to texts. *For the Learning of Mathematics, 5* (1), 21-23.

Borasi, R., & Sigel, M. (2001). *Reading counts: Expanding the role of reading in mathematics classrooms.* New York: Teachers College Press.

Bradbury, R. (2002). *Fahrenheit 451.* [Narrated by Paul Hecht] Cassette Recording No. RC-842-DJ. Prince Frederick, MD: Recorded Books, LLC.

Britton, J. (1982). *Prospect and retrospect: Selected essays of James Britton.* Montclair, NJ: Boynton-Cook.

Brouse, D. E. (1990). Population education: Awareness activities. *The Science Teacher,* 57 (9), 31-33.

Brown, H. D. (1987). Learning a second culture. In H. D. Brown's *Principles of language learning and teaching* (pp. 129-144). Englewood, NJ: Prentice-Hall.

Brown, R. (1991). Group work, task difference, and second language acquisition. *Applied Linguistics, 1* (1), 1-12.

Brozik, D., & Zapalska, A. (1999). Interactive classroom economics: The market game. *Social Studies, 90* (6), 278-282.

Bruner, J. (1990). *Acts of meaning.* Cambridge, MA: Harvard University Press.

Burdett, L. (1998). *Shakespeare can be fun! Romeo and Juliet for kids.* New York: Firefly Books Inc.

Butler, F. A., & Stevens, R. (2001). Standardized assessment of the content knowledge of English language learners K-12: Current trends and old dilemmas. *Language Testing, 18* (4), 409-427.

Call, P. E. (1991). SQ3R+what I know sheet=one strong strategy. *Journal of Reading, 35* (1), 50-52.

Campbell, A. (1979). How readability formulae fall short in matching student to text in the content areas. *Journal of Reading, 22* (8), 683-89.

Campbell, R. (1992). *I won't bite.* Union City, CA: Pan Asian Publications.

Cantoni-Harvey, G. (1987). *Content-area language instruction.* Reading, MA: Addison-Wesley.

Carrasquillo, A. L., & Rodriguez, V. (1995). *Language minority students in the mainstream classroom.* Clevedon, UK: Multilingual Matters.

Carroll, J. B. (Ed.) (1956). *Language, thought, and reality: Selected writings of Benjamin Lee Whorf.* Cambridge, MA: MIT Press.

Carson, J. G. (1992). Becoming biliterate: First language influences. *Journal of Second Language Writing, 1* (1), 37-60.

Castantino, R. (1995). Learning to read in a second language doesn't have to hurt: The effect of pleasure reading. *Journal of Adolescent & Adult Literacy, 39* (1), 68-69.

Cather, M. (2002). *My Antonia.* [Narrated by George Guidall] Cassette Recording No. RE-906-DJ. Prince Frederick, MD: Recorded Books, LLC.

Cervantes, R., & Gainer, G. (1992). The effects of syntactic simplification and repetition on listening comprehension. *TESOL Quarterly, 26* (4), 767-70.

Chamot, A. U., & O'Malley, J. M. (1994). *The CALLA handbook: Implementing the cognitive academic language learning approach.* Reading, MA: Addition-Wesley.

Chappell, F., & Thompson, D. R. (1999). Modifying our questions to assess students' thinking. *Mathematics Teaching in the Middle School, 4* (7), 470-74.

Chinese Department of Education. (1982). *Senior high world history text: Vol. 2.* China, P. R.

Ching, E., et al. (1991). *Two bushels of grain: Forget the turnips!* Cerritos, CA: Wonder Kids Publications.

Ching, E., et al. (1991). *The blind man & the cripple.* Cerritos, CA: Wonder Kids Publications.

Ching, E., et al. (1991). *Sun valley: A stone carver's dream = Thai yang kuo ti chin tzu: Shig chiang ti meng.* Cerritos, CA: Wonder Kids Publications.

Cho, K., & Krashen, S. (1994). Acquisition of vocabulary from the sweet valley kids series: Adult ESL acquisition. *Journal of Reading, 37* (8), 662-667.

Chomsky, N. (1959). A review of B. F. Skinner's verbal behavior. *Language, 35* (1), 26-58.

Christensen, F. (1968). *The Christensen rhetoric program: The sentence and the paragraph.* New York: Harper & Row.

Cisnero, S. (1991). *The house on Mango street.* New York: Knopf Publishing Group.

Clark, L. E. (2000). Other-Wise: The case for understanding other cultures in a unipolar world. *Social Education, 64* (7), 448-53.

Cline, P. C. (1996). Using symbolism to enhance government studies. *The Social Studies, 87* (4), 182-184.

Coburn, J. R., & Lee, T. C. (1996). *Jouanah, a Hmong Ciderella.* Arcadia, CA: Shen's Books.

Collard, S. (1996). *Our natural homes.* Watertown, MA: Charlesbridge Publishing, Inc.

Collie, J., & Slater, S. (1999). *Literature in the language classroom: A resource book of ideas and activities.* Cambridge, UK: Cambridge University Press.

Collier, V. P. (1987). Age and rate of acquisition of second language for academic purposes. *TESOL Quarterly, 21* (4), 617-641.

Collier, V. P. (1989). How long? A synthesis of research on academic achievement in a second language. *TESOL Quarterly, 23* (3), 509-531.

Collier, V. P. (1992). A synthesis of studies examining long-term language minority student data on academic achievement. *Bilingual Research Journal, 16* (1 & 2), 187-212.

Collier, V. p., & Thomas, W. P. (1998). Assessment and evaluation. In C. J. Ovando and V. P. Collier (Eds.) *Bilingual and ESL classrooms: Teaching in multicultural contexts* (pp. 240-268). Boston, MA: McGraw-Hill.

Colosi, J. C., & Zales, C. R. (1998). Jigsaw cooperative learning improves biology lab courses. *Bioscience, 48* (2), 118-125.

Cormier, R. (2002). The chocolate war. [Narrated by George Guidall] Cassette Recording No. RE-125-DJ. Prince Frederick, MD: Recorded Books, LLC.

Countryman, J. (1992). *Writing to learn mathematics.* Portsmouth, NH: Heinemann.

Crandall, J., ed. (1987). *ESL through content area instruction: Mathematics, science, social studies.* Englewood, NJ: Prentice Hall.

Crane, S. (2002). *The red badge of courage.* [Narrated by Frank Muller] Cassette Recording No. RE-921-DJ. Prince Frederick, MD: Recorded Books, LLC.

Cullum, A. (1985). *Shake hands with Shakespeare: Eight plays for elementary schools.* New York: Scholastic, Inc.

Cummins, J. (1980). The exit and entry fallacy of bilingual education. *NABE Journal, 4* (3), 25-59.

Cummins, J. (1981). Age on arrival and immigrant second language learning in Canada: A reassessment. *Applied Linguistics, 11* (2), 132-149.

Cummins, J. (1984). Language proficiency, bilingualism, and academic achievement. In J. Cummins *Bilingualism and special education: Issues in assessment and pedagogy* (pp. 136-151). San Diego, CA: College-Hill.

Cummins, J. (1986). Empowering minority students: A framework for intervention. *Harvard Educational Review, 56* (1), 18-36.

Cummins, J. (1994). The ESL students IS the mainstream: The marginalization of diversity in current Canadian educational debates. *English Quarterly, 26* (3), 30-33.

Dawe, L. (1986). Teaching and learning mathematics in a multicultural classroom: Guidelines for teachers. *The Australian Mathematics Teacher, 42* (1), 8-18.

Day, R. R., Omura, C., & Hiramutsu, M. (1991). Incidental vocabulary learning and reading. *Reading in a Foreign Language, 7* (2), 541-51.

Derwing, T. M., et al. (1999). Some factors that affect the success of ESL high school students. *The Canadian Modern Language Review, 55* 4, 533-547.

Dong, Y. R. (2002). Integrating language and content: How three biology teachers work with non-English speaking students. *International Journal of Bilingual Education and Bilingualism, 5* (1), 40-57.

Dong, Y. R. (1999a). The need to understand ESL students' native language writing experiences. *Teaching English in the Two-Year College, 26* (3), 277-285.

Dong, Y. R. (1999b). The impact of native language literacy on ESL college freshmen's writing of argumentative essays. *Journal of Teaching Writing, 17* (1 & 2), 88-117.

Dong, Y. R. (1998). From writing in their native language to writing in English: What ESL students bring to our writing classrooms? *College ESL, 8* (2), 87-102.

Douglass, B. (1987). Sociocultural factors in teaching language minority students. In B. *Douglass principles of language learning and teaching* (pp. 122-145). Englewood Cliffs, NJ: Prentice Hall, Inc.

Duin, A. H., & Graves, M. F. (1987). Intensive vocabulary instruction as a prewriting technique. *Reading Research Quarterly, 22* (3), 311-330.

Dunn, S. (1989). *Between angels: The poems.* New York: Alfred. A. Knorpf.

DuPlass, J. A. (1996). Charts, tables, graphs, and diagrams: An approach for social studies teachers. *Social Studies, 87* (1), 32-38.

Durgunoglus, A. Y. (1997). Bilingual reading: Its components, development, and other issues. In A. M. B. De Groot and J. F. Kroll (eds.) *Tutorials in bilingualism: Psycholinguistic perspectives* (pp. 255-276). Mahwah, NJ: Lawrence Erlbaum.

Echevarria, J., & Graves, A. (1998). *Sheltered content instruction: Teaching English-language learners with diverse abilities.* Boston, MA: Allyn and Bacon.

Eckman, F. (1977). On the naturalness of interlanguage phonological rules. *Language Learning, 31* (1), 195-216.

Edwards, V., & Walker, S. (1996). Some status issues in the translation of children's books. *Journal of Multilingual and Multicultural Development, 17* (5), 339-48

Enright, D. S., & McClosky, M. L. (1988). *Integrating English: Developing English language and literacy in the multicultural classroom.* Reading, MA: Addition-Wesley.

Esty, W. W. (1992). Language concepts of mathematics. *Focusing on Language Problems in Mathematics, 14* (4), 31-54.

Esty, W. W., & Teppo, A. R. (1994). A general-education course emphasizing mathematical language and reasoning. *Focus on Learning Problems in Mathematics, 16* (1), 13-35.

Evered, L. J. (2001). Riddles, puzzles, and paradoxes: Having fun with serious mathematics. *Mathematics Teaching in the Middle School, 6* (8), 458-461.

Faltis, C., & Wolfe, P. (1999). *So much to say: Adolescents, bilingualism, & ESL in the secondary school.* New York: Teachers College Press.

Fichtner, D. & Peitzman, F., & Sasser, L. (1994). What's fair? Assessing subject matter knowledge of LEP students in sheltered classrooms. In F. Peitzman & G. Gadda's *With different eyes: Insights into teaching language minority students across the disciplines* (pp. 114-123). Reading, MA: Addison-Wesley.

Field, R. J. (2000). *World history volume 1: Understanding our past.* New York: Educational Services, Inc.

Fitzgerald, F. S. (1995). *The great Gatsby.* New York: Simon & Schuster Inc.

Frank, A. (2002). *The diary of a young girl.* [Narrated by Susan Adams] Cassette Recording No. RD-093-DJ. Prince Frederick, MD: Recorded Books, LLC.

Freeman, D., & Freeman, Y. (1994). *Between the worlds: Access to second language acquisition.* Portsmouth, NJ: Heinemann.

Fry, E. (2000). *25 mini-plays world history.* New York: Scholastic Professional Books.

Fu, D. (1995). *"My trouble is my English" Asian students and the American dream.* Portsmouth, NH: Boyton/Cook Publishers

Gaines, E. J. (1993). *A lesson before dying.* New York: Vintage Books.

Garcia, G. E. (1994). Assessing the literacy development of second language students: A focus on authentic assessment. In K. Spangenberg-Urbschat & R. Rpitchard (Eds.) *Kids come in all languages: Reading instruction for ESL students.* Newark, DE: International Reading Association.

Garcia, M. (1992). *The adventures of Connie and Diego (Las adenturas de connie y diego).* New York: Children's Book Press.

Garrod, A., & Davis, J. (1999). *Crossing customs: International students write on U.S. college life and culture.* New York, NY: Falmer Press.

Genesee, F. (1976). The role of intelligence in second language learning. *Language Learning, 26* (3), 267-280.

Genesee, F. (1993). All teachers are second language teachers. *The Canadian Modern Language Review, 50* (1), 47-53.

Genesee, F. (1995). ESL and classroom teacher collaborations: Building futures together. *TESOL Matters, 4* (6), 1-2.

Gerofsky, S. (1996). A linguistic and narrative view of work problems in mathematics education. *For the Learning of Mathematics, 16* (2), 36-45.

Ghaith, G. M. (2002). The Relationship between Cooperative Learning, Perception of Social Support, and Academic Achievement. *System, 30* (3), 263-73.

Gibbs, A. & Lawson, A. E. (1992). The nature of scientific thinking as reflected by the work of biologists and by biology textbooks. *American Biology Teacher, 54* (3), 137-152.

Gonzalez, V. (1996), Theoretical and practical implications of assessing cognitive and language development in bilingual children with qualitative methods. *The Bilingual Research Journal, 20* (1), 93-131.

Golding, W. (1997). *The lord of the flies.* New York: Riverhead Books.

Gonzales, N., & Schallert, D. L. (1999). An integrated analysis of the cognitive development of bilingual and bicultural children and adults, In V. Gonzales (ed.) *Language and cognitive development in second language learning,* pp. Needham, MA: Allyn and Bacon.

Goodman, Y. M., & Watson, D. J., & Burke, C. L. (1987). *Reading miscue inventory: Alternative procedures.* Richard C. Owen Publishing, Inc.

Gottlieb, M. (1999). Assessing ESOL adolescents: Balancing accessibility to learn with accountability for learning. In C. J. Faltis & P. Wolfe (Eds) *So much to say: Adolescents, bilingualism, & ESL in the second school* (pp. 176-201). New York: Teachers College Press.

Graham, C. (1996). *Singing, chanting, telling tales: Arts in the language classroom.* Orlando, FL: Harcourt Brace & Company.

Green, B. (2002). *Summer of my German soldier.* [Narrated by Dale Dickey] Cassette Recording No. RE-246-DJ. Prince Frederick, MD: Recorded Books, LLC.

Gross, E. R. (1996). The United States as presented in Chinese texts. *The Social Studies, 87* (3), 133-141.

Gunderson, L. (1991). *ESL literacy instruction: A guide to theory and practice.* Englewood Cliffs, NJ: Prentice Hall.

Hancin-Bhatt, B., & Nagy, W. (1994). Lexical transfer and second language morphological development. *Applied Psycholinguistics, 15* (3), 289-310.

Harste, J., Short, K., & Burke, C. (1988). *Creating classrooms for authors.* Portsmouth, NH: Heinemann.

Hasegawa, T., Gundykunst, W. B. (1998). Silence in Japan and the United States. *Journal of Cross-cultural Psychology, 29* (5), 668-684.

Hennessey, G. S. (1994). Reliving colonial days in your classroom. Curriculum Boosters. Social Studies *Learning, 23* (3), 66-68.

Hernandez, R. D. (1994). Reducing bias in the assessment of culturally and linguistically diverse populations. *The Journal of Educational Issues of Language Minority Students, 14* (3) 269-300.

Herrell, A. L. (2000). *Fifty strategies for teaching English language learners.* Upper Saddle River, NJ: Merrill.

Hinston, S. E. (2002). *The outsiders.* [Narrated by Spike McClure] Cassette Recording No. RE-279-DJ. Prince Frederick, MD: Recorded Books, LLC.

Holyoak, S., & Piper, A. (1997). Talking to second language writers: Using interview data to investigate contrastive rhetoric. *Language Teaching Research, 1* (2), 122-148.

Hoobler, T. (1997). *Confucianism.* New York: Facts on File, Incorporated.

Horwitz, E. K. (1983). The relationship between conceptual level and communicative competence in French. *Studies in Second Language Acquisition. 5,* (1), 65-73.

Howarth, P. (1998). Phraseology and second language proficiency. *Applied Linguistics, 19* (1), 24-44.

Jameson, J. H. (1998). Simplifying the language of authentic materials. *TESOL Matters, 8* (3), 13.

Johannessen, L. R. (2000). Using a simulation and literature to teach the Vietnam War. *The Social Studies, 91* (2), 79-83.

Johnson, D. (1994). *Cooperative learning in the classroom.* Alexandria, VA: Association for Supervision and Curriculum Development.

Johnston, T. (1996). *My Mexico—Mexico mio.* New York: G. P. Putnam's Sons.

Jones, J. F. (1999). From silence to talk: Cross-cultural ideas on students' participation in academic group discussions. *English for Specific Purposes, 18* (3), 243-259.

Joseph, G. G. (1991). *Crest of the peacock.* Princeton, NJ: Princeton University Press.

Joyce, B., M. Weil, and B. Showers. 1992. *Models of teaching.* Boston: Allyn & Bacon.

Kaplan, R. B. (1966). Cultural thought patterns in inter-cultural education. *Language Learning, 16,* (1), 1-20.

Kaplan, R. B. (1988). Contrastive rhetoric and second language learning: Notes toward a theory of contrastive rhetoric. In A. Purves (ed.) *Writing across languages and cultures: Issues in contrastive rhetoric* (pp. 274-304). Newbury Park, CA: Sage.

Keating, J. F. (1997). Harvesting cultural knowledge: Using ethno-botany to read the benefits of ethnic diversity in the classroom. *The Science Teacher, 64* (2), 22-25.

Keenan, & Dressler (1990). *Integrated mathematics: Course II.* New York: AMSCO School Publications.

Kern, R. G. (1989). Second language reading strategy instruction. *Modern Language Journal, 73* (2), 135-49.

Khattri, N., Kahe, M. B., & Reeve, A. L. (1995). How performance assessments affect teaching and learning. *Educational Leadership, 53* (3), 80-83.

Kindcaid, J. (1997). *Annie John.* New York: Farrar, Straus, and Girous.

Kirby, D., & Liner, T. (1987). *Inside out: Developing strategies for teaching writing.* Upper Montclair, NJ: Boynton/Cook Publishers, Inc.

Kirman, J. M. (1996). Urban map tag: An elementary geography game. *Journal of Geography, 95* (5), 211-12.

Krashen, S. (1981). The case for narrow reading. *TESOL Newsletter, 15* (6), 23.

Krashen, S. (1982). *Principles and practice in second language acquisition.* Oxford, UK: Pergamon Press.

Krashen, S., & Terrell, T. D. (1983). *The natural approach: Language acquisition in the classroom.* Oxford: Pergamon Press.

Lachtman, O. (1998). *Big enough—Bastante grande.* Hoston, TX: Pinata Books.

Lakoff, G., & Johnson, M. (1980). *Metaphors we live by.* Chicago, IL: The University of Chicago Press.

Lam, T. C. M. (1993). Testability: A critical issue in testing language minority students with standardized achievement tests. *Measurement and Evaluation in Counseling and Development, 26* (2), 179-191.

Lamb, C., & Lamb, M. (1987). *Tales from Shakespeare.* England: Puffin Books.

Larson, R., & Hostetler, R. P. (1993). *Precalculus.* Lexington, MA: Washington, D.C. Health and Company.

Lauber, P. (1995). *Who eats what? Food chains and food webs.* New York: HarperCollins Publishers.

Lee, H. (1960). *To kill a mockingbird.* A Time Warner Books.

Lee, H. (2002). *To kill a mockingbird.* [Narrated by Sally Darling] Cassette Recording No. RC-069-DJ. Prince Frederick, MD: Recorded Books, LLC.

Lee, L. (1994). *Stella: On the edge of popularity.* Chicago, IL: Polychrome Publishing.

Leki, I. (1992). *Understanding ESL writers: A guide for teachers.* Portsmouth, New Hempshire: Boynton/Cook Publishers.

Lemke, J. L. (1990). *Talking science language learning & values.* CT: Greenwood Publishing Group, Inc.

Leonard, W. H., & Penick, J. E. (1993). What's important in selecting a biology textbook? *American Biology Teacher, 55 (1),* 14-19.

Lie, A. (1993). Paired storytelling: An integrated approach for EFL students. *Journal of Reading, 36* (8), 656-657.

Lightbown, P. M., & Spada, N. (1993). *How languages are learned?* Oxford, UK: Oxford University Press.

Lindfors, J. W. (1989). The classroom: A good environment for language learning. In P. Rigg and V. G. Allen (eds.) *When they don't speak English: Integrating the ESL student into the regular classroom* (pp. 39-54). Urbana, IL: National Council of Teachers of English.

Lipsyte, R. (2002). *The contender.* [Narrated by Peter Fracis James] Cassette Recording No. RE-397-DJ. Prince Frederick, MD: Recorded Books, LLC.

London, J. (2002). *The call of the wild.* [Narrated by Frank Muller] Cassette Recording No. RE-992-DJ. Prince Frederick, MD: Recorded Books, LLC.

Lowry, L. (2002). *Number the stars.* [Narrated by Christina Moore] Cassette Recording No. RE-408-DJ. Prince Frederick, MD: Recorded Books, LLC.

Lozano, G. (1979) *Suggestology and outlines of suggestopedy.* New York: Gordon and Breach Science Publishers.

Lumpe, A. T., & Beck, J. (1996). A profile of high school biology textbooks using scientific literacy recommendations. *The American Biology Teacher, 58* (3), 147-153.

Manzo, A. V. (1975). Guided reading procedure. *Journal of Reading, 18* (4), 287-290.

Masingila, J. O., & Prus-Wisniowska, E. (1996). Developing and assessing mathematical understanding in calculus through writing. In P. C. Elliott and M. J. Kenney (Eds.) *Communication in mathematics, K-12 and beyond,* pp.95-104. Reston, VA: The National Council of Teachers of Mathematics, Inc.

Matalene, C. (1985). Contrastive rhetoric: An American writing teacher in China. *College English, 47* (8), 789-808.

Mayer, M. (1955). *They thought they were free: The Germans,* Chicago, IL: University of Chicago Press.

McCauley, J. K., & McCauley, D. S. (1992). Using choral reading to promote language learning for ESL students. *The Reading Teacher, 45* (7), 526-533.

McDonell, T. B. (1998). Closed captioning opens doors to learning. *ESL Magazine, 1* (5), 17.

McIntosh, M. E. (1994). Word roots in geometry. *Mathematics Teacher, 87* (7), 510-515.

McIntosh, M. E., & Draper, R. J. (2001). Using learning logs in mathematics: Writing to learn. *Mathematics Teacher, 94* (7), 554-557.

McKeon, D. (1994). When meeting "common" standards is uncommonly difficult. *Educational Leadership, 51* (8), 45-49.

Menon, R. (1996). Mathematical communication through student-constructed questions. *Teaching Children Mathematics, 2* (9), 530-32.

Miller, A. (1976). *Death of a salesman.* New York: Penguin Books.

Miller, L. D. (1991). Writing to learn mathematics. *Mathematics Teacher, 84* (7), 516-521.

Miller, J. (1998). *If the earth were a few feet in diameter.* The Greenwich Workshop Press.

Miriam, M. (1994). The effects of metacognitive reading strategy training on the reading performance and student reading analysis strategies of third grade bilingual students. *Bilingual Research Journal, 18* (1-2), 83-97

Miura, I. T. (2001). The influence of language on mathematical representations. In Cuoco, A. A., & Curcio, F. R. (ed.). *The roles of representation in school mathematics* (pp. 53-62). Teston, VR: National Council of Teachers of Mathematics.

Mohan. B. (1986). *Language and content.* Reading, MA: Addison-Wesley.

Mohan, B. A. (1986). What are we really testing? In B. Mohan *Language and content* (pp. 122-135). Reading, MA: Addition-Wesley.

Monterosso, A. (1983). The eclipse. In I. Howe and I. W. Howe (Eds.) *Short shorts: An anthology of the shortest stories* (pp. 179-180). New York: Bantam Books.

Morache, J. (1987). Use of quotes in teaching literature. *English Journal, 76* (6), 61-63.

Moschkovich, J. (1999). Supporting the participation of English language learners in mathematics discussions. *For the Learning of Mathematics, 19* (1), 11-19.

Moulton, L., & Tevis, C. (1991). Making history come alive: Using historical photos in the classroom. *Social Studies and the Young Learner, 3* (4), 13-14.

Muriel, J. (1990). *Shakespeare made easy.* Portland, ME: J. Weston Walch Publisher.

Nagy, W., & Anderson, R. C. (1984). How many words are there in printed school English? *Reading Research Quarterly, 19* (3), 304-30.

Nation, I. S. P., & Deweerdt, J. P. (2001). A defense of simplification. *Prospect, 16* (3), 55-67

Neihardt, J. G. (1998). *Black Elk speaks.* Lincoln, Nebraska: University of Nebraska Press.

Nesbit, E. (2002). *Beautiful stories from Shakespeare for children.* Totowa, NJ: Barnes & Noble Books.

New York City Board of Education. (2000). *Regents biology test result comparing ELL and English proficient students.* Division of Assessment and Accountability.

New York City Board of Education. (2003). *Statistical summaries: 2002-2003.* www.nycenet.edu.

Noden, H. R. (1999). *Image grammar: Using grammatical structures to teach writing.* Portsmouth, NH: Boynton/Cook.

Norwood, K., & Carter, G. (1994). Journal writing: An insight into students' understanding. *Teaching Children Mathematics, 1* (3), 146-148.

Odean, P. M. (1987). Teaching Paraphrasing to ESL Students. *MinneTESOL Journal, 6,* 15-27

O'Dell, S. (1971). *Island of the blue dolphins.* New York: Bantam Books.

Odijk, P. (1991). *The Chinese.* Englewood Cliffs, NJ: Silver Burdett Press.

Oh, S. (2001). Two types of input modification and EFL reading comprehension: Simplification versus elaboration. *TESOL Quarterly, 35* (1), 69-96.

Oller, J. W., & Nagato, N. (1974). The long-term effect of FLES: An experiment. *Modern Language Journal, 58* (1), 15-19.

Olmedo, I. M. (1996). Creating contexts for studying history with students learning English, *The Social Studies, 87,* (1), 39-43.

Olmedo, I. M. (1993). Junior historians: Doing oral history with ESL and bilingual students. *TESOL Journal, 2* (4), 7-10.

O'Malley, J. M., & Pierce, L. V. (1996). *Authentic assessment for English language learners: Practical approaches for teachers.* Reading, MA: Addison-Wesley.

Orwell, G. (2002). *Animal farm.* [Narrated by Patrick Tull] Cassette Recording No. RF-015-DJ. Prince Frederick, MD: Recorded Books, LLC.

Paulson, F. L., Paulson, P. R., & Meyer C. A. (1991). What makes a portfolio a portfolio? *Educational Leadership, 48* (5), 60-63.

Paz, A. (1983). The blue bouquet. In I. Howe and I. W. Howe (Eds.) *Short shorts: An anthology of the shortest stories* (pp. 163-165). New York: Bantam Books.

Peizman, F., & Gadda, G. (1994). *With different eyes: Insights into teaching language minority students across the disciplines.* Reading, MA: Addison-Wesley.

Penfield, J. (1987). *The media: Catalysts for communicative language learning.* Reading, MA: Addison-Wesley.

Perfetti, C. A. (1995). Cognitive research can inform reading education. *Journal of Research in Reading, 18* (2), 106-15.

Perry, M., Scholl, A. H., Davis, D. F., Harris, J. G., & Von Laue, T. H. (1995). *History of the world.* Evanson, IL: McDougal Littell Inc.

Peyton, J. K., et al. (1990). The influence of writing task on ESL students' written production. *Research in the Teaching of English, 24* (2), 142-71

Philipp, R. A. (1996). Multicultural mathematics and alternative algorithms. *Teaching Children Mathematics, 3* (3), 128-133.

Piaget, J. (1947). *The psychology of intelligence.* New York: Harcourt, Brace.

Piaget, J. (1972). Intellectual evolution from adolescence to adulthood. *Human Development, 15* (1), 1-12.

Pignatiello, J., (1998). *Essentials of biology.* New York: Holt, Rinehart and Winston.

Pirie, B. (1995). Meaning through motion Kinesthetic English. *English Journal, 84* (8), 46-51.

Pittman, H. C. (1996). *A grain of rice.* New York: Bantam Doubleday Dell Books for Young Readers.

Powell, A. B., Ramnauth, M. (1992). Beyond questions and answers: Prompting reflections and deepening understandings of mathematics using multiple-entry logs. *For the Learning of Mathematics, 12* (2), 12-18.

Pugh, S. L., Hicks, J. W., & Davis, M. (1997). *Metaphorical ways of knowing: The imaginative nature of thought and expression.* Urbana, IL: National Council of Teachers of English.

Purves, A. (1986). Rhetorical communities, the international student, and basic writing. *Journal of Basic Writing, 5* (1), 38-51.

Raphan, D. (1996). A multimedia approach to academic listening. *TESOL Journal, 6* (2), 24-28.

Rawls, W. (2002). *Where the red fern grows.* [Narrated by Frank Muller] Cassette Recording No. RE-551-DJ. Prince Frederick, MD: Recorded Books, LLC.

Rees, R. (1997). *The ancient Greeks.* Portsmouth, NH: Heinemann.

Reilly, K. (1997). *The West and the World: A History of Civilization from the Ancient World to 1700.* Princeton, NJ: Markus Wiener Publishers.

Reisin, G. (1993). Experiencing Macbeth: From text rendering to multicultural performance. *English Journal, 82* (4), 52-53.

Reisner, L. (1998). *Tortillas and lullabies—Tortillas y cancioncitas.* New York: Greenwillow Books.

Reisner, L. (1993). *Margaret and Margarita—Margarita y Margaret.* New York: Greenwillow Books.

Richard-Amato, P. A., & Snow, M. A. (1992). *The multicultural classroom: Readings for content-area teachers.* Reading, MA: Addison-Wesley.

Richter, C. (2002). *The light in the forest.* [Narrated by Frank Muller] Cassette Recording No. RE-992-DJ. Prince Frederick, MD: Recorded Books, LLC.

Richter, C. (1981). *The light in the forest.* New York: Fawcett Juniper.

Robinson, F. P. (1961) *Effective study.* New York: Harper & Row, Publishers.

Rosenblatt, L. (1978). *The reader, the text, the poem: The transactional theory of the literary work.* Carbondale, IL: Southern Illinois University Press.

Rowland-Entwhistle, T. (1987). *Confucius and ancient China.* Danbury, CT: Watts Franklin.

Samuel, M. (1995). Using versions of literary texts to improve comprehension. *TESOL Journal, 4* (3), 21-23.

Samway, K. D., & McKeon, D. (1999). *Myths and realities: Best practices for language minority students.* Portsmouth, NH: Heinemann.

Sandberg, C. (1989). Chicago. In R. DiYanni (Ed.) *Reading poetry: An anthology of poems* (pp. 248-249). New York: Random House.

Santiago, E. (1993). *When I was Puerto Rican.* New, York: Random House.

Scarcella, R. (1990). Providing culturally sensitive feedback. In R. Scarcella's *Teaching language minority students in the multicultural classroom* (pp. 130-145). Englewood Cliffs, NJ: Prentice Hall, Inc.

Schmitt, N., & Carter, R. (2000). The lexical advantages of narrow reading for second language learners. *TESOL Journal, 9* (1), 4-9.

Schraer, W. D., & Stoltze, H. J. (1995). *Biology: The study of life.* Englewood, NJ: Prentice Hall, Inc.

Schumann, J. (1978). Second language acquisition: The pidginization hypothesis. In E. Hatch (Ed.) *Second language acquisition.* (pp. 181-190). Rowley, MA: Newbury House.

Schwab, P. N., Coble, C. R. (1985). Reading, thinking, and semantic webbing. *Science Teacher, 52* (5), 68-71

Scott, J. E. (1994). Teaching Nonfiction with the Shared Book Experience. *Reading Teacher, 47* (8), 676-78.

Shakespeare, W. (2003). *Hamlet.* New York: Simon & Schuster.

Shakespeare, W. (2003). *Macbeth.* New York: Washington Square Press.

Shakespeare, W. (1976). *Romeo and Juliet.* New York: Simon & Schuster.

Shen, F. (1989). The classroom and the wider culture: Identity as a key to learning English composition. *College Composition and Communication, 40* (4), 459-466.

Shepard, A. (2001). *Lady white snake: A tale from Chinese opera.* Union City, CA: Pan Asian Publications.

Short, R. J. (1994a). The challenge of social studies for limited English proficient students. *Social Education, 58* (1), 36-38.

Short, R. J. (1994b). Expanding middle school horizons: Integrating language, culture, and social studies. *TESOL Quarterly, 28* (3), 581-608.

Short, R. J. (1997). Reading, writing, and ...social studies: Research in integrated language and content secondary classrooms. In D. Brinton & M. A. Snow (eds.) *The Content-based classroom: Perspectives on integrating language and content* (pp. 213-232). Reading, MA: Addison-Wesley Longman.

Short, R. J. (1999). Integrating language and content for effective sheltered instruction programs. In C. J. Faltis & R. Wolfe (eds.) *So much to say: Adolescents, bilingualism & ESL in the secondary school* (pp. 105-137). NY: Teachers College, Columbia University.

Soyibo, K. (1995). Using concept maps to analyze textbook presentations of respiration. *The American Biology Teacher, 57* (6), 344-351.

Spivey, N. N. (1997). *The constructivist metaphor: Reading, writing and the making of meaning.* San Diego, CA: The Academic Press.

Spurlin, Q. (1995). Making science comprehensible for language minority students. *Journal of Science Teacher Education, 6* (2), 71-78.

Staples, S. F. (2002). *Shabanu: Daughter of the wind.* [Narrated by Christina Moore] Cassette Recording No. RE-648-DJ. Prince Frederick, MD: Recorded Books, LLC.

Staples, S. F. (1991). *Shabanu: Daughter of the wind.* New York: Random House.

Steinbeck, J. (2002). *The pearl.* [Narrated by Frank Muller] Cassette Recording No. RF-039-DJ. Prince Frederick, MD: Recorded Books, LLC.

Steinbeck, J. (1994). *Of mice and men.* New York: The Penguin Group.

Stone, A. H., & Collins, S. (1973). *Populations: Experiments in ecology.* New York: Franklin Watts, Inc.

Stubbs, M. (1995). Collocations and cultural connotations of common words. *Linguistics and Education, 7* (4), 379-390.

Sullivan, P. N. (1996). Sociocultural influences on classroom interactional styles. *TESOL Journal, 6* (1), 32-34.

Taylor, K. L., & Sobota, S. J. (1998). Writing in biology: An integration of disciplines. *The American Biology Teacher, 60* (5), 350-353.

Todd, L. P., & Curti, M. (1986). *Triumph of the American nation.* Chicago: Harcourt Brace Jovanovich.

Tovani, C. (2000). *I read it, but I didn't get it: Comprehension strategies for adolescent readers.* Portland, Maine: Stenhouse Publishers.

Toumasis, C. (1995). Concept worksheet: An important tool for learning. *Mathematics Teacher, 88* (2), 98-100

Trugen, T. (1987). *The little weaver of Thai-yen village—Co be tho-det lang thai-yen.* San Francisco, CA: Children Books Press.

Twain, M. (2002). *The adventure of Huckleberry Finn.* [Narrated by Norman Dietz] Cassette Recording No. RF-058-DJ. Prince Frederick, MD: Recorded Books, LLC.

Twain, M. (2002). *The adventure of Tom Sawyer.* [Narrated by Norman Dietz] Cassette Recording No. RC-090-DJ. Prince Frederick, MD: Recorded Books, LLC.

Usiskin, Z. (1996). Mathematics as a language. In P. C. Elliott and M. J. Kenney (eds.) *Communication in mathematics, K-12 and beyond* (pp. 231-243). Reston, VA: National Council of Teachers of Mathematics.

Vizmuller-Zocco, J. (1987). Derivation, creativity and second language learning. *Canadian Modern Language Review, 43* (4), 718-30.

Vygotsky, L. S. (1978). *Mind in society,* MA: Harvard University Press.

Wharton, E. (1987). *Ethan Frome and other short fiction by Edith Wharton* (pp. 5, 10). New York: Bantam Books.

White, E. B. (1949). Here is New York. In *Essays of E. B. White.* New York: Harper Collins Publishing.

Whitman, G. (2000). Teaching students how to be historians: An oral history project for the secondary school classroom. *History Teacher, 33* (4), 469-81

Wiggins, G. (1992). Creating tests worth taking. *Educational Leadership, 49* (8), 26-33.

Wilker, J. D. (1999). *Confucius: Philosopher and teacher.* New York: Scholastic Library.

Wilson, J., & Dilulio, J. (1999). *American government: Institutions and policies.* Boston, MA: Houghton Mifflin Company College Division.

Wylie, E. (1921). Puritan sonnet. In *Collected poems of Elinor Wylie.* New York: Alfred A. Knopf, Inc.

Yee, I. (1999). Names, names—What strange creatures they are. But could we live without them? *The Social Studies, 90* (1), 25-27.

Zarnowski, M. (1990). *Learning about Biographies: A reading-and-writing approach for children.* Urbana, IL: National Council of Teachers of English.

Zarnowski, M. (1991). Wait!...before you throw out that outdated textbook. *Social Studies and the Young Learner, 3* (4), 3-31.

Zaslavsky, C. (1999). *African counts: Number and pattern in African cultures.* (3rd ed.) Chicago, IL: Lawrence Hill Books.

Zaslavsky, C. (1991). World cultures in the mathematics class. *For the Learning of Mathematics, 11,* (2), 32-36.

Zevin, J. (1993). World studies in secondary schools and the undermining of ethno-centrism. *The Social Studies, 84*, (2), 82-87.

Zevin, J. (2000). *Social studies for the twenty-first century: Methods and materials for teaching middle and secondary schools.* Mahwah, NJ: Lawrence Erlbaum Associates Publishers.

Zhao, Q. (1998). *Liang Shanbo and Zhu Ying Tai.* Beijing, China: New World Press.

SUBJECT INDEX

Adolescent second language learning, 1-18,
    acculturation, 5-7, 24-25, 27, 36
    cognitive developmental factor, 11-15
    native culture impact, 5-6, 7, 10-11, 17, 26-28, 36, 199-203
    native language impact, 1-3, 5, 7-18, 20-21, 32, 36, 37, 41, 42, 47
Affective filter, 4-6
Age difference in language acquisition, 2, 11-12
Assessment, 38-65
    cultural bias in standardized tests, 53-57
    language issues in standardized tests, 53, 56-59
    miscue analysis, 47-49
    of beginning ELL students, 40-45
    of intermediate or advanced ELL students, 46-47, 50-51
    performance assessment, 60, 62-65
    standardized tests, 52-59

Basic Interpersonal Communication Skills (BICS), 2-6
Bilingual reading (*See* Dual language reading), 41

Cognitive Academic Language Proficiency (CALP), 2-6
Collaboration with ESL/Bilingual teachers, 16, 21, 23, 34-36, 41-43, 56
Comparing second language acquisition and first language acquisition, 1-2
Culturally oriented ways of teaching, 67-95
    in English classes, 79-89
    in mathematics classes, 72-79
    in science classes, 67-72
    in social studies classes, 89-95, 199-202
Culturally varied ways of learning, 10-11, 26-28, 72-74, 199-202
Culture shock, 6, 36

Teaching Language and Content to Linguistically and Culturally Diverse Students: Principles, Ideas, and Materials; pages 255–259.
A Volume in: Language Studies in Education
Copyright © 2004 by Information Age Publishing, Inc.
All rights of reproduction in any form reserved.
ISBN: 1-59311-088-X (paper), 1-59311-089-8 (cloth)

Effective ELL assessment, 39-52
  in science classes, 42-43, 46-47
  in social studies classes, 41, 42-43, 46-
    47, 52
Effective ELL instructional examples,
  19-38, 60-62
  in English classes, 20-21, 22-25, 26-
    31, 60
  in mathematics classes, 31-33
  in science classes, 21-22, 62
  in social studies classes, 20-21, 25-26,
    61
ELL placement. 40-41
ELL students' stories, 15, 19-37, 40-42,
  46
  about English language and content
    learning, 19-38
    Argentine student, 25-26
    Bangladeshi student, 20-21
    Chinese student, 26-28, 40, 42, 46
    Colombian student, 23-25
    Egyptian student, 40, 41
    Haitian student, 31-33
    Mexican student, 28-31
    Nicaraguan student, 22-23
    Pakistani student, 21-22
  comparing ESL and mainstream
    classes, 15
English listening and speaking
  instruction, 214-219
  choral reading, 215-216
  dramatic adaptations, 214-215
  music story telling, 218-219
  speaking with a subtext, 216-217
  talk show, 217-218
  tongue twister, 216
English reading instruction, 144-154
  dual-language reading, 146-147 (*See
    also* Bilingual reading)
  graphic organizers in reading, 147-
    149
  jigsaw reading, 152-154
  multicultural literature, 86-88
  parallel reading, 144-145
  quotation collage, 149-150
  slow-paced audio book reading, 145-
    146
  text transformation, 150-152

English vocabulary instruction, 110-116
  character physicalization, 111
  connotation and collocation, 114-
    115
  dictionaries and thesauri, 113-114
  human tableau, 110
  metaphorical ways of thinking, 115-
    116
  sensory imagery, 114
  word pictures, 111-112
  writer's word palette, 113
English writing instruction, 186-197
  comparative writing, 28-30
  clustering, 186-188
  cross-cultural writing, 88-89
  "I am . . ." poem, 196-197
  in-role writing, 188-189
  literature double-entry journals, 186
  literature mimic writing, 193-195
  multilingual text exploration, 190-192
  picture poetry, 189-190
  word association poem, 195-196
  writing for a different audience, 192-
    193
ESL oriented lesson planning, 60-62
  English, 60
  science, 62
  social studies, 61

Home Language Identification Survey
  (HLIS), 41

Input principle, 4
Internet ESL resources, 239
Involving ELL students in class
  discussions, 27, 46, 87

Language and mathematics integration,
  31-33
Language Assessment Battery Revised
  (LABR), 40
Language and content teaching, 4-5, 12,
  15-18, 20-22, 31-38, 43, 58, 140
Listening/speaking instructional
  strategies, 207-224
  in English classes, 214-219
  in mathematics classes, 211-214
  in science classes, 207-211
  in social studies classes, 219-226

Mainstream content classes, 17, 20, 27,
28, 31, 35, 41, 42, 44, 227
Mainstream content teachers, 15, 16,
18, 21, 28, 34, 35, 36, 37, 39,
40, 41, 42, 43, 46, 47, 49, 52,
53, 58, 60, 109
Mainstreaming ELL students, 22, 28,
42, 47, 49
Mathematics listening and speaking
instruction, 211-214
fishing for questions, 212-213
homework challenger, 212
say something, 213-214
speak in a full sentence, 214
Think-Pair-Share (TPS), 211-212
Mathematics reading instruction, 134-
144
fictional reading, 137-138
guided reading, 142-144
logical connectors, 139
non-fictional reading, 229-231
providing a roadmap for textbook
reading, 135-136
textbook simplification, 136-137, 138
word problem trouble shooter, 139-
142
Mathematics vocabulary instruction,
103-110
everyday words and mathematical
words, 103-104
graffiti mathematics, 106-107
mathematical language and English
swapping, 105-106
multilingual mathematics glossary,
104-105
vocabulary diagram, 107-109
word building using prefixes and
suffixes, 109-110
Mathematics writing instruction, 176-
186
concept comparisons, 185
double-entry journal, 177, 179
language translation, 176-177
learning autobiography, 183
personalizing mathematics text, 178,
180-182
reader response, 184
real-world mathematics application,
182-183

riddle writing, 184-185
word problem questions, 178, 180
Multicultural literature reading, 233-
238
advanced level reading, 236-238
beginning level reading, 233-235
intermediate level reading, 235-236

Native language and literacy skills
transfer, 9, 10, 12, 17, 18, 51,
62, 79, 102
New York State English as a Second
Language Achievement Test
(NYSESLAT), 41

Performance assessment, 60, 62-65
Preparing to teach ELL students, 56-62
cultural notes, 56, 58, 60, 61, 62
ESL anticipated difficulties, 58, 60,
61, 62
language objective, 58, 60, 61, 62
Providing culturally sensitive feedback,
17

Reading instructional strategies, 125-
165
in English classes, 144-154
in mathematics classes, 134-144
in science classes, 125-134
in social studies classes, 154-165

Schumann's social distance hypothesis,
6-7
Science listening and speaking
instruction, 207-211
conversational cooperative learning,
210-211
guess who I am, 208-209
how to . . . , 208
tongue twister, 207-208
Science reading instruction, 125-134
guessing the unknown from the
context, 131-133
jigsaw reading, 128
matching headlines with articles, 134
organizational links, 133
parallel reading, 125-128
reading and diagramming, 129-131
scrambled sentences, 128-129

Science vocabulary instruction, 97-103
  concept probing before definition, 98-100
  elaborated semantic webbing, 97-98
  matching synonyms/antonyms, 100-101
  multilingual science glossary, 102-103
  word building using prefixes and suffixes, 101-102
Science writing instruction, 167-176
  from a headline to an article, 172
  journal writing, 64-65, 173
  picture captions, 167-168
  poem writing, 168-170
  reader response, 174-176
  sentence combining, 174
  writing for a different audience, 171-172
Silent period, 20, 23, 25, 40
Social studies listening and speaking instruction, 219-226
  closed captions, 225-226
  group decision making, 219-221
  guessing who s/he is, 221-222
  how to . . . , 222-223
  role play, 223-224
  simulation game, 224-225
Social studies reading instruction, 154-165
  focused reading, 156-157
  graphic organizers, 159-160
  jigsaw reading, 160-162
  note-taking, 52
  organizational links, 157, 158
  parallel reading, 154-156
  SQ2R reading, 162-165
  text simplification, 157, 158
  using internet sources, 25-26
Social studies vocabulary instruction, 116-124
  class vocabulary calendar, 122-123
  concept exploration through senses, 116-117
  concept maps, 121
  concept physicalization, 118-119
  concept visualization, 117-118
  group mime game, 119-120
  historian's word journal, 122

  realias for symbolism, 119
  semantic differential scale, 120-121
  tràcing the word family, 123-124
Social studies writing instruction, 197-205
  biographical interview report, 204, 205
  cross-cultural perspective comparison, 201-202
  "In other words . . . ", 199-201
  media analysis, 203-204
  photo essays, 198-199
  sentence combining, 198
  timeline caption, 197-198
  written debate, 202-203

Tapping into ELL students' prior knowledge in English instruction, 79-89
  cross-cultural writing, 88-89
  cross-cultural language and literacy comparisons, 83-86
  Bangla vs. English, 83
  Chinese vs. English, 84
  Greek vs. English, 84
  Japanese vs. English, 84
  Korean vs. English, 84-85
  Urdu vs. English, 85
  Polish vs. English, 85
  Russian vs. English, 85-86
  Spanish vs. English, 86
  home language and literacy survey, 81-86
  journey to America, 79-81
  multicultural literature, 86-88
Tapping into students' prior knowledge in mathematics instruction, 72-79
  cross-cultural mathematics, 75-76, 77-78
  culturally varied ways of learning mathematics, 72-74
  home country learning experiences with mathematics, 76, 78-79
Tapping into students' prior knowledge in science instruction, 67-72
  exotic habitats, 70-71
  home science learning survey, 68-69
  home country biomes, 69

home culture food chains, 70
immigrant population growth
      patterns, 71-72
Tapping into students' prior knowledge
      in social studies instruction,
      89-95
   cross-cultural name investigation, 95
   cultural history study, 92, 93
   family history interview, 91-92
   home culture connection, 13
   multicultural and multilingual map
      study, 90
   theme-based social studies
      instruction, 92, 93-94
Teacher reflections on ELL instruction,
      37-38
   English teacher, 37

science teacher, 37
social studies teachers, 37-38

Vocabulary instructional strategies, 97-
      124
   in English classes, 110-116
   in mathematics classes, 103-110
   in science classes, 97-103
   in social studies classes, 116-124

Whorfian hypothesis, 8-10
Writing instructional strategies, 167-204
   in English classes, 186-197
   in mathematics classes, 176-185
   in science classes, 167-176
   in social studies classes, 197-205